TELEVISION STUDIES

Media and Society Series
J. Fred MacDonald, General Editor

TELEVISION STUDIES
Textual Analysis

Edited by
Gary Burns and Robert J. Thompson

Media and Society Series

PRAEGER

New York
Westport, Connecticut
London

Copyright Acknowledgment

John Hartley, "Invisible Fictions: Television Audiences, Paedocracy, Pleasure," *Textual Practice* 1, No. 2 (Summer 1987): 121–138. Reprinted with permission.

Library of Congress Cataloging-in-Publication Data

Television studies : textual analysis / edited by Gary Burns and
   Robert J. Thompson.
         p. cm. — (Media and society series)
         Bibliography: p.
         Includes index.
         ISBN 0-275-92745-8
         1. Television broadcasting. I. Burns, Gary, 1952–
  II. Thompson, Robert J., 1959–   . III. Series.
PN1992.5.T38 1989
791.45'0973—dc 19   88-23170

Library of Congress Catalog Card Number: 88-23170
ISBN: 0-275-92745-8

First published in 1989

Praeger Publishers, One Madison Avenue, New York, NY 10010
A division of Greenwood Press, Inc.

Printed in the United States of America

The paper used in this book complies with the Permanent Paper Standard issued by the National Information Standards Organization (Z39.48-1984).

10 9 8 7 6 5 4 3 2 1

To William E. Burns and to
the memory of Beatrice Burns

To the memory of
Roy and Joan Thompson

Contents

Part III: Critical Studies of Nonfiction Television

Part IV: Audience as Text

Acknowledgments

The editors gratefully acknowledge the assistance of Linda Thompson and Beth Kizer at the University of Missouri-St. Louis, and of Adele Gmoser at the State University of New York at Cortland. We also thank our editors, J. Fred MacDonald and Alison Bricken, for their unfailing encouragement and support.

TELEVISION STUDIES

Introduction
Gary Burns and Robert J. Thompson

The impetus for this volume was our realization that there was no regular forum for current research on television. Many film journals have broadened their scope to include television and video, and more and more anthologies of TV research are being published. Still, the development of television studies as a discipline, or even as an inter-disciplinary area, has been inhibited by the lack of a specialized journal or annual. Our plan is for the present volume to be the first in a series of anthologies (annual, we hope) that will provide an outlet for some of the best recent research in television studies.

Each volume will have a theme chosen to reflect some current trend we perceive or wish to encourage in television studies. We assume that trends in scholarship will, in turn, be influenced to some extent by developments in television itself, so that in many cases our volumes will be as timely as the most recent TV season. That does not mean, however, that we are unconcerned with TV's history, or that we plan to publish essays that will hold no interest a decade from now. Although TV series come and go, often with dizzying rapidity, there are, nonetheless, enduring issues of many sorts—theoretical, methodological, political—that enliven the best work in television studies, even work whose main concern is to document or interpret an esoteric, unavailable, forgotten, or disparaged televisual text. We intend to publish studies that have the sort of lasting value associated with the best scholarly work in other fields, but at the same time we hope to avoid stodginess, methodological fetishism, and pedantry.

The present volume exemplifies the balance we hope to maintain between timely interest and lasting relevance. Most of the dramatic series discussed here are either still running or have left the air only recently. The news, sports, and documentary programs examined should also still be fresh in the minds of many readers. But in most cases, it is not necessary to have seen the series or program in order to follow the author's argument and absorb the flavor of the show. In addition, the analysis of specific TV texts is complemented, especially in Sections I and IV, but also throughout the volume, by rigorous theoretical argumentation. We trust that a reader encountering this volume several years hence will find both that the theory has lost none of its edge and that the exegeses are still comprehensible and evocative, even though the particular programs discussed may by then be quite unfamiliar.

The book is divided into four parts:

    I. Political Economy vs. Cultural Studies
   II. Critical Studies of Dramatic Series
 III. Critical Studies of Nonfiction Television
 IV. Audience as Text.

Part I is a two-chapter "debate" about several issues, the largest of which is definitional: What is the field of television studies? What should it be? Mike Budd and Clay Steinman argue that it is impossible to arrive at an adequate understanding of television without examining, closely and critically, the capitalist institutions that dominate television as an industry. Cultural studies contributes to this enterprise only to the extent that it considers "texts as institutions . . . and institutions as texts . . . ."

More typically, the authors assert, cultural studies ascribes too much autonomy to audiences, and too little importance to institutional entities such as networks and sponsors. Central to Budd and Steinman's critique of the political economy of television, and of particular importance in a volume on textual analysis, is Dallas Smythe's notion of the audience as commodity. According to this view, television viewing as an economic transaction is much different from, say, purchasing and reading a book. In the latter case, a publisher sells a book to a reader. The book is both a literary text and the commodity in an economic transaction. In the case of television, a network sells an audience to an advertiser. The audience is the principal commodity, while the television program, whatever its aesthetic merits may be, serves primarily as a facilitative mechanism by means of which capital acquires the attention (a form of intellectual labor) of viewers to commercials and ideology.

John Fiske defends cultural studies by identifying a "cultural economy" in addition to the financial economy emphasized by Budd and Steinman. In the cultural economy, audiences are both producers and consumers of meanings and pleasures derived from television programs or other texts. To view audiences as passive receptacles, powerless because of their status as commodities, is elitist and defeatist, says Fiske. Far from being "cultural dupes," audiences are active participants in the production of meaning in texts.

Popular texts—those that appeal to a large, heterogeneous audience (such as most television shows)—must of necessity be polysemic, full of a variety of potential meanings. The proper task of textual analysis is to discover and illuminate the polysemy within texts. Fiske, like Budd and Steinman, sees criticism as a political activity—an intervention. Unlike Budd and Steinman, his preference is to intervene at the site of reception by encouraging and creating "readings" (of TV shows and other texts) grounded in resistance to domination.

Part II of the book consists of five chapters devoted to analysis of dramatic television series. Marsha F. Cassidy examines the development of the lengthy serial text of "Dallas" as a process of "refiguration." Murray Smith proposes a nasty metaphor (vomiting) as an aid to understanding a nasty show, "The Young Ones." Robert J. Thompson follows a similar path in uncovering overlooked filth in "Hill Street Blues" and other series. Arthur Asa Berger performs a semiological and structural analysis of the pilot episode of "Cheers," concluding that it is very much like a fairy tale. Wende Vyborney Dumble argues that "The People's Court," "Divorce Court," and "Superior Court" encourage a positive view of the American justice system while at the same time discouraging actual participation in the system.

Among the commonalities discernible in the studies in Part II, perhaps the most significant is the drawing of insights through means that, at the most general level, can be called dialectical. The two most influential approaches in this category are the notions of Fiske and John Hartley concerning polysemy and the open text, and the "dialogic" view adapted by Horace Newcomb from Mikhail Bakhtin. Both perspectives treat TV (or other) texts as evolutionary entities rather than as immutable objects containing a finite meaning waiting to be discovered through "correct" interpretation.

Cassidy uses both theories to show that "Dallas" is not mere ideology, but an "ideological forum" that presents "multilayered hypotheses about social behavior to which viewers or groups of viewers can respond actively and richly."

This view of television as text-in-flux is developed elsewhere by Hartley in a discussion of TV as a "dirty category."[1] Hartley's point is to celebrate the failure of analytical boundaries and binary logic to contain television (and many other things). But the idea of television as "dirt" has appeal beyond Hartley's terminological probe, as Smith and Thompson demonstrate. Smith's spicy account of "The Young Ones" reveals the program's dialectical challenge to the sit-com genre. Similarly, Thompson's discovery of surprising quantities of scandalous material amid what has lately been known as "quality television" suggests that the boundaries of good taste are, so to speak, fluid.

Berger's analysis of "Cheers" reveals a dialectic located especially in character—"He's everything you're not." Through a study of codes and their violation, and of the interplay of opposites, Berger arrives at an understanding of "Cheers" as a sort of modern-day fairy tale in which a beauty and a beast live in a state of alternating contradiction and resolution in wide-ranging areas of interest and identity including, most prominently, class and gender.

Dumble's essay is placed last in Part II because it explores the borderline between fiction and nonfiction, and might almost as well have been included in Part III. The dialectical foundation of Dumble's analysis is the tension between fact and fiction in the genre she calls "prototrial" programs.

Part III of the book contains five essays on nonfiction television. Meg Moritz presents an insider's view of the production and promotion of local TV news, particularly during "sweeps" periods. Herbert Zettl explains how manipulation of pictorial components in TV news can enhance the "personification" of the anchor. Wendy Kozol analyzes CBS's and ABC's TV news coverage of South Africa over a two-week period in 1987, concluding that the coverage sent mixed messages but most often reinforced racist stereotypes. Martin J. Medhurst provides a rhetorical analysis of PBS's "Vietnam: A Television History" and the Accuracy in Media (AIM) response program, "Television's Vietnam: The Real Story." He finds that the PBS series is effective as propaganda, while the AIM program is not. Jimmie L. Reeves examines televised sports as athletic performances filtered through a presentational system that has many functions, including the dialogic one of describing present performances in relation to those of the past (statistics, records, etc.).

Each of the studies in Part III concerns the *construction* of programs that are usually presented, and are often accepted, as objective reality. The contrived nature of fictional programs is something the viewer takes for granted. In the case of nonfiction, most audience members probably understand that a similar process of fabrication or editorial tampering occurs, but the extent and effectiveness of the deception are easily overlooked and seldom exposed. Examining nonfiction programs as constructed texts, rather than as "20/20" refractions of reality, reveals part of a vast apparatus of institutions and practices lurking behind the programs. If, as George Gerbner argues, control of stories constitutes power, then control of "true" stories is surely one of the greatest powers of all. The chapters in Part III are studies of this power in action.

Moritz demonstrates the alarming extent to which local news is neither local nor news. Focusing on "sweeps" rating periods, she shows how ideas, and often footage, are imported from other cities, and how stories are frequently chosen on the basis of their potential for promotional tie-ins with network dramatic series.

Zettl develops a theory of "graphication" of video images—the suggestion of a two-dimensional area within the larger picture ordinarily perceived as three-dimensional. He shows how use of the two-dimensional area ("second-order space") to contain location reports, satellite interviews, and the like has the curious effect of making the occupant of "first order," three-dimensional space seem more "corporeal" and real, more "personified." Zettl suggests a connection between graphication, personification, and ratings. Methodical construction of visual spectacle may be instrumental in "constructing" a large audience.

Kozol argues that TV news stories about South Africa are ideologically unstable constructions grounded in discourses of capitalism, racism, violence, and news objectivity, among others. Through an analysis of the interaction of visual and verbal codes, she demonstrates how a contradictory, polysemic image of South Africa emerges from CBS and ABC news coverage.

Medhurst identifies nine propaganda techniques often used in documentary films and TV programs, and grades the PBS and AIM Vietnam documentaries on their skill in using these devices. In addition to illuminating how different producers can create radically different and opposed renderings of the same topic, Medhurst challenges the ethics of "skillful" propaganda and, implicitly, of documentary as a form and polysemy as an ideal.

Reeves looks at TV's role in the construction—or, more accurately, reconstruction—of sport forms. He identifies TV as one of the forces behind changes in the rules, style of play, and popularity of many sports.

Section IV consists of one chapter, John Hartley's refutation of conventional wisdom concerning "the audience." Hartley sees "the audience" as a construct based on essentialist assumptions about other constructs, particularly television and nation. In his view, "the audience" is never "external to its discursive construction," but is always a fiction, rooted in ideology and the self-interest of the institution promulgating the fiction.

We hope it is clear from this introduction, and from the chapters in the book, that we see textual analysis of television developing along a path that is not much like that taken by literary criticism or cinema studies, even though television studies borrows many concepts from these fields. Just as television is not a clearly demarcated phenomenon, neither is television studies. With 40 years' worth of programming to choose from, one is hard pressed to identify a canon of masterpieces in TV; by the same token, the scattered serious writings on the medium, from the 1940s to the 1980s, are so variegated as to make it difficult even to enumerate the major schools of thought. Both TV itself and television studies are still, and perhaps forever, dirty categories.

However, dirty categories are still categories, and all the more interesting for being dirty. The present anthology will, we hope, provide valuable insights not only into specific series, genres, news reports, and so forth, but also into television and television studies in the current state of their evolution.

NOTE

1. John Hartley, "Encouraging Signs: Television and the Power of Dirt, Speech and Scandalous Categories," *Australian Journal of Cultural Studies* 1, no. 2 (1983): 62–82.

I
POLITICAL ECONOMY
VS. CULTURAL STUDIES

1
Television, Cultural Studies, and the "Blind Spot" Debate in Critical Communications Research

Mike Budd and Clay Steinman

"Little known" in Great Britain[1] and invisible in film-TV studies in the United States, the Canadian-initiated "blind spot" debate over leisure as labor and audiences as commodities indicates how we might develop analyses linking institutions of production and audiences to texts that are, socially, in movement.

Generated within the left wing of North American mass communication studies, the "blind spot" position argues that those who stress the ideological in their critiques of television and other mass media too often lose sight of the political-economic. "The first question that historical materialists should ask about mass communications is *what economic function for capital do they serve*," Dallas Smythe wrote in the article that opened the debate in 1977.[2] Although working within a traditional Marxist paradigm that distinguishes capitalism's "base" (mode of production) from its "superstructure" (roughly, culture and ideology), Smythe does not "[reject] the existence of a superstructure and [collapse] consciousness itself into the economic base."[3] Rather, he argues that ideological processes cannot be separated from economic ones; that, however audiences see them, television programs should be seen as what A. J. Liebling once called the "free lunch," which gathers consumers into audiences for sale to advertisers.[4]

An earlier version of this chapter was presented to members of the Society for Cinema Studies, May 22, 1987, in Montreal.

The mass media of communications are *simultaneously* in the superstructure *and* engaged indispensably in the last stage of infrastructural production where demand is produced and satisfied by purchases of consumer goods.[5]

Qualifying the argument increases its force: Packaged as individuals and in groups, we may or may not buy what is pitched to us; but in general the television business addresses us as objects for sale, and this (but not this alone) structures the address and helps construct our subjectivity as gendered consumers and workers. The lunch may be free for the poor who cannot buy and for the rich who pay others to shop for them.[6] But for the rest of us, whatever else goes on, "The work which audience members perform for the advertiser to whom they have been sold is to learn to buy particular 'brands' of consumer goods, and to spend their income accordingly"[7]—and to work producing goods and services to earn the income to spend. What might otherwise seem happy hours in front of the set become grotesque to the extent that criticism breaks out their costs and beneficiaries from their usual obscurity.

Yet the power of the industry's bottom line seems at best on the rim of consciousness of the vast majority of consumers (and critics and makers) of television. Reading criticism, and listening to what people say when they talk about TV, leads us to believe that the majority of producers, critics, and viewers imagine television as discrete programs (or commercials). This underscores the necessity for analysis beyond the uses and gratifications, the pleasures of texts, to their complex connections in an economy of domination and waste. Critical mass communications research in North America for three decades has been developing approaches that seek to avoid isolation of elements of media processes. Central has been the work of Smythe, Thomas Guback, Herbert Schiller, and their students. In their macroanalyses of international media institutions, stressing state-corporate relations, these scholars have, virtually alone in North America, sustained a radical critique of capitalist mass communication.

Quite different from this primarily institutional work, radical film/TV scholarship has been mostly tied to texts or to rigorous metatheoretical debates, emphases that reproduce those of our leading schools, where political commitments tend to be sublimated. The lack of attention to texts in most radical mass communications research follows the lead of major graduate schools in that field as well; what we in cinema studies see as vast and varied territory becomes simplistically mapped out as "content." But just as their social science training too often leads to superficial handling of media products, so our humanities backgrounds tend to make our handling of social, economic, and political issues cursory except as abstractions.

Fortunately, this academic division of labor, this debilitating alienation from those we could learn from and teach, may be changing. In the last few years, the political-economic work in radical communications research has been challenged by a critical version of cultural studies, influenced by Stuart Hall and the Centre for Contemporary Cultural Studies at the University of Birmingham in England, itself influenced by the continental theory that has so transformed our field. With the growth of interest in cultural studies, critical mass communications scholars have become increasingly attracted to semiotics and to various kinds of textual analysis. And the dynamic of contemporary film/TV theory has carried it away from formalist and auteurist assumptions, away from "the text itself," to larger concerns with ideology and psychoanalysis, narrative and reception, to a matrix of texts and technologies, subjectivities and social formations. Most important, feminist concerns have politicized what many of us do; in a sense, they have polarized our field in productive ways, making research that ignores feminism anti-feminist.

There is a limited but clear movement in film/TV studies toward a new integration of sophisticated economic, social, and technological history with gender-sensitive textual and other analyses, earlier traces of this integration having been marginalized during the revolution of French high theory in the mid- and late 1970s and the early 1980s. The best work we have of this new integration is the monumental study by David Bordwell, Janet Staiger, and Kristin Thompson, *The Classical Hollywood Cinema: Film Style and Mode of Production to 1960*.[8] Drawing on the Russian formalist tradition for their account of stylistic norms in the Hollywood cinema, and on recent neo-Marxist work on the mode of production by Harry Braverman, David Noble, and others,[9] the authors trace a complex set of reciprocal determinations between signifying and economic practices. Mode of production, style, and technology form the conditions for one another's existence and change, are both cause and effect of one another. So intense is the interdetermination, so intertwined the different modes and moments, and so concrete the activity of making texts and institutions, that one gets a real sense of a relatively integrated (though hardly uncontradictory) mode of film practice, of a social practice and its conditions. *The Classical Hollywood Cinema* is not so much the definitive work on

Hollywood as a tremendously generative one. Regardless of one's agreement or disagreement with particular arguments, the book redefines the problematic of film/TV studies—and by extension of other critical and cultural studies—in a synthesis of materialist institutional history and textual analysis of a corporate style.

Whereas Bordwell, Staiger, and Thompson focus on the relations of texts to the institutions of production, British cultural studies concentrates on the relations of texts to reception and consumption; it is interested less in particular economic institutions, and more in the power struggles of texts with social classes and subcultures. Stuart Hall, Dick Hebdige, Angela McRobbie, and David Morley live and work in an active socialist and feminist political culture. This shapes their research, contributing to an interplay of theory and practice few critical scholars in North America can claim. What is crucial about British cultural studies now is not only its particular formulation of the relation of institutions and texts, but also its increasing influence both on film/TV scholars whose object is primarily texts and on critical mass communications researchers whose object is mostly political-economic or social institutions. Broadening the conception of text, style, and discourse to include clothing, music, and all sorts of cultural artifacts, while similarly finding quotidian institutions in the *bricolage* of oppositional subcultures, cultural studies at its best explores texts as institutions (as social organizations) and institutions as texts (as symptomatic discourses and practices).[10] Here culture is a material process made by women and men, but not under conditions of their choosing—culture as contested terrain, as a battle over the meanings that help define the social.

A crucial text in the development of cultural studies is Morley's *The 'Nationwide' Audience*.[11] Though not the most valuable or accomplished work in this tradition, it shows Morley struggling with a central set of questions: In the encounter between TV viewers and TV texts, how are power relations articulated? In the struggle over meaning, how does the process of determination work? Hall had argued that meanings are not structured into texts themselves, but are subject to different kinds of readings by people in different social situations—readings that could be generally classified as dominant, negotiated, or oppositional.[12] When Morley talked with groups of people from different classes and occupations about the BBC program "Nationwide," he found it difficult to interpret the results using Hall's scheme. The reasons are instructive for cultural studies in general, indicating the enormous problems in articulating social and semiotic processes. A full exposition of the issues is beyond the scope of this chapter, though Morley himself has critiqued the effort and indicated more productive lines of inquiry.[13] These would involve, among other things, more attention to the professional ideologies of broadcasters and to discursive practices of the text as a cultural form, the ways the text organizes its processes of making meaning and pleasure; both of these help determine the conditions under which viewers make meanings.

Clearly the work of Bordwell, Staiger, and Thompson is relevant here as a more complete model of determination, though it does not treat meaning or reception. The differences in the two approaches are evident in their contrasting treatment of function. *The Classical Hollywood Cinema* argues that the Hollywood stylistic paradigm assimilates new techniques by assigning them familiar functions:

> Both the alternatives and the limitations of the style remain clear if we think of the paradigm as creating *functional equivalents*: a cut-in may replace a track-in, or color may replace lighting as a way to demarcate volumes, because each device fulfills the same role. Basic principles govern not only the elements in the paradigm but also the ways in which the elements may function.[14]

In contrast, Morley concludes, following V. N. Vološinov and discourse analysis, that "the same linguistic form can have different discursive functions in different contexts, and conversely, that different linguistic forms can have the same discursive function in particular contexts."[15] Where Bordwell, Staiger, and Thompson explore the functions of particular techniques within the limits of a mode of film practice, Morley and others tend to treat linguistic or other signifying forms as relatively undifferentiated wholes, exploring their differential social functions through the articulation and mediation of discourse. This "articulation theory" seems to have replaced the encoding/decoding model in recent cultural studies work.[16]

British cultural studies remains very much a product of a particular political situation in Britain, one that has no equivalent in the United States. Cultural studies enters the North American academy largely divorced from this concrete situation, as a set of generalized methods and analytical strategies. To examine the representation of British cultural studies to North American readers, we'll look at an article on the subject by John Fiske, in an anthology on television, *Channels of Discourse*.[17] Fiske's essay is in many ways a good introduction to cultural studies, but it raises important problems, too; we choose it because Fiske is quickly becoming a major interpreter and popularizer of cultural studies in North America. From this side of the Atlantic, it's difficult to tell whether the problems are with one or more of the various versions of cultural studies, or with Fiske's presentation. These problems tend to revolve around the text-institution relation, a central issue for cultural studies.

Glossing Hall's essay "Encoding and Decoding in the Television Discourse,"[18] Fiske argues:

Reading or viewing television, then, becomes a process of negotiation between the viewer and the text. Use of the word "negotiation" is significant, for it implies both that there is a conflict of interests that needs to be reconciled in some way, and that the process of reading television is one in which the reader is an active maker of meanings from the text, not a passive recipient of already constructed ones.[19]

But negotiation also implies a conscious and critical viewer, aware of the political implications of television discourses and prepared to define and defend her or his interests. Negotiation takes place between parties who are aware that negotiations are occurring and of what's at stake. Does anyone really believe that this situation obtains with the majority of North American TV viewers? Can all those network executives and advertisers who are buying and selling audiences by the millions be wrong? We need not subscribe to an elitist theory that TV viewers are stupid, or cultural dupes, to be skeptical of the idea of negotiation. Capital has bought itself an enormous advantage in the struggle over meaning, for its hegemony over the realm of signifiers is nearly total—Fiske's battle over signifieds must be waged largely with *their* signifiers, the rationalized capitalist production institutions largely elided as concrete influences in the work of cultural studies.

Similar problems emerge in Fiske's assertion of the active status of TV viewers. One of the critiques of Althusserian *Screen* theory is that its subject interpellated by ideology is merely passive, leaving no room for human action, will, or choice. The answer is usually to show how the film or TV viewer you theorize is active. *The Classical Hollywood Cinema* responds in typically concrete fashion by describing the activities engaged in by viewers of classical Hollywood cinema as "gap-filling": "Just as we project motion on to a succession of frames, so we form hypotheses, make inferences, erect expectations, and draw conclusions about the film's characters and actions. . . . The spectator must cooperate in fulfilling the film's form."[20]

While this begins to specify kinds of activity, it conceives of activity in a quite limited sense. Looked at more broadly, and confounding

Manichaean oppositions, most film or TV viewers seem to be actively passive—active makers of form and meaning that, however, come mostly prefabricated. A genuinely active viewer, like one who negotiates, would be conscious and critical, aware of the power of discursive and economic practices, able to gauge the freedom and domination in her or his own specific activities of viewing. How many people possess these skills? Do they choose to exercise them for 4 hours and 20 minutes a day watching television? What about the unconscious? Clearly, the vexing issue of viewer activity or passivity has only begun to be investigated, though we know more about the functions of viewers in texts than we do about the institutions that constrain and enable the functions of texts for viewers. Meanwhile, assertions of viewer activity, in the most important sense of critical consciousness and democratic control, seem to be largely wishful thinking, motivated mostly by political hope.

Fiske ends his article on British cultural studies with this summary:

Despite the cultural pessimism of the Frankfurt School, despite the power of ideology to reproduce itself in its subjects, despite the hegemonic force of the dominant classes, the people still manage to make their own meanings and to construct their own culture within, and often against, that which the industry provides for them. Cultural studies aims to understand and encourage this cultural democracy at work.[21]

Some of this is true, but it also blunts cultural studies' critical, negative edge. Despite several qualifications, Fiske tends throughout his article and elsewhere to collapse the complex, active interdetermination of people, texts, and institutions into a David-and-Goliath battle between two relatively monolithic entities: the people, plucky underdogs; and the culture industry, big, bad, and hegemonic. Fiske's use of the term "the people" is uncomfortably reminiscent of Ma Joad's speech at the end of the film *The Grapes of Wrath* ("We're the people who live"), Hollywood's appropriation of the popular front discourse of the 1930s. This romantic relapse is possible partly because of the pseudo-Althusserian overemphasis on ideology: For Fiske, capitalism as a social and economic system immediately becomes the capitalist ideology of individualism and competition.[22]

In cultural studies generally there is little attention to the concrete historical institutions of capitalist television—the economic structure of networks, which sell audiences to advertisers; the marketing; the demographics; the flow of commercials and programs. "Nationwide," for example, was made for the noncommercial BBC.[23] As cultural studies gains influence outside of Great Britain, its work will be increasingly vitiated if it cannot break through the detailed intellectual division of labor that so uncannily resembles that of the capitalist society it seeks to understand. The political economists and others who study concentration of ownership, economic imperialism, and other institutional questions may have the mistaken notion that texts, and culture generally, don't matter very much, but that doesn't mean we can ignore economic determination. In our haste to separate ourselves from vulgar Marxism, we needn't throw out the Marxism with the vulgarity.

Smythe argues that mass media consumers are workers, that we are on the job as long as we are awake.[24] To recast the argument slightly: Outside of the comparatively few liberated zones of the society (communal households and work places and other alternative institutions, time we can win for emancipatory struggles), we spend our working hours selling our labor power for the profit of others, in terms others ultimately control; we spend our remaining hours recovering from and preparing to go back to work, in some cases producing the next generation of workers, and consuming and playing within and against structures profound and resilient in ways that continually confound us. Of course, this isn't true of everyone all of the time. But the argument maintains that however aspects of our lives appear to us, looked at radically, they must be seen within this process in order to avoid the blind spot. As Bill Livant puts it, "This totality of time as labour time is not homogeneous; there are qualitative divisions within it, but they are precisely *within* it."[25]

Discussing advertisers' manipulations and resistance to them is not enough, suggests Smythe.[26] Whatever we think, we still buy the goods and work to buy them, and if we devote our 40 hours to getting ahead and our leisure to accumulation, nothing more is asked. To the extent that it separates out the ideological and the economic, theory here lags behind late capitalist social relations by decades. The link between labor and leisure was forged more than 60 years ago, when, following costly battles with militant workers, corporate owners and their managers "modernized" the work place as well as the marketplace.[27] With the help of management experts and psychologists like Frederick W. Taylor and Hugo Münsterberg, they created incentive systems to change attitudes toward work and management. Writes Smythe:

People learned . . . that work under monopoly capitalism involves competition between individuals whose possessive needs necessarily set them in conflict with each other rather than with the owners of the means of their (concealed) cooperative production. The carrot which systematically motivated them was the pursuit of commodities, which joined this half of the ideological exercise with the next.[28]

"In this context," he says, "the work of the audience members . . . is learning cues which are used when the audience member makes up his/her mental shopping list and spends his/her income"[29]—and makes decisions about her/his life.

Developing the argument, Livant defines the "audience" not as a group of receivers of messages but as a commodity form developed to be sold on the market. "It is precisely the subordination of the making of messages to the making of audiences which marks the modern media."[30] Analysis sensitive to the production of audience-commodities puts textual processes within complex, ongoing histories, histories that need complementing by those of textual production. What might otherwise be static, idealizing analysis becomes analysis of processes in motion, part of the *"motion* of the media *as a whole."*[31]

We can see the contribution this perspective can make by briefly reconsidering concepts of "flow." As analyzed somewhat differently by Raymond Williams and by Rick Altman, flow is the heterogeneous text of commercial television, the seemingly unrelated ribbon of fragments—commercials, programs, and promotional material.[32] Once we defamiliarize this television text by seeing how virtually everything is at least partly designed to sell us something, similarities between programs and ads emerge with startling force. By breaking flow out of its isolation (in the text, in the home), we can redefine it to include connections available elsewhere in public and private life—on the street or in the work place, for example. Beyond its links with other texts, we can see how flow articulates with desires, practices, and productions throughout the waking day, and into the night. We can see how flow helps produce the audience as commodity, is integral to its marketability, and how it is produced by the organization of people into audiences.

Thinking in terms of audience-as-commodity also allows us to differentiate between people organized as demographic commodities and people who try to organize themselves into groups. According to Livant, "Their struggle for group membership goes on under the difficult condition that they are being traded as audience commodities, but the groups that *actually emerge* in the audience sometimes hold surprises for the bourgeoisie."[33] This enables us to envision what collective resistance to the culture industry might look like without underestimating the difficulties of subverting interpellated social positioning.

The pertinence of this approach seems clearer when we look at Fiske's analysis of "Miami Vice" in the first issue of *Cultural Studies*.[34] The article shows how glib, how abstract, cultural studies can become when it separates a culture industry text from social relations. Jane Gaines calls this kind of abstraction "textual detachment": "concentration on the functioning of discourse [that] creates the impression that developments in an ideological realm are unrelated to developments elsewhere in social life."[35]

In a perverse use of Laura Mulvey's "Visual Pleasure and Narrative Cinema,"[36] Fiske treasures a nonnarrative song segment from one of the show's episodes. The song does not relate specifically to the narrative, Fiske says, but refers to what he calls the "extra-diegetic world—that is, to the viewer's previous experience of it [presumably the song], and the domain of pop in general." As such,

It disrupts not only the narrative but also television. Its voice is that of a black urban subculture and is thus more likely to articulate the hoods than the agencies of law and order. It loosens Crockett and Tubbs momentarily from their diegetic social authority and allows their style and masculinity to become freely available pleasures, not the free lunch of hegemony.[37]

Inside the text, the lunch may be free, but the cost of the analysis is blindness to the context of audience-commodity production, the show's repressive desublimation of conventional TV narrative and genre. Fiske's own pleasure in identification with a "black urban subculture . . . more likely to articulate the hoods" and his celebration of an unabashed "masculinity" in which the "feminine is written out" provides symptomatic testimony to the show's power to produce its audience for sale to the advertisers Fiske ignores. The song over a series of shots of Ferraris, credit cards, big rings, aftershave, and guns produces what Fiske calls "that frozen moment when the subject and object of desire merge . . . the moment of *jouissance*, when power, pleasure and affect liberate the masculine self."[38] In this discourse, racism becomes solidarity; patriarchal totems, signs of liberation.

In this world the boundaries are blurred between the good and the bad, the power of the dominant to control slips away as pleasure and style produce a multivocality in which commodities are anybody's speech and not the bearers of a capitalist economy. It's a world of fragments whose democracy lies in their fragmentation.[39]

The argument has an emancipatory pedigree—the 1960s aspiration for eroticization of aesthetic experience, as well as the 1970s valorization of subcultures.⁴⁰ But—emblematic of these times—Fiske's writing here adds the new and terrifying twist of postmodern theory. Hey, guys, it's OK to feel good about masculinity, Ferraris, guns. Forget your troubles, come on, get happy. It's democratic. The "extra-diegetic" matters only as a term of textual analysis. Behind our backs, it's the aestheticization of politics 50 years after Benjamin's critique.⁴¹ When cultural studies, like film/TV studies, abstracts texts from the social and economic institutions of consumer capitalism, it imitates rather than critiques their decontextualization, their commodification of experience. Blinded to the socioeconomic, media studies all too easily slips into celebration, missing the urgent critique of domination's newest forms.

NOTES

1. David Buckingham, "Against Demystification: A Response to 'Teaching the Media,'" *Screen* 27, no. 5 (1986):85.
2. Dallas Smythe, "Communications: Blindspot of Western Marxism," *Canadian Journal of Political and Social Theory* 1, no. 3 (1977):1; emphasis in original. Other articles on the "blind spot" debate include Graham Murdock, "Blindspots About Western Marxism: A Reply to Dallas Smythe," *Canadian Journal of Political and Social Theory* 2, no. 2 (1978):109–119; Dallas Smythe, "Rejoinder to Graham Murdock," *Canadian Journal of Political and Social Theory* 2, no. 2 (1978):120–127; Bill Livant, "The Audience Commodity: On the 'Blindspot' Debate," *Canadian Journal of Political and Social Theory* 3, no. 1 (1979):91–106.
3. Buckingham, "Against Demystification," p. 85n.
4. Smythe, "Communications," p. 23n.
5. Ibid., p. 3; emphasis in original.
6. Ibid., pp. 13–14.
7. Ibid., p. 6.
8. David Bordwell, Janet Staiger, and Kristin Thompson, *The Classical Hollywood Cinema: Film Style and Mode of Production to 1960* (New York: Columbia University Press, 1985).
9. Harry Braverman, *Labor and Monopoly Capital: The Degradation of Work in the Twentieth Century* (New York: Monthly Review Press, 1974); David F. Noble, *America by Design: Science, Technology, and the Rise of Corporate Capitalism* (New York: Alfred A. Knopf, 1977).
10. Dick Hebdige, *Subculture: The Meaning of Style* (London: Methuen, 1979); Angela McRobbie, "Settling Accounts with Subcultures: A Feminist Critique," *Screen Education* 34 (1980):37–49.
11. David Morley, *The 'Nationwide' Audience: Structure and Decoding* (London: British Film Institute, 1980).
12. Stuart Hall, "Encoding/Decoding," in *Culture, Media, Language,* ed. Stuart Hall et al. (London: Hutchinson/Centre for Contemporary Cultural Studies, 1980), 128–38.

13. David Morley, "The 'Nationwide' Audience—A Critical Postscript," *Screen Education* 39 (1981):3–14.

14. Bordwell, Staiger, and Thompson, *Classical Hollywood Cinema*, p. 5; emphasis in original.

15. Morley, "The 'Nationwide' Audience," p. 7.

16. Larry Grossberg, "On Postmodernism and Articulation: An Interview with Stuart Hall," *Journal of Communication Inquiry* 10, no. 2 (1986):45–60.

17. John Fiske, "British Cultural Studies and Television," in *Channels of Discourse*, ed. Robert C. Allen (Chapel Hill: University of North Carolina Press, 1987), 254–298.

18. Stuart Hall, "Encoding and Decoding in the Television Discourse," Centre for Contemporary Cultural Studies Media Series Stencilled Paper no. 13 (September 1973), excerpted as "Encoding/Decoding," in Hall et al., eds., *Culture, Media, Language*, 128–138.

19. Fiske, "British Cultural Studies," p. 260.

20. Bordwell, Staiger, and Thompson, *Classical Hollywood Cinema*, p. 8.

21. Fiske, "British Cultural Studies," p. 286.

22. Ibid., p. 285.

23. See Charlotte Brunsdon and David Morley, *Everyday Television: 'Nationwide'* (London: British Film Institute, 1978).

24. Smythe. "Communications," p. 7.

25. Livant, "The Audience Commodity," p. 103; emphasis in original.

26. Smythe, "Communications," p. 6.

27. See Braverman, *Labor and Monopoly Capital*, as well as Stuart Ewen, *Captains of Consciousness: Advertising and the Social Roots of the Consumer Culture* (New York: McGraw-Hill, 1976).

28. Smythe, "Communications," p. 18.

29. Ibid., p. 14.

30. Livant, "The Audience Commodity," p. 98.

31. Ibid., p. 95; emphasis in original.

32. See Raymond Williams, *Television: Technology and Cultural Form* (New York: Schocken Books, 1975); Rick Altman, "Television Sound," in *Television: The Critical View*, 4th ed., ed. Horace Newcomb (New York: Oxford University Press, 1987), 566–584.

33. Livant, "The Audience Commodity," p. 101; emphasis in original.

34. John Fiske, "*Miami Vice*, Miami Pleasure," *Cultural Studies* 1, no. 1 (1987):113–119.

35. Jane Gaines, "White Privilege and Looking Relations: Race and Gender in Feminist Film Theory," *Cultural Critique* 4 (1986):59–79.

36. Laura Mulvey, "Visual Pleasure and Narrative Cinema," *Screen* 16, no. 3 (1975):6–18.

37. Fiske, "*Miami Vice*," p. 116.

38. Ibid., p. 117.

39. Ibid., p. 118.

40. See Susan Sontag, "Against Interpretation," in her *Against Interpretation* (New York: Delta, 1966), 3–14; Herbert Marcuse, "The New Sensibility," in his *An Essay on Liberation* (Boston: Beacon Press, 1969), 23–48; Hebdige, *Subculture*.

41. Walter Benjamin, "The Work of Art in the Age of Mechanical Reproduction," trans. Harry Zohn, in *Illuminations*, ed. Hannah Arendt (New York: Schocken Books, 1969), 241–242.

2
Popular Television and Commercial Culture: Beyond Political Economy

John Fiske

Budd and Steinman's well-argued case for the centrality of political economy to the study of television contains a critique of British cultural studies for failing to recognize this centrality. Accepting for a moment their flattering nomination of me as the approach's transatlantic popularizer, I would like to make a defensive point before engaging more positively with some of the issues they raise. The work by me that they cite[1] was commissioned to explain and demonstrate the cultural studies approach to television; it is hardly surprising, then, that it did not deal with political economy. It is one of the ironies of the exportability of scholarship that work from the Birmingham Centre for Contemporary Cultural Studies has become relatively widely known in the United States, whereas that from the equivalent center at Leicester University has received less recognition—which, considering that one of its main strengths is its contribution to the understanding of the political economy of British media, is a pity. The work of the two centers in Britain is both complementary and contradictory, and each precedes along its own path in the knowledge of where the other is going. The comparative absence of the political economic perspective in cultural studies is perhaps less disabling in the United Kingdom than it is in the United States, and Budd and Steinman have done us a service by pointing this out so cogently.

Many of my colleagues in the area would be uneasy with my nomination as their spokesperson, so I must, with thanks, reject the role and enter the debate on my own responsibility, though from a background of cultural studies, however eccentrically I may make use of it.

Mainstream, commercial television is the arena in which the struggle for popularity is fought, and central to my work at the moment is the problem of understanding popular culture within a late capitalist economy. Although no cultural text can be adequately described in terms of commodity theory, clearly the role of economics is vital. There is almost no popular culture today that does not survive and exist solely because it makes money. It is only highbrow culture that needs subsidizing. People who automatically think that profit-making culture is bad need to rethink, because they can arrive at that conclusion only from an extremely elitist and, for those of us on the left, untenable position. To argue that anything that makes a profit is therefore socially or politically undesirable leaves us in the position of allowing for no contemporary popular culture, or only paternalistically or politically produced popular culture, which, if history is any guide, will inevitably be *un*popular.

This is an uncomfortable position for anyone on the left to occupy. Unfortunately, it is a position that much traditional Marxist cultural theory, particularly that of the Frankfurt School and of political economy, and much post-Althusserian ideological theory has promoted. And the end point of such theories is that, whatever we mean by "the people"—I'll address that in a moment—they are, in some way, cultural dupes. The necessary implication is that they are the dupes of the industry or of ideology, and that there can be no such thing in their position as popular discrimination; there can be no such thing as popular taste or as popular cultural capital. These are all issues that I think are crucially important to investigate, issues that contradict a lot of the last generation of ideological and cultural theory.

So I want to address the following questions: Why is commercial art popular (and it *is*)? What do we mean by popularity? and Why is its description in terms of its profit motive entirely inadequate? What I want to get away from is the idea that the people are in any way the dupes of the industry. They're not; the television audience is not adequately described by the metaphor of the couch potato. Equally, I want to reject an even more insidious assumption, which is that the culture industries produce an essentially singular audience. Whether we conceive of this audience in terms of the one-dimensional man of Marcuse or the commodity of political economy, the concept is still one of a singular, homogenized mass audience.

So what do I mean by "the people," then? First of all, "the people" is an abstract potential concept. It is not an empirical one; it does not exist in objective reality. The people, the popular, the popular forces, are a shifting set of allegiances that cross all social categories; various individuals belong to different popular formations at different times, often shifting between them quite fluidly. By "the people," then I refer to this shifting set of social formations or social allegiances, which are described better in terms of people's felt collectivity than in terms of external sociological factors such as class, gender, age, race, region, or what have you. Cultural allegiances can, and often do, coincide with class and other social categories, but they don't necessarily; they can often cut across them, they can often ignore them. Thus, while there clearly are interrelationships between the structure of the social system and cultural allegiances, they are not rigidly determinate.

Next, I must specify what I mean by "culture." A simple, workable definition is that culture is the circulation of meanings and pleasures that people give to and gain from their social experience. While the socioeconomic and political systems may provide the material basis for our social experience, the meanings that we give to that experience, and the meanings of ourselves and our social relations within it, are the product of culture.

I find it helpful here to conceive of two parallel, semiautonomous economies whose interrelationships are shifting and varied. I call these economies the financial (which circulates wealth in two subsystems) and the cultural (which circulates meanings and pleasures). They can be modeled as in Table 2.1.

Table 2.1
The Two Economies of Television

	Financial Economy		Cultural Economy
	I	*II*	
PRODUCER: produces a	Production Studio	Program	Audience
COMMODITY: which is sold/circulated to a	Program	Audience	Meanings/Pleasures
CONSUMER:	Distributor	Advertiser	Itself

The production houses produce a commodity, which is a program, and in the first circulation it is sold to the distributors, the broadcasting or cable networks, for profit. This is nothing more than a financial economic exchange. But immediately problems occur. The television program does not seem to me to be a commodity of the same sort as a can of beans or a machine gun. It is very much harder to define the use value of a television program than it is of other, more material, commodities.

Marx suggests that the use value of art is its production of aesthetic pleasure, but this seems to be a metaphoric use of the term "use value," compared with the much more material uses of more material commodities. To trace a cultural commodity's "use value," we need to enter the second circulation within the financial economy, in which the program shifts its role and becomes a producer. What it produces is an audience, which is the measure of its use value, and which is then sold to advertisers. Here again, this is a straightforward economic transaction. And many of the positions that I reject, such as those of political economy or the Frankfurt school, tend to concentrate on the model up to here. They are finally content to rest with the idea that the audience is commodified, reduced to a commodity to be sold to advertisers.

In order to maintain this view, they have to ignore the second economy that occurs after this—the cultural economy. Within the cultural economy what is produced and circulated is a series of meanings and pleasures. The audience now becomes the producer. The commodity it produces, if we can use that term, is meanings and pleasures. And the consumer becomes very difficult to envisage, for in this economy there is no valid distinction between production and consumption.

Political economy is at its strongest where cultural studies is at its weakest, and vice versa. Thus political economy is good at analyzing the two circulations of the financial economy, but in order to demonstrate the adequacy of its conception of the audience as a commodity, it has to deny the audience's role as a producer of meanings and pleasures from the commodity or text (see chapter 1). It cannot conceive of the audiences (a) as differentiated and thus capable of producing different meanings and pleasures from the same commodity, (b) as producers of their own culture from the resources provided in part by the cultural industries and in part by their nonmass-mediated sociocultural experience, and (c) as discriminatory, able to choose between cultural commodities and to make some popular and others not; and (d) it cannot conceptualize the cultural commodity as a text that requires "reading."

It is these and related issues that I believe are most important. Any scholarly or research agenda has ideological and political assumptions built into it, and I would like to make mine explicit.

First, assumptions of "the popular." The people make their own popular culture out of the offerings of the industry. Culture can be made and circulated only from within; it cannot be imposed from without. Thus the Reithian enterprise of using the BBC to improve the tastes and the educational level of the British people foundered when the people chose to use the products of the commercial, (initially) American industries for the resource bank of their popular culture.[2] The people are not cultural dupes and are not readily manipulable, either by the greedy barons of the industry or by benevolent paternalists who claim to have their interests at heart. Stuart Hall argues:

> Now, if the forms and relationships, on which participation in this sort of commercially provided "culture" depend, are purely manipulative and debased, then the people who consume and enjoy them must either be themselves debased by these activities or else living in a permanent state of "false consciousness." They must be "cultural dopes" who can't tell that what they are being fed is an up-dated form of the opium of the people. That judgment may make us feel right, decent and self-satisfied about our denunciations of the agents of mass manipulation and deception—the capitalist cultural industries: but I don't know that it is a view which can survive for long as an adequate account of cultural relationships; and even less as a socialist perspective on the culture and nature of the working class. Ultimately, the notion of the people as a purely *passive*, outline force is a deeply unsocialist perspective.[3]

Equally, the people in capitalist societies are not in touch with some "authentic" folk culture that can be used as a touchstone against which to measure the inauthenticity of mass culture.

In the cultural domain, the term "people" refers to social groups that are relatively powerless and may be addressed as consumers, but do not necessarily respond in that way. They have cultural forms and interests of their own that differ from, and often conflict with, those of the producers of cultural commodities. The autonomy of these social formations from the dominant is only relative, and never total, but it originates in their marginalized and repressed histories that have intransigently resisted incorporation, and have retained material, as well as ideological, differences. For some groups these differences from the dominant may be small and the conflicts muted, but for others the gap is enormous. For a cultural commodity to be popular, then, it must be able to meet the various cultural interests of the people among whom it is popular as well as the economic interests of its producers.

In capitalist societies, popular culture is made out of those cultural commodities that a large number of the various and shifting formations of the people have chosen as the resource from which to make meanings that are pertinent to their social position and in the making of which they can find pleasure. Popular culture is created at the interface between the products of the mass media and the material social experiences of the subordinate.

Second, assumptions of the audience. I respect popular audiences because they are diversified, discriminatory, and productive. Let me elaborate briefly on each adjective in turn. The audiences, and I stress the plural form of the word, come from the huge diversity of social groups and subcultures that constitute the social formations of late capitalist societies. The people, as argued above, are diversified socially along many interfacing axes, of which some of the most instrumental are gender, class, race, age, nation, education, religion, occupation, region, and marital status. The social position of any one person within this network of axes is nomadic, unstable, and thus the social alliances he or she forges shift as different axes are granted different priorities at different times.[4]

The audiences are discriminatory. The only way the culture industries can accommodate popular discrimination is to produce a repertoire of products from which the people choose. Twelve out of 13 pop records fail to make a profit; the vast majority of films fail to make a profit on their first release, and many fail even to cover their advertising budget.[5] Television series are axed by the dozen in midseason despite all the efforts of promoters and schedulers. Far from being among the most powerful of the capitalist industries, the culture industries are, I would argue, capitalism at its most vulnerable.

In television, popular choice is exercised not only among genres, programs, and commercials, but also within programs. Altman[6] characterizes "Dallas" as a "menu" from which people choose their meanings and pleasures.[7]

An example of audience productivity is Hodge and Tripp's work on children and "Prisoner."[8] In Australia, in the early 1980s "Prisoner" was either first or second in popularity with young teenagers, particularly girls. Hodge and Tripp investigated this popularity, and found that one of the underlying reasons was that the students were able to read the program as a metaphor for school. This metaphoric relationship between prison and school is actually very precise: both are total institutions, and both exist to turn their inmates into the sort of people that society thinks they ought to be, which may not coincide with the sort of people they think they are or wish to be. There are parallels between the wardens and school staff—for instance, the wardens included most stereotypes of schoolteachers: the tough, unfeeling bullying one; the young, nice one the students could get around; the decent one who treated them well but who came down hard if they stepped out of line; and so on. There were also strategies of resistance in "Prisoner"; the prisoners were good at communicating under the eyes of the warders with a secret language of nudges and winks and slang, just like students. There were struggles over cultural control of various domains within the prison. The laundry, where a lot of the program was set, was a site of constant struggle as to whether it was in the control of the prisoners or the warders; the same sort of territorial battle goes on in the school toilets and bicycle sheds during recess.

Throughout, "Prisoner" was being read and used by the schoolchildren to articulate and make their own sense of their experience of subordination and powerlessness within an institutional social structure. The students were reading it in a very active way, articulating it with their social experience and thus making it their popular culture, not because they had been turned into a commodity by it but because it provided them with a discursive repertoire from which to make their popular culture. This sometimes spilled over into their schoolyard games. Palmer,[9] for instance, investigated a case in which a friendly teacher was co-opted to play the role of a particularly unpleasant warden—it was the social role of teacher-warden, and it was the power inscribed in it that was significant, not the personality of the individual filling it.

Popular culture is made popular by the people because of the meanings and pleasures they produce from it. As we go beyond textual analysis and ideological theory, move into realms of cultural ethnography, and start investigating why audiences find certain programs popular, why audiences choose to buy certain cultural commodities rather than others, we begin to find that these meanings and pleasures are immensely diverse. They can be understood only in terms of the social situation of the group or people among whom they're popular. Thus, Ien Ang, in her study of Dutch viewers of "Dallas,"[10] found Marxists who read its excessiveness as a critique of capitalism and other viewers who liked it precisely for its glorification of Americanness, of modernity, of plate glass, of the fast-lane life-style.[11] "Dallas" is a remarkably "open" program: Rick Altman's description of it as a "menu" from which various, differently socially situated viewers choose different "meals" is a productive one. It is certainly much more productive than seeing the text as a singular determinate, closing down its meanings and producing a singular dominant ideology.

This reader activity may be a process of selection, as the menu metaphor implies, of attending to some parts of the text and not to others. The woman soap opera fan[12] who taped her show so that she could fast forward through the "boring" bits was only using technology to enhance the process that Gans noticed among Italians in Boston's West End. Arguing that "[t]he West Enders make highly selective use of the popular culture," Gans concluded: "In using the mass media, West Enders are accepting themes from the outside world. Whether or not they are also accepting its values, however, is doubtful. . . . West Enders are careful to select from the large variety of themes those which support their own values."[13]

This selection does not just choose some meanings from a set of relatively equal ones on the program's "menu." Television programs do not offer meanings as equally and freely as supermarket shelves offer goods. They are always structured in dominance, though in some programs, such as "Dallas" or a soap opera, this structure is minimized. Lewis,[14] for example, found that even in as tightly structured a program as TV news, viewers could and did pay selective attention to segments such as a vox pop insert and ignore the narrative that framed them. They thus diametrically changed the "meaning" of the story. Such selection is a generative semiotic process because it changes the syntagmatic relations within the text— and therefore its structure of meanings.

The audiences may also engage in an active reinterpretation[15] of actions or motives represented in the text, or an active writing in of motives not given, reactions not fleshed out in full. They fill these and other syntagmatic gaps in many ways.[16] This "writing" by the audience may go beyond selection and actually change diegetic details, as was the case with Katz and Liebes's[17] Arabic viewers who rewrote the script of "Dallas" into their own culture by making Sue Ellen return with her baby to her father rather than to her brother, or Michaels's[18] Aboriginals who rewrote Rambo into a tribal or kinship, rather than a nationalistic, relationship with those he was rescuing.

This audience activity of producing a variety of socially pertinent meanings from a single text is motivated by the diversity of subordinate positions in society. It is thus an activity structured along lines of domination and subordination. The text is no do-it-yourself meaning kit from which any meaning can be made, nor one in which all meanings are equal. The text not only delimits the arena within which this production of meaning occurs, it also attempts to guide and control this process. Equally, however, the text offers its "weak points," its contradictions and gaps, its heteroglossia and multiaccentuality, which present opportunities to resist or evade its own control and enable it to be made popular among the diversity of the social formations of the subordinate, a diversity that political economy can account for only in terms of market segmentation, and that it therefore cannot see as productive of semiotic difference or resistance.

Despite nearly two centuries of capitalism, and all the ideological power that that entails, our societies have not been totally homogenized, either materially or subjectively. We have to be able to account for diversity and difference within the structures of capitalist societies. We have to be able to recognize that people are socially situated quite differently and that hegemony has to work so hard because the forces of difference and resistance are so intransigently present. Political economy has no theory of resistance. Much previous theorizing on ideology, particularly when it received the psychoanalytic support of Freud and Lacan, is useful only for explaining the forces of homogenization. But what these theories are not good at is accounting for the intransigence, the resistance, the diversity of social groups that still exists despite the power of these homogenizing forces. It is productive to model late capitalist societies along the opposing forces of homogeneity on the one hand and of heterogeneity on the other, of unity and difference. Theories that concentrate on the financial side of my model are ones that concentrate on the homogenizing forces, the unifying forces. When we go out and investigate the meanings and pleasures that people actually get from those commodities, we are shifting the theoretical impulse toward investigating the diversity, the forms of resistance, the intransigence of the different formations of the people who make up television's popular audiences.

The culture industries have often been cast as the almost irresistible villains of capitalism; they are seen as the agents who sell this unfair socioeconomic system to the people. But, conversely, it is arguable that the culture industries are among the least efficient and the least effective of all capitalist industries. The record industry's ability to produce only a single financial success for every 12 failures is hardly the sign of a terrifyingly efficient or hegemonically powerful industry. The record of the cinema industry is, if anything, worse; and even in television, with its "captive" audiences, expensively produced and promoted failures are at least as common as the successes. And the producers don't know which commodity is going to be chosen, which will be made popular; they are relatively powerless in the face of popular choice.

We must, therefore, be able to account for popular discrimination. Far from being passive dupes, the people are highly discriminatory in the cultural commodities that they choose to make into their popular culture. For generations we have had an academic industry devoted to establishing and exploring the process of critical discrimination. But as yet we have hardly begun to investigate popular discrimination, even though we do know[19] that one of the defining characteristics of a fan is the drawing of strong critical lines between what one is a fan of and what one is not. Being a fan requires making very firm and very precise critical judgments. We know very little about how such popular critical judgments are made, though we are beginning to realize that they are made quite differently from judgments in the "official" critical industry. Popular discrimination is less concerned with the structure of the text than with the social uses it can be put to, and with the pertinence of the meanings that any one audience can activate from it and use in ways that are culturally specific to itself.

The power of the people to influence the industry, rather than vice versa, is also the origin of cultural innovation. The industry's needs would be best served by constantly reproducing what has gone before. The motivation for change, for new cultural forms, comes solely from the people. If it weren't for this, the industry would simply do what suits its economic interest, which is reproducing and recycling old material all the time. And it doesn't, because it isn't allowed to. The cultural industries are heavily generic because they believe that genre can minimize their market risk by identifying previously successful forms and audience expectations. But what is interesting is that the people, the audiences, seem to want to cut across genre boundaries and to deny the effectiveness of genre as a limiting strategy of both production and reception; the new popular shows are nearly always ones that confuse genres. "Hill Street Blues" is a clear example, uncertainly poised between the genres of soap opera and cop show. "Cagney and Lacey" is similar. "Moonlighting" is ambivalently a romance, a sit com, and a detective show. In order to keep up with the changing social formations, to produce polysemic texts that can be read in different ways, the industry is forced by popular taste to go beyond its safe, generic habits and conventions. Reproducing last year's popular taste is a sure way to lose popular audiences.

Cultural change is built into the system because, as I argued earlier, we must understand "the people" as a consistently shifting set of cultural allegiances. Social formations are changing all the time. "The people" is not a static or reactionary concept; it is not a solid, immovable mass; it is a highly dynamic set of social formations. And it is the main source of social change. We need to reevaluate our notion of "the people"—and therefore of television audiences. Far from seeing them as the weakest, most powerless, commodified end of the economic chain, we actually need to see them as the driving force behind the cultural industries. They constitute the force that keeps the industries on their toes, that keeps them uncertain, that keeps them moving.

Popular texts, then, in order to be popular, in order to meet the diverse needs of a diversity of audiences, have to be polysemic. They have to be full of a variety of potential meanings. Recognizing this requires a shift in the dominant modes of textual analysis because textual analysis and textual theory have traditionally concentrated on recovering from the depth of the text the final, "true," ideological, latent meaning. Textual analysis has concentrated on the forces of closure within the text, the forces of homogenization. We need to take a leaf from the book of deconstructionism (without going far along that road at all) and to shift the focus of textual analysis toward the gaps and spaces, the contradictions and differences within a text that open it up to polysemic readings, rather than toward the forces of homogenization. If we understand society as being in a constant tension between forces of homogeneity and forces of heterogeneity, we need to think of texts in precisely the same way. Texts, too, have structures that attempt to close them down and homogenize their meanings, but if they are to be popular, they must also have the resisting elements within them that open them up, that diversify them, that oppose the forces of closure.

The notion of popularity and the popular commodity that I want to put forward, then, is one that comes back constantly to this opposition between homogeneity and heterogeneity, between unity and difference. The popular must always occur within the negotiation of this field of force. This is, of course, a particular inflection of the constant interplay of powers and resistances, of domination and subordination. As Stuart Hall says, "[T]he people versus the power-bloc: this, rather than 'class-against-class', is the central line of contradiction around which the terrain of culture is polarized. Popular culture, especially, is organized around the contradiction: the popular forces versus the power-bloc."[20] This leads Hall to conclude that the study of popular culture should always start with "the double movement of containment and resistance, which is always inevitably inside it."[21]

If cultural theory is to move into the realms of social and political action, then the theory I'm proposing suggests that the site of intervention should not be only the moment of production but should also include the moments of reception. Intervention in the consciousness and readings of audiences may be much more effective than in the processes of production. The trouble is, of course, that intervention at the level of policy and production is comparatively easy to operationalize, and it is all too tempting to argue that where we ought to intervene is where we can easily intervene. Intervention at the reception end is much harder to operationalize, though schools, families, and community groups offer possibilities. But one should not let one's assessment of the effectiveness of intervention be swayed by the ease of intervention. Such instrumentalism has misdirected communication studies for too long.

Running throughout my argument has been the notion of resistance. I think it is helpful to separate resistance into two basic types, a political or social or organized resistance that is active, that works in the domain of the political or the social, and an interior, internalized resistance that works within the realm of the cultural. Though the two are separate, they are also interrelated—sometimes directly, more often indirectly.

Janice Radway[22] found that her fans of romance novels discriminated in favor of those novels in which the hero started off cruel, insensitive, unthinking, aloof, distant. The heroine was a feisty, spunky sort of girl who fought this. She suffered, and through her suffering the male was feminized into becoming more caring, sensitive, aware of others, less aloof, less distant. Not until he had been adequately feminized would she marry him. Their readings and pleasures in the romance quite contradicted the patriarchal, ideological view of it as a training of women for marriage. The fans' readings were ideologically resistant, even though these resistances were essentially interior. But some women reported first that the reading of romances was disapproved of by their husbands and that this was part of their pleasure in reading them—the act of reading itself was a resistance to husbandly power. And, second, after reading the romances, some felt more self-confident, their self-esteem had been increased, and they felt more able to stand up against the demands of their husbands and families, and to resist them.

We have to be chary about saying that popular culture provides escape or fantasy that leads one away from the real. Rather, we need to understand that the escapes and fantasies that people choose to indulge in are very often ones that enable them to return to the real and to be more effective in it. An example similar to Radway's is provided by Ellen Seiter's[23] study of soap opera fans in Oregon. Some of these women reported their enjoyment of a character's extramarital affair, their husband's disapproval of this enjoyment, and their use of this to threaten, albeit playfully, his power to demand fidelity from them. But even where this interior semiotic resistance does not translate directly into social resistance—whether in the politics of the family or in the wider political domain—it should not be dismissed or undervalued. The power to think differently, to think resistingly, is crucial to social change. Only a minority of people ever act collectively in the social realm, but the effectiveness of their social action depends upon all those interior semiotic resistances, for it is the existence of these resistances that makes them into social spokespeople, rather than eccentric, isolated activists. The interior is political.

This leads us to raise again the role of ideology in culture. Stuart Hall recognizes how valuable political economy is in explaining the "external" aspects of communication, but he argues that its contribution cannot carry much conviction until it addresses more adequately the ideological character of the communication system it investigates. His exposure of its failure to deal properly with ideology is so cogent that I can do no better than quote it at length:

The reflective model of ideology which the "political economy" approach conceals is a source of its continuing crudity and reductionism, which exposes it to the critique of the practitioners of the dominant paradigm. Its model of class relations and of the class origin of ideology is out of date, inherited not produced as genuine scientific knowledge of present social realities. Its view of the conspiratorial and class-originated source of ideology, which does not match the necessity of a theory of articulations, is itself woefully inadequate. Its notion of the ideological field being already prescribed, in place, by the givenness of a class structure is exposed to the critique of teleology. It has no conception of the struggle for meaning. It has no idea of how ideology constructs social subjects or positions them in relation to social and political practices. It still believes that hegemony is another word for the ideological incorporation of the masses. And against the real reconceptualization of what the struggle over meaning implies, it stitches into place instead an equally inert model of the passive consumers.[24]

To explore further ways in which television viewers are more than such "passive consumers" possessing nothing but their buying power, I would like to develop the notion, raised earlier, of cultural capital. The term comes originally from Bourdieu,[25] who used it to liken cultural capital to economic capital, in that both serve discriminatory purposes in society; they are unequally distributed and draw clear distinctions between those who possess them and those who do not. Cultural capital underwrites the social differences produced by economic capital by grounding them in a "natural" taste. Cultural discrimination, which includes both "abilities," such as literary taste, and more external factors, such as habituated access to cultural institutions like art galleries and theaters, is a way of validating class difference. Cultural capital works to support and naturalize economic capital by locating its consequent social differences not in economics but in discrimination and taste, so that it is the "naturally" finer, more sensitive people who can understand and appreciate art, opera, classical music and literature. And capital, which is the result of this "natural" discrimination, works to validate their equal possession of economic capital.

I wish to extend the notion of cultural capital to include that of a *popular* cultural capital that is consistently nagging away at the validated cultural capital in a way that does not happen in the economic sphere. There is no popular economic capital to keep bourgeois economic capital under pressure, but in the sphere of culture there is such a force. There is a variety of popular discursive competencies through which popular audiences engage with the text, fill its gaps and spaces, and activate its meaning potential in socially pertinent ways. These competencies, tastes, and pleasures that constitute popular cultural capital are essentially ideologically resistant, and have been maintained through academically ignored and invalidated forms found in oral culture and in the culture of everyday life. Television is an enormous provoker of conversation, people talk about it endlessly, and through their talk they incorporate it into the culture of their everyday lives. The meanings of television are not just reference points for comparative judgments, not just shared cultural experience, though they are, of course, both of these; they are as "real" a part of everyday experience as doing the shopping, playing with the kids, or mowing the lawn. Ethnographic research[26] has shown the immense variety of roles that watching television can play in the culture and politics of the family, how it is inserted into everyday life by a variety of popular social practices. Its diversity of roles in the cultural economy is far greater than its commodification process in the financial.

To conclude, I would like to reiterate that commercial television is very much more than the profit it makes for its producers, distributors, and advertisers, and watching it is equivalently more than being subjected to a commodification process. There is a real paradox here that left-wing academic theories have been inclined to avoid—partly, I suspect, because it is discomforting to face up to. This paradox is that in nations where there is a choice between public television (with its ethos of "service," of the "national good," and so on) and commercial television, popular tastes are always better met by the commercial system. The profit motive appears to be more effective in producing cultural commodities out of which the various formations of the people can constitute their popular culture than do apparently "purer" motives, whether these be moral, political, aesthetic, or nationalist.[27] As yet, public television, with its noneconomic motives, has tended to serve middle-class interests and definitions of culture: those who wish to develop an intentional, programmatic, and "responsible" cultural policy, however benevolent, altruistic, and politically correct their intentions, are noticeably reluctant to submit such a policy to the test of popular pleasures and popular discrimination.

The culture industries, on the other hand, depend for their very existence upon their ability to meet these tastes, to survive this discrimination. They may not, and they do not, fully understand how such pleasures and tastes operate; they may not, and they do not, understand how the people make popular culture out of their products, or which of their products will be chosen for this purpose—but they have evolved a series of hit-and-miss production strategies that enable them to meet popular taste in some fashion, however limited. Those of us who wish to broaden and extend the range of cultural products in our society, who would like to see greater cultural and social diversity and the empowerment of the subordinate that this entails, have more to learn from the cultural industries, and from their competent, literate popular viewers, than we do from many traditional academic and economic theories whose central position in academia is now being challenged.

NOTES

1. John Fiske, "British Cultural Studies," in *Channels of Discourse: Television and Contemporary Criticism*, ed. Robert Allen (Chapel Hill: University of North Carolina Press, 1987), 254–289.

2. Dick Hebdige, "Towards a Cartography of Taste 1935–1962," in *Popular Culture, Past and Present*, ed. Bernard Waites, Tony Bennett, and Graham Martin (London: Croom Helm/The Open University Press, 1982), 194–218; Richard Hoggart, *The Uses of Literacy* (Harmondsworth, England: Penguin, 1957).

3. Stuart Hall, "Notes on Deconstructing 'The Popular'," in *People's History and Socialist Theory*, ed. Robert Samuel (London: Routledge and Kegan Paul, 1981), p. 232.

4. David Morley, *Family Television* (London, Comedia, 1986), 42–43. Morley gives a clear hypothetical example:

Perhaps this issue can be made clearer if we take a hypothetical white male working-class shop steward (identified in the *Nationwide* project) and follow him home, and look at how he might react to another *Nationwide* programme, this time in his home context. First, it would seem likely that in his domestic context, away from the supportive/regulative mores of the group of fellow shop stewards with whom he viewed the "News" tape in the *Nationwide* interviews, the intensity of his "oppositional" readings will be likely to diminish. But let us also look at how he might respond to a few items in this hypothetical *Nationwide* on different topics. So, his working-class position has led him to be involved in trade union discourses and thus, despite the weaker frame supplied by the domestic context, he may well still produce an oppositional reading of the first item on the latest round of redundancies. However, his working-class position has also tied him to a particular form of housing in the inner city, which has, since the war, been transformed before his eyes culturally by Asian immigrants, and the National Front come closest to expressing his local chauvinist fears about the transformation of "his" area; so he is inclined to racism when he hears on the news of black youth street crimes—that is to say, he is getting close to a dominant reading at this point. But then again his own experience of life in an inner city area inclines him to believe the police are no angels. So when the next item on the programme turns out to be on the Brixton riots he produces a negotiated reading, suspicious both of black youth and also of the police. By now he tires of *Nationwide*, and switches over to a situation comedy in which the man and woman occupy traditional positions, and his insertion within a working-class culture of masculinity inclines him to make a dominant reading of the programme.

5. Graeme Turner, *Film as Culture* (London: Methuen, in press).

6. Rick Altman, "Television/Sound," in *Studies in Entertainment: Critical Approaches to Mass Culture*, ed. Tania Modleski (Bloomington: Indiana University Press, 1986), 39–54.

7. For further examples of the audiences choosing meanings from a program, see Ien Ang, *Watching Dallas* (London: Methuen, 1985); Elihu Katz and Tamar Liebes: "Once upon a Time in Dallas," *Intermedia* 12, no. 3 (1984):28–32; "Mutual Aid in the Decoding of *Dallas*: Preliminary Notes from a Cross-Cultural Case Study," in *Television in Transition*, ed. Philip Drummond and Richard Paterson (London: British Film Institute, 1985), 187–198, also in *Television: The Critical View*, 4th ed., ed. Horace Newcomb (New York: Oxford University Press, 1987), 419–432; and "On the Critical Ability of Television Viewers," in *Rethinking the Television Audience*, ed. Ellen Seiter (London: Methuen, in press).

8. Robert Hodge and David Tripp, *Children and Television* (Cambridge: Polity Press, 1986). Some of their work is summarized in greater detail than here in John Fiske, *Television Culture: Popular Pleasures and Politics* (London: Methuen, 1987).

9. Patricia Palmer, *The Lively Audience: A Study of Children Around the TV Set* (Sydney: Allen and Unwin, 1986).

10. Ang, *Watching Dallas*.

11. See also Katz and Liebes, "Once upon a Time," "Mutual Aid," and "Critical Ability."

12. In conversation with the author.

13. Herbert Gans, *Urban Villagers: Group and Class in the Life of Italian Americans* (New York: The Free Press, 1962), 193–194.

14. Justin Lewis, "Decoding Television News," in *Television in Transition*, ed. Philip Drummond and Richard Paterson (London: British Film Institute, 1985), 205–234.

15. John Tulloch, *Television Drama: Agency, Audience and Myth* (London: Methuen, in press), gives the example of a plot line in the Australian soap "Country Practice" that dealt with youth unemployment. Viewers in a working-class school found that it confirmed their social experience: that there was a shortage of jobs, school qualifications were irrelevant, and unemployment was a fact of their class life. Boys in a middle-class school, however, also found that the plot confirmed their social experience: that unemployment was largely the fault of the unemployed, and that if they stayed in school and got good grades, there would inevitably be good jobs for them.

16. Robert C. Allen, *Speaking of Soap Operas* (Chapel Hill: University of North Carolina Press, 1985), argues that the episodic, segmented form of soap opera produces many and large syntagmatic gaps that the "reader" has to fill. Fiske, *Television Culture*, elaborates this and gives examples, such as that of Charlotte Brunsdon, "Writing About Soap Opera," in *Television Mythologies: Stars, Shows & Signs*, ed. Len Masterman (London: Comedia/MK Media Press, 1984), 82–87.

17. Katz and Liebes, "Mutual Aid."

18. Eric Michaels, "Aboriginal Content," paper presented at the Australian Screen Studies Association Conference, Sydney, December 1986.

19. See Lawrence Grossberg, "Another Boring Day in Paradise: Rock and Roll and the Empowerment of Everyday Life," *Popular Music* 4 (1984):225–257; and Janice Radway, *Reading the Romance: Feminism and the Representation of Women in Popular Culture* (Chapel Hill: University of North Carolina Press, 1984).

20. Hall, "Deconstructing 'The Popular'," p. 238.

21. Ibid., p. 228.

22. Radway, *Reading the Romance*.

23. Ellen Seiter, Gabriel Kreutzner, Eva-Marie Warth, and Hans Borchers, "'Don't Treat Us like We're so Stupid and Naive': Towards an Ethnography of Soap Opera Viewers," in *Rethinking the Audience*, ed. Ellen Seiter (London: Methuen, in press).

24. Stuart Hall, "Ideology and Communication Theory," in *Paradigm Dialogues: Theories and Issues*, ed. Brenda Dervin, Lawrence Grossberg, Barbara O'Keefe, and Ellen Wartella (Beverly Hills, CA: Sage, in press).

25. Pierre Bourdieu, "The Aristocracy of Culture," *Media, Culture and Society* 2 (1980):225–254.

26. See Morley, *Family Television*; Palmer, *Lively Audience*; Tulloch, *Television Drama*; John Tulloch and Albert Moran, *A Country Practice: Quality Soap* (Sydney: Currency Press, 1986); Dorothy Hobson, *Crossroads: The Drama of a Soap Opera* (London: Methuen, 1982), and "Housewives and the Mass Media," in *Culture, Media, Language*, ed. Stuart Hall, Dorothy Hobson, Andrew Lowe, and Paul Willis (London: Hutchinson, 1980), 105–114; and Ian Uwe Rogge, "The Media in Everyday Family Life: Some Biographical and Typological Aspects," in *Rethinking the Television Audience*, ed. Ellen Seiter (London: Methuen, in press).

27. See Ien Ang, "The Vicissitudes of 'Progressive Television,'" paper presented at the International Television Studies Conference, London, July 1986; Simon Blanchard and David Morley, eds., *What's This Channel Fo(u)r? An Alternative Report* (London: Comedia, 1982); Nick Garnham, "Concepts of Culture: Public Policy and the Cultural Industries," *Cultural Studies* 1, (1987):23–37, for further discussion of the problems of cultural policy and popular tastes.

II
CRITICAL STUDIES OF DRAMATIC SERIES

3
"Dallas" Refigured
Marsha F. Cassidy

In 1980, *Time* magazine called the plot of "Dallas" "a Rube Goldberg machine of the seven deadly sins."[1] Since then, the plot has more than quadrupled in length, and the metatext[2] has turned its way through a vast maze of virtue and vice. Although 1985 was the last year the series ranked either first or second among the top-rated programs in the United States, "Dallas" held steady as America's tenth most popular program in 1986–1987,[3] and the 1987 cliff-hanger placed third across the nation for the week of May 11.[4] Some 25 million viewers still tune in "Dallas" every Friday night.[5] No longer a fad, "Dallas" has survived the uncertainties of network television to become a staple of American popular culture.

The great length of the "Dallas" text and its duration since the pilot season in the spring of 1978[6] offer a new perspective from which the series can be refigured. Questions about "Dallas" as a transforming and unfolding saga can be studied in retrospect after more than a decade. Over the years, what formal properties and fundamental narrative structures have been expressed in the metatext? And, related to this, how does the narrative form of "Dallas" shape both the ideological issues that have dominated "Dallas" criticism and the process by which audiences understand these issues?

The purpose of this chapter is not to reveal the "true meaning" of "Dallas" for all viewers, however. Formalists have been criticized, and rightly so, for presuming to discover the secret design hidden in the carpet,[7] forgetting that viewer responses are varied and negotiated. When a television text is seen as a "dialogic" mechanism,

as Horace Newcomb argues it is, the viewer is assumed to be active—
"accepting, rejecting, and modifying what is offered."[8] A textual
approach to "Dallas" is the first step in a "reader-oriented
criticism," however, in which the text is studied as a schematic for
meaning production but the viewer is presumed to make sense of the
text by filling in "gaps,"[9] the narrative connections the text omits.
While John Fiske argues that the text on the television screen is "a
potential of meanings that can be activated in a number of ways,"
he adds that "this potential is proscribed and not infinite."[10]
Because the text delimits readings, it becomes an important object
for study.

No matter how objectively the responses of actual viewers are
critiqued, they take on meaning in the interaction with a textual interpretation.[11] Ien Ang, for example, based her arguments about the
early seasons of "Dallas" upon an analysis of 42 Dutch viewers'
responses to a feminist hypothesis she constructed about the text.[12]
The work now of Elihu Katz and Tamar Liebes, which analyzes the
responses of matched focus groups in Israel and the United States to
a single episode of "Dallas," interprets these responses in light of
issues addressed by the text: "value questions about family life, living by the rules, loyalty, money vs. happiness, civilisation vs. 'the
frontier,' the invasion of the family by business, and vice versa."[13]
Likewise, my own study of viewer reactions to the controversial
"dream solution" that brought Bobby back to the series[14] necessarily reflects my textual assumptions about "Dallas." Any criticism,
including this study, is an "ideological bid" for the meaning of a
text.[15]

My approach here designates "Dallas" as a special kind of
melodrama whose serial properties heighten its effect as an
ideological forum. Its value as a "dialogic" text springs from a plot
that expresses multilayered hypotheses about social behavior to
which viewers or groups of viewers can respond actively and richly.
The work of Katz and Liebes verifies that "the reading" of
"Dallas" "is a process of negotiation between the story on the
screen and the culture of the viewers, and it takes place in interaction among the viewers themselves."[16] In their study, "Dallas"
stimulates literal interpersonal dialogue; in my own study, too, the
"dream solution" evoked public (and emotion-charged) dialogue
within the social forum of a popular radio call-in show.[17] In each of
these examples, viewers are in part testing ways of filling in
ideological gaps in the text. It is not within the scope of this chapter
to discuss the literal dialogues that "Dallas" provokes within the

culture, except through brief examples. Rather, I am interested here in what Newcomb calls, metaphorically, the "internal dialogue"[18] of the text, particularly the visual treatment in the series and its plot "machine."

In the process of making sense out of "Dallas," viewers can and must refer to "ideological codes"[19] outside the text. The "ideological problematic" Charlotte Brunsdon discovers in the British serial "Crossroads" also frames the subject matter of "Dallas." She says the "field in which meanings are made . . . is that of the 'personal'; more particularly, personal life in its every-day realization through personal relationships." The action in "Dallas," like the action in "Crossroads," is a "dialogue of emo-tional and moral dilemmas."[20] In "Dallas," these predicaments speculate about what the acceptable modes of conduct are in business and family life.

Functioning like traditional melodrama to reward right-minded behavior and to punish the antisocial, "Dallas" offers the viewer "solutions" to the ethical problems developed in the text. The viewer is then free to accept or reject in varying degrees the norms expressed within these outcomes. Unlike melodrama that is more simply structured, however, the superstructure of "Dallas" requires the viewer to fill in more gaps on every level, to participate actively in what Peter Brooks calls "the play of the ethical mind."[21] It is in this play that the dialogic function of the text is realized.

Before I turn to the structural foundation of "Dallas"—the multiplication of story lines, the delay and staggering of subplot closure, and the text's extravagant "duration"[22]—I want to discuss another aspect of the series that foregrounds the dialogic process: the set of stylized visual conventions that make up the "Dallas" lexicon.

In the framing, location, and movement of the camera, the "Dallas" viewer is literally "positioned" to see what is meaningful in the text. The camera spotlights character interactions and the moral conflicts raised within them. Through framing, the camera directs the viewer to the relationships under scrutiny, most often between two people, frequently among three, sometimes among many more. The often repeated zoom-in signals a close inspection of the human face, the fast zoom-in connoting the additional element of surprise, the slower zoom-in suggesting a special intensity in the emotional content. The repetition of the medium close-up and the close-up, especially in combination with the lengthened duration of these shots,[23] invites the viewer to "gaze"[24] upon the performer's face. So, too, does the now-conventional freeze frame that completes each episode at that very moment when a character is landed "in a new, psychologically conflictual situation."[25] Each of these techniques rivets attention upon the emotional action that lies beneath the surface and the string of moral choices that make up the story.

While words are often privileged in "Dallas"—when Bobby asks Pam to remarry him, for example, or when Sue Ellen angrily accuses Kristin of shooting J. R., or when Ellie declares J. R. will no longer be the president of Ewing Oil—they are but a clue to the true locus of meaning—the feelings, motives, and moral deliberations of the characters, accentuated by a purposeful camera. Visual representations create dialogue "even when characters do not speak."[26]

The most direct way the "Dallas" visual style sets up dialogue is through the "quasi-omniscient" vantage point[27] in the series that fosters what Tania Modleski calls "multiple identification."[28] This shifting perspective encourages the viewer to accept the "interest-vantage"[29] of many different players and allows the spectator a privileged "inside view" of each player's private world. Wayne Booth argues that the inside view in literary narrative works rhetorically to "build sympathy even for the most vicious characters."[30] In "Dallas," too, the inside view diffuses a black-white assessment of a character's conduct during private scenes with the camera. Ellie sits alone at the dining room table, and the viewer can read in her face her renewed determination to fight Jock on the Takapa project, despite her fear that she will lose her husband; Cliff paces nervously in his office as he is about to consummate the biggest business deal of his life; in the depth of her alcoholism, Sue Ellen struggles not to take that first drink.

Importantly, the text favors inside views of J. R., which sometimes disclose a sinister glee or a wicked thought but at other times betray a vulnerability, a secret doubt. One of the best examples occurs when J. R. learns for sure that John Ross is his son. Only the camera watches as J. R. privately embraces the baby for the first time, with a look of relief and tenderness upon his face. When the episode ends in a freeze frame of this picture, the spectator is asked to consider J. R. in a new way. The frequent use of the inside view throughout the series undermines the simple polarization of good and bad associated with conventional melodrama. In "Dallas," there are contradictions—refinements. The viewer must look carefully to interpret what is seen.

The narrative structures underpinning the series further encourage active interpretation. "Dallas" is a "polyphonic story,"[31] expressed through the interweaving of multiple story lines, repeated closure delay, and the repetition and expansion of material over time. Each of these formal characteristics privileges a dialogic reading of the text as questions of personal conduct are inextricably interlinked and compared.

The "multiplicity principle" David Thorburn has found in nonserial melodrama[32] generates in "Dallas" a text that redoubles ethical considerations. That multiple stories are told "all at once" suggests that no subplot can be decoded except in juxtaposition to other story lines. This web enfolds narrative meaning within a vast plot system that the viewer must unravel to "read." Because the subplots in "Dallas" are not merely contiguous, but convergent and divergent as well, each intersection of subplots demands the reassessment of the characters in light of their shifting relationships, alliances, and enmities. In "Dallas," the multiplicity principle is multiplied many times over.

The most frequent discussions regarding the serial structure of "Dallas" have focused upon a second principle of storytelling: narrative closure. Critical consensus has been that, like daytime soap opera, "Dallas" is an endless narrative that is devoid of closure. This absence of closure in both daytime and prime-time serial drama has become the assumption upon which important ideological conclusions have been based. Critics have cogently argued that without final closure, the "hermeneutic" code of narrative is subverted, and the adventure-story ending associated with nonserial melodrama, in which good reliably triumphs over evil, is voided.

How can a narrative "predicated upon the impossibility of closure"[33] demonstrate what Thorburn calls melodrama's "reassurance-structure"?[34] If the work of melodrama is to rehearse the confrontation between virtue and vice, and to expunge the villain again and again,[35] then, it is argued, soap opera undermines the possibility for melodramatic expression because the form "has no *telos* from which meaning can be retrospectively constructed."[36] As Jane Feuer observes, the "moral universe of the prime-time serials is one in which the good can never ultimately receive their just reward, yet evil can never wholly triumph."[37]

Continuing this line of argument, serial dramas are viewed as either "open" and morally ambiguous texts that allow for multiple aberrant readings, or as static works that imitate women's forever frustrated expectations in a patriarchal world. Feuer concludes that the prime-time family sagas, including "Dallas," represent "a[n] expression of cultural contradictions . . . bearing what appears to be a right-wing ideology by means of a potentially progressive narrative form."[38] Ang discovers in "Dallas" a "tragic structure of feeling," resulting from the viewer's perception that the characters "live in the prison of an eternally conflictual present,"[39] the confines of the patriarchal family.

A study of "Dallas" as it has evolved since 1978 makes clear that narrative closure is not absent in the metatext, however. While certainly "Dallas" has not reached any final resolution, it is equally obvious that the series is replete with subplot endings, or what Allen has dubbed "mini-closures,"[40] and that these endings are meaningful markers. It is also apparent that a certain number of conflictual "givens" in "Dallas" formulate overarching plot lines that resist resolution: the feud between Cliff and J. R., for example, or the love-hate relationship between Sue Ellen and J. R., or the star-crossed love of Bobby and Pam. I will explain more later about how these ongoing conflicts are integrated into the melodramatic structure of "Dallas" through amplification. It is important to stress, however, that even though the series as a whole has no final resolution, and even though some plot lines appear at first glance to be static, subplots do end in "Dallas," and it is within subplot closure that meanings can be inferred.

As in traditional melodrama, the characters in "Dallas" are held accountable for their moral actions, and the text supplies its version of retribution in subplot closure. The fate of Jeff Farraday illustrates this point at its simplest extreme. Farraday is a character presented to be at the "bad-bad" end of the moral spectrum.[41] He has helped Kristin extort money from both J. R. and Jordan Lee; worse still, he is abusive with Bobby, a favored character, in a blackmail scheme against the Ewings, and Bobby says directly that he doesn't like Farraday and will kill him if he ever approaches Pam again. Farraday is also a drug abuser and a drug dealer; his final villainy is that he sells his own son to Bobby for $30,000. These acts do not go unpunished, however. In a resolution that functions as it might in traditional melodrama, Farraday is murdered by his drug suppliers. Although Bobby is suspected and questioned in the murder, he is eventually released, and Farraday is obliterated as a threat to Bobby and Pam.

Other master villains in "Dallas" meet their deserved fates: Kristin Shepard, who, high on drugs, falls to her death from the Southfork balcony; Rinaldo Marchetta, who is murdered by rival drug smugglers; and, more recently, B. D. Calhoun, a soldier of fortune killed by Bobby and Ray moments before he attempts to murder John Ross before J. R.'s eyes.

Viewed in retrospect, the "Dallas" text can be shown to stagger and delay subplot resolution, but not to void it. Because each episode of "Dallas" ends with a "hook" suspended in a freeze frame—rather than with the conventional resolving climax—scenes of narrative closure are pushed into unconventional positions. They can and do occur almost anywhere within an episode: in the first scene of the first act (when J. R. is vindicated in Kristin's death), in the second scene of the fourth act (when Edgar Randolph evens the score with J. R.), or in the next-to-last scene of the last act (when Sue Ellen is able to nurture John Ross for the first time). Subplot closure may be deemphasized by its unconventional placement, but it is not missing.

Once the convention of weekly closure was put aside in "Dallas," the program became a real serial, free to arch irresolution across many, many episodes or even over many seasons. The uncertainty about John Ross's paternity, for example, was the first continuing subplot in the series.[42] It began in episode 15, when Sue Ellen discovered she was pregnant—and taunted J. R. with the line, "Chances are, it's yours"—but wasn't resolved until the Ewings learned the conclusive results of a second blood test in episode 44. Other story lines stretch across many seasons. The fate of Rebecca Barnes Wentworth, Pam and Cliff's lost mother, began in the fourth season and ended in the sixth. Closure delay in "Dallas" leads directly to the text's fictional "duration," the final property of serial narrative.

Although real time and story time are not identical in "Dallas"—the passage of time in the summer months being virtually ignored in the series, for example—references in the text remind us that the two chronologies are roughly concurrent. For example, when Wes Palmerlee tells Ellie in the episode aired October 11, 1986, that he is really her husband Jock, she replies that Jock died five years earlier. (More specifically, Jock is presumed dead in "The Search," first aired January 8, 1982). A continuous, long-running narrative like "Dallas" gives characters "both histories and memories,"[43] making possible a "multiplication of motives and antecedents"[44] across time. "Dallas" uses television's formal potential for duration to complicate ethical dilemmas diachronically.

To read "Dallas," codes of conduct must be brought into play, but the narrative form of the series requires a constant testing and retesting of normative solutions offered by the text. The discourse of "Dallas" conjectures that right and wrong are interlocked, that virtue is flawed and vice is tempered. A spectrum of values is constructed and reconstructed. A version of retributive closure governs the "Dallas" text—but with a twist. While simpler straight-line melodrama defeats objectified evil, "Dallas" is a kind of melodrama that figures an order of moral norms; recompense is made proportionally, in a hierarchy of virtue and villainy. The interwoven and ongoing text of "Dallas" constructs a system that portrays the moral predicaments of the characters, always in relationship to each other, and then metes out the complicated requitals they have earned.

In the resolution of the simple Farraday subplot, for example, a whole set of cultural values is asserted by the text: extortion is wrong; blackmail is wrong; drug abuse and drug dealing are wrong; it is wrong to sell a child for profit. I think it would be difficult to find many "Dallas" viewers who believe Farraday deserved a better fate. In this case, the narrative solution presented by the text is probably close to a "consensus."

Many subplot endings produce requitals that are grounded in a much more complex moral interplay of the characters, however. In the intricate structuring of the subplots, the viewer is called upon to fill in the "gaps," to make sense of the text by supplying the implied set of values, and then to negotiate a reading of the text's solution from personal experience. This is the dialogic process.

J. R. is the figure in "Dallas" whose conduct most consistently calls for an active reading. Although his actions are frequently presented as immoral, they are often situated within a set of motives that the viewer can approve or at least understand. This is not to say that J. R. doesn't deserve punishment or get it. Again and again his schemes backfire, his parents step in to take away his power, Bobby foils his malicious designs, or he is tormented in those relationships in which he is most vulnerable.

J. R., like the other characters in "Dallas," cannot be evaluated at any given time except in relation to the conduct of the characters around him. The Edgar Randolph subplot is a good example. Randolph is the government official whom J. R. successfully blackmails into revealing the sealed bids for a valuable offshore oil tract in the Gulf of Mexico. In an escalation of the Barnes-Ewing feud, J. R. schemes to trick Cliff into buying the tract for an exorbitant price, hoping to force Cliff into financial ruin. J. R.'s sleazy method is mitigated in the text, however, when Cliff is portrayed as ambitious, vain, and greedy, and when it turns out that the crime J. R. is blackmailing Randolph to keep secret is child molesting. The story of the molestation is first revealed by the victim's mother to Ray and Donna, structuring an abhorrence for the deed that Ray himself verbalizes. Where do the viewer's sympathies lie now? With J. R.? with Randolph? with Cliff? with Donna, who is sympathetic to Randolph? with Ray? It is the posing of these questions that invigorates "Dallas" as a value-charged forum, placing in the foreground "the moral and ideological frameworks"[45] that inform the action.

In the closure of these subplots a normative reading is suggested, although the viewer is free to reject it. As the camera slowly and sympathetically zooms in on Randolph, he tells Donna and Ray that the shame of his past crime drove him to a lengthy reformation through psychoanalysis. He also explains that because he broke the law in revealing the bids, he has voluntarily resigned his government position. Ray is won over, and Donna urges Randolph to confess everything to his wife so that no one can ever blackmail him again. In the next act, Randolph, accompanied by his wife (who clearly has forgiven him), forces his way into J. R.'s office and punches him in the stomach. On the one hand, then, Randolph, who is guilty of child molesting and revealing a sealed bid, "punishes" himself by resigning, but in doing that and in confessing his crime to Donna, Ray, and his wife, he is rewarded on the other hand by freedom from a dark secret. J. R. has earned the blow, but his other punishments are more severe. His scheme immediately effects an angry promise of increased vigilance from Bobby. More important, in the long run, his plan backfires and catapults Cliff into wealth. After a period of unnerving uncertainty that serves as a just penalty to Cliff for his greed, and only hours before Cliff faces complete financial ruin, the offshore wells come in, making Cliff a multimillionaire and a more formidable enemy than ever to J. R.

If Peter Brooks is right that melodrama has become "the principal mode for uncovering, demonstrating, and making operative the essential moral universe in a post-sacred era,"[46] then "Dallas" can be seen as a melodramatic forum for value speculation. Its polyphonic plot necessarily elicits reflection about the conduct of one's life. Its structure generates a fabulous interplay of characters as personal ethics are tested and retested, measured and remeasured, as subplots converge, separate, and converge again, formulating a grand scheme of dilemmas and solutions.

Because "Dallas" has endured on network television for so many years, its dialogic potential has been enhanced in one final and important way. The duration of the series across fictional time has created a plot in which each episode that is added makes more and different interpolations possible. This diachronic potential creates a fluid metatext. As the series evolves, the plot is continually revised and "refigured."[47]

In the simplest form of refiguration, important value-charged elements of the back story are brought into the present and retold by a "disguised narrator"[48] in a way that is technically redundant but that suggests the rightness of a subplot resolution. When Cliff and Jamie attempt to seize control of Ewing Oil, for example, the company is saved when Jock's first wife, Amanda, insane and institutionalized for years (last seen in episode 51, aired March 14, 1980), produces the necessary document to disprove Jamie's claim (in the May 3, 1985, episode). The viewer is reminded through dialogue that Jock's morally correct decision to tell Ellie and his sons about Amanda and to support Amanda financially for the rest of her life after their divorce pays off for his heirs when Ewing Oil is rescued.

The extended duration of the text not only permits the surprise convergence of old subplots with new ones but, more important, offers a progressive enrichment of meanings through "amplification," a "horizontal . . . expansion or an unrolling" of themes and events, "charged with echoes of the past and premonitions of the future."[49] In those overarching plot lines that resist final resolution in the series (even though subplots within them are temporarily solved), amplification is a way of layering new meanings upon conflicts that are superficially repetitive. Executive producer Leonard Katzman calls this development "variations on a theme."[50] Refiguration opens up even more gaps in the text. As Allen suggests in his study of daytime soap opera, "The text might initiate [a] movement back across portions of the text already read . . . but it cannot specify what will be recalled. The text provides the reference, but the reader provides the context within which the recalled event is embedded."[51] The "Dallas" viewer is given considerable room to participate actively in meaning production in the varied repetitions of events.

The dissolution of Ewing Oil that concluded the 1986–87 season is a case in point. In the summer of 1985, *TV Guide* said "Dallas" was "showing the strain of recycled plots: how often can Ewing Oil be up for grabs?"[52] But the varied repetitions of subplots that threaten the survival of Ewing Oil time and again constitute patterns that culminate in the loss of Ewing Oil in the tenth season. In each of the subplots, J.R. puts Ewing Oil at risk either because he uses corporate money to fight personal battles or because he schemes to guarantee the survival of the company in an underhanded and dangerous way.

In the fifth season, for example, he risks $100 million of company money to pressure Clayton Farlow into returning John Ross to Southfork, a scheme that fails when Ellie steps in and removes J. R. as president. He also repeatedly uses the resources of Ewing Oil to undo Cliff Barnes. Dangerous foreign oil schemes form another pattern. In the third and fourth seasons, J. R. barely escapes losing the company in an illegal Asian oil enterprise that includes the toppling of a foreign government; and in the sixth season, an equally corrupt Cuban oil deal is foiled (and Ewing Oil saved) by Bobby and Ray. In J. R.'s third attempt at an illegal and unsavory plan to boost oil prices—the destruction of oil fields in the Middle East—Bobby and Ray can avert tragedy only within the family (when they rescue John Ross from B. D. Calhoun), but they cannot prevent the demise of Ewing Oil. Jeremy Wendell, an oil tycoon who has been trying to buy out Ewing Oil since the fourth season, outsmarts J. R. When the government forces the Ewings to sell the company at a fraction of its real value, Wendell is ready to buy. The pattern of three is completed, and J. R.'s luck runs out.

In a similar way, refiguration works in "Dallas" to effect what Katzman calls "character realization."[53] The extended plot of the series becomes character descriptive, circumscribing in the main characters the ethical boundaries for each personality. Through repetition, characters express the possible variations of behavior innate to their psychological makeup, incrementally changing but also remaining true to themselves. Because virtue and vice are contained to some degree within each main character, and because this balance is always changing, the audience's response is under constant revision. Philip Capice, Katzman's predecessor, said about the continuing characters in "Dallas," "There are no traditional heroes. . . . Our characters are multidimensional and flawed. Just like real people."[54] Pressured hard enough by a justifiable cause, for example, even virtuous Bobby resorts to forgery and blackmail in the sixth season. This inherent duality of the main characters in "Dallas" complicates even further the reading of ethical issues.

Refiguration also helps to explain the repetitive behavior in some characters akin to a tragic flaw: Sue Ellen's long-running compulsion to drink, or Lucy's persistent misjudgment of lovers, or J. R.'s drive for power and profit that motivates his dangerous alliances with villains who ultimately threaten the Ewing family. While it is true that "Dallas" expresses no single reversal that effects an immutable revision of character, subplot endings do accomplish a transformation of characters over time. When viewed across ten seasons, the expression of character is not merely repetitive but forward-moving.

J. R.'s succession of sexual alliances, for example, collectively delineates Sue Ellen as the one woman J. R. cannot leave behind. His sexual affairs form several different associations in the metatext. There are women J. R. shares with Cliff Barnes, for example: Julie, Sue Ellen, Afton Cooper. There are women J. R. exploits to gain a business or personal advantage: Holly Harwood, Katherine Wentworth, Marilee Stone, Sue Ellen, April Stevens, Kimberly Cryder. There are women who give J. R. a satisfying chase: Leslie Stewart, Sue Ellen, Mandy Winger. Taken together, these patterns of association describe a man who is incapable of using sex for love and, conversely, women who variously use J.R. for reasons of ambition or personal weakness.

Emerging from these patterns, and ultimately standing apart from them, is Sue Ellen, the one woman in his life he does love, in his own way. And certainly Sue Ellen has been gradually transformed across the series from a childish and materialistic "Mrs. J. R. Ewing" into an integrated person who can put aside her own compulsions (including her compulsion to drink) for the well-being of herself first, and then of others (Peter Richards, Dusty Farlow, and her own son).

Because refiguration assumes that past events will be remembered, a crucial problem is imposed upon the text as it continues to expand over the years. How much can a viewer be expected to recall? Certainly when elements of a "back story" are reiterated in dialogue, this accommodates a viewer who may or may not remember the complex antecedents of a story line. In this way, the text is constructed to allow for a complete reading but also to provide enough information in summary for the less frequent viewer to make sense of it.

In the episode aired November 14, 1986, for example, when Bobby and Pam discover on their wedding day that Jenna is pregnant with Bobby's child, Pam explains that what hurts the most is knowing she can never give Bobby the child they both want. Through this dialogue, even a newcomer to the series can understand why Jenna's pregnancy is an especially painful problem for Pam. For the competent "Dallas" viewer, however, the associations are more poignant. In my viewer-response study, 21 of 115 long-time fans cited subplots in which Pam had been unsuccessful in bearing a child when asked to write down any episodes or story lines that especially stood out in their minds. Since the survey was conducted in late November and December 1986, it seems likely that Jenna's pregnancy and its consequences for Pam evoked these earlier associations. In this case, at least, many long-time viewers spontaneously contextualized Jenna's pregnancy in terms of Pam's desperate unhappiness more than six seasons earlier.

The most publicized and most controversial example of refiguration in "Dallas," however, is the reconstruction of the entire 1985–86 season as Pam's nightmare, a simple narrative trick that rectified "good" Bobby's death (although his sacrificial death to save Pam's life was melodramatically allowable because it was heroic). The refiguration of an entire season of subplots, some resolved, many still unresolved, opened up tremendous gaps in the text that the viewers were expected to interpolate actively. It is no wonder that viewers reported feeling angry, betrayed, confused, and duped; the "Dallas" text was provoking the ultimate dialogue. What is interesting, however, is that the pool of fans I surveyed quickly recovered from this narrative jolt; they accepted the dream solution because it brought the beloved Bobby back. More important, however, their attentions were adroitly diverted to a possible new refiguration, one that the viewers in my study found as threatening as Bobby's return: Had Jock come back from the dead?

To my surprise, the viewers I surveyed strongly disliked the possibility of Jock's return. One viewer said the old Jock could never be as "wishy-washy" as Wes Palmerlee; another said, "Wes Palmerlee looks like a wimp compared to the original . . . Jock Ewing."

These responses gave me an insight into how "Dallas" as a whole has been refigured over the years. The possibility of Jock's return exposed a fundamental change in the ethical balance point of "Dallas." His return would destroy Ellie's "tent-pole" relationship with Clayton. Since the death of actor Jim Davis in 1981 and the loss of Jock as Ellie's foil, "Dallas" has drifted slightly to the left of where it began. A frontier man and a man of action—like the traditional western hero—Jock lived by a tough code of personal ethics; he was a rugged individualist whose values were sometimes out of step with the new Dallas. He was power-hungry, hot-tempered, pragmatic; but he was a devoted father and husband, deeply in love with Ellie, and his handshake was his word. His powerful personality and the forceful influence he wielded over his sons created in the early years of "Dallas" an alignment with a code of conduct that tilted the series to the right of center.

When "Jock" reentered the text in the tenth season, it became obvious that the series had shifted its consensual center point; its values had moved closer to a sentimentalized ethical humanism balanced upon the more liberal codes of Ellie-Clayton. In order for "Jock" to fit in, he had to be softened, as Wes Palmerlee was, or he had to turn out not to be Jock, which he did. The ideological baseline of "Dallas" had been altered too much for viewers to reincorporate Jock easily. But Wes Palmerlee promised Ellie he would return someday. Perhaps in a future season he will come back as Jock Ewing and refigure the Ewing saga yet again.

NOTES

1. Richard Corliss, "Larry Hagman: *Vita Celebratio Est*," *Time*, August 11, 1980, p. 64.

2. Robert C. Allen considers the metatext of a daytime soap opera to be "the sum of all its episodes broadcast since it began." See his "On Reading Soaps: A Semiotic Primer," in *Regarding Television: Critical Approaches—An Anthology*, ed. E. Ann Kaplan (Frederick, MD: University Publications of America, 1983), 98.

3. Lee Winfrey, "'Cosby' Tightens Grip on the Nielsen Ratings," *Chicago Tribune*, December 10, 1986, sec. 5, p. 13.

4. *Electronic Media*, May 25, 1987, p. 28.

5. *Pocketpiece Report: Nielsen People Meter*, November 9–15, 1987, p. 13. This figure represents the average audience projection of persons age 2 and older for the first eight telecasts of "Dallas" in the 1987–88 season.

6. "Dallas" premiered on the CBS network April 2, 1978, in the first episode of a five-part pilot series that is counted as the first season. (Thus, 1978–1979 is considered the second season, although it was the first full year. The 1987–1988 season was the eleventh). The principal cast included Jim Davis as Jock Ewing; Barbara Bel Geddes as Eleanor Ewing (Miss Ellie); Larry Hagman as J. R. Ewing; Linda Gray as Sue Ellen Ewing; Patrick Duffy as Bobby Ewing; Victoria Principal as Pamela Barnes Ewing; Charlene Tilton as Lucy Ewing; Ken Kercheval as Cliff Barnes; David Wayne as "Digger" Barnes (later replaced by Keenan Wynn); David Ackroyd as Gary Ewing (later replaced by Ted Shackelford); Joan Van Ark as Valene Ewing; and Steve Kanaly as Ray Krebbs. Larry James Gianakos, *Television Drama Series Programming: A Comprehensive Chronicle, 1975–80* (New York: Scarecrow Press, 1981), and *Television Drama Series Programming: A Comprehensive Chronicle, 1980–82* (Metuchen, NJ: Scarecrow Press, 1983), lists air dates, numbers, and titles for each episode of "Dallas" through 1982. Episode titles and plot summaries through 1986 are in *The Complete Book of "Dallas": Behind the Scenes at the World's Favorite Television Show*, ed. Suzy Kalter (New York: Harry N. Abrams, 1986), 68–200. In this chapter, all episode numbers are from Gianakos; other references are to Gianakos, to Kalter, and to my own records.

7. See Robert C. Allen, "Reader-Oriented Criticism and Television," in *Channels of Discourse: Television and Contemporary Criticism*, ed. Robert C. Allen (Chapel Hill: University of North Carolina Press, 1987), 74.

8. Horace Newcomb, "On the Dialogic Aspects of Mass Communication," *Critical Studies in Mass Communication* 1 (1984): 46–47.

9. See Allen, "Reader-Oriented Criticism," pp. 74–112.

10. John Fiske, "British Cultural Studies and Television," in *Channels of Discourse: Television and Contemporary Criticism*, ed. Robert C. Allen (Chapel Hill: University of North Carolina Press, 1987), 269.

11. See John Cawelti, "The Question of Popular Genres," *Journal of Popular Film and Television* 13 (Summer 1985):55–61.

12. Ien Ang, *Watching Dallas: Soap Opera and the Melodramatic Imagination*, trans. Della Couling (London: Methuen, 1985).

13. Elihu Katz and Tamar Liebes, "Once upon a Time, in Dallas," *Intermedia* 12 (May 1984):29.

14. Marsha F. Cassidy, "Viewer-Response Criticism and Bobby Ewing's 'Return' to *Dallas*," unpublished paper.

15. Fiske, "British Cultural Studies," p. 284.

16. Katz and Liebes, "Once upon a Time," p. 28. See also Liebes and Katz, "Dallas and Genesis: Primordiality and Seriality in Popular Culture," *Media, Myths, and Narratives: Television and the Press*, ed. James W. Carey. Newbury Park, CA: Sage Publications, 1988, pp. 113–26.

17. "The Roy Leonard Show," WGN, Chicago, September 26, 1986.

18. Newcomb, "Dialogic Aspects of Mass Communication," p. 42.

19. Robert C. Allen, *Speaking of Soap Operas* (Chapel Hill: University of North Carolina Press, 1985), 89.

20. Charlotte Brunsdon, "*Crossroads*: Notes on Soap Opera," in *Regarding Television: Critical Approaches—An Anthology*, ed. E. Ann Kaplan (Frederick, MD: University Publications of America, 1983), 79.

21. Peter Brooks, *The Melodramatic Imagination: Balzac, Henry James, Melodrama and the Mode of Excess* (New Haven, CT: Yale University Press, 1976), 15.

22. Jane Feuer, "Film Theory/Television Theory," paper presented at the Fourth International Conference on Television Drama, Michigan State University, East Lansing, May 20, 1985.

23. See Jane Feuer, "Melodrama, Serial Form, and Television Today," *Screen* 25 (January–February 1984):10–11.

24. John Ellis, *Visible Fictions: Cinema, Television, Video* (Boston: Routledge & Kegan Paul, 1982), 24. He says television is for "glancing," not "gazing," but at least in this case "Dallas" is an exception.

25. Ang, *Watching Dallas*, p. 53.

26. Newcomb, "Dialogic Aspects of Mass Communication," p. 41.

27. Allen, *Speaking of Soap Operas*, p. 64.

28. Tania Modleski, "The Search for Tomorrow in Today's Soap Operas," *Film Quarterly* 33 (1979):14.

29. Seymour Chatman, *Story and Discourse: Narrative Structure in Fiction and Film* (Ithaca, NY: Cornell University Press, 1978), 152.

30. Wayne C. Booth, *The Rhetoric of Fiction* (Chicago: University of Chicago Press, 1961), 378.

31. C. S. Lewis, *Studies in Medieval and Renaissance Literature* (Cambridge: Cambridge University Press, 1966), 134.

32. David Thorburn, "Television Melodrama," in *Television: The Critical View*, 3rd ed., ed. Horace Newcomb (New York: Oxford University Press, 1982), 539.

33. Allen, *Speaking of Soap Operas*, p. 13.

34. Thorburn, "Television Melodrama," p. 531.

35. Caren J. Deming, *"Hill Street Blues* as Narrative," *Critical Studies in Mass Communication* 2 (March 1985):6.

36. Allen, *Speaking of Soap Operas*, p. 14.

37. Feuer, "Melodrama, Serial Form, and Television Today," p. 12.

38. Ibid., p. 16.

39. Ang, *Watching Dallas*, p. 75.

40. Allen, *Speaking of Soap Operas*, p. 75.

41. Nora Scott Kinzer, "Soapy Sin in the Afternoon," in *Mass Media and Society*, ed. Alan Wells (Palo Alto, CA: Mayfield, 1975), 78, quoted in Mary B. Cassata, "The More Things Change, the More They Are the Same: An Analysis of Soap Operas from Radio to Television," in *Life on Daytime Television: Tuning-in American Serial Drama*, ed. Mary B. Cassata and Thomas Skill (Norwood, NJ: Ablex, 1983), 92.

42. See Marsha F. Cassidy, "The Duke of *Dallas*: Interview with Leonard Katzman," *Journal of Popular Film and Television* 16 (Spring 1988), p. 17.

43. Allen, *Speaking of Soap Operas*, p. 72.

44. Eugene Vinaver, *The Rise of Romance* (Totowa, NJ: Barnes and Noble, 1984), 89.

45. Brunsdon, *"Crossroads*: Notes on Soap Opera," p. 79.

46. Brooks, *The Melodramatic Imagination*, p. 15.

47. Ellis, *Visible Fictions*, p. 147.

48. Booth, *The Rhetoric of Fiction*, p. 152.

49. Vinaver, *The Rise of Romance*, pp. 75, 92.

50. Quoted in Cassidy, "The Duke of *Dallas*," p. 12.

51. Allen, *Speaking of Soap Operas*, p. 72.

52. Dick Friedman and Mike Lipton, "The Worst and the Best We Saw," *TV Guide*, June 29, 1985, p. 4.

53. Quoted in Cassidy, "The Duke of *Dallas*," p. 14.

54. Quoted in *The Complete Book of "Dallas,"* ed. Suzy Kalter (New York: Harry N. Abrams, 1986), 34.

4

Flatulent Conceptions: "The Young Ones," Inoculation, and Emesis

Murray Smith

At the 1985 Edinburgh Festival, the ballet dancer Michael Clark performed with his small company at the Royal Lyceum Theatre. Though Clark's training is in classical ballet,[1] since the mid-1980s he has been incorporating elements of popular culture into his performances: the use of rock music (T. Rex, the Fall), elements of popular dance styles (disco, slam), and subcultural dress styles (glam-rock, punk). He has embraced this collaborative effort further by appearing in the Fall's musical at the Riverside Studios in London, *Hey, Luciano*. In this incorporation of popular styles and mass cultural products, Clark is certainly the most radical dancer to emerge from the classical tradition in Britain (at least in terms of the unexpected audiences he has reached). Along with the fragmentation of classical decorousness through subcultural interruptions there is a profanation of the image and use of the body in classical ballet. In one dance, garbed in lurid red ski pants and a woman's platform shoe, Clark struts across stage to the incantations of the Fall's "New Puritan" while a fellow dancer holds the end of a ticker tape apparently being produced by Clark's rectum (arse).[2] Clearly, we have moved a long way from *The Nutcracker*, or even Merce Cunningham.

The Lyceum is a "major" venue in the hierarchies of the Edinburgh Festival: a voluminous Victorian proscenium, a far cry from the squalid spaces that most fringe groups inhabit. Apparently, then, Clark's performance in the Lyceum perfectly demonstrated the power of the art world to incorporate avant-garde experimentations and flirtations with popular culture. During the performance I attended, however, something strange and exhilarating occurred. As the show mounted to its climax, two young punks started to dance in the central aisle of the orchestra section. One of these demotic dancers was a capable body-popper; the other flailed around in the preferred punk mode. As the Italian suits of the art establishment started to twitch with discomfort, and affronted glances were exchanged across the auditorium, I became aware of the limits of the subversive elements (listed above) as purely formal devices. The threat of Clark's postmodern ballet was effectively bracketed and anesthetized by the institution in which it was performed, reflected in the very design of the building—until the punks broke into their dance. Althusser describes this institutional unity thus:

> Before becoming the occasion for an identification (an identification with self in the species of another), the performance is, fundamentally, the occasion for a cultural and ideological recognition. This self-recognition presupposes as its principle an essential identity . . . : the identity uniting the spectators and actors assembled in the same place on the same evening.[3]

As the extemporizing punks gained confidence—there were, of course, no bouncers on hand, such physical regimentation being a feature only of football matches, rock concerts, and the like—they veered toward the stage, and finally they ascended to it. Now there was almost a literal collision between two cultures on stage: the sophisticated, mannered pyrotechnics of the high avant-garde and the simpler (but no less exhilarating) impulse to shake the body free of, or at least in resistance to, all those social conventions that restrict physical expression in everyday life. This collision, and the transgression of the spatial restrictions of the bourgeois theater, indicate a fundamental contrast between "popular" and "bourgeois" entertainment:

> "Nothing," argues Pierre Bourdieu, "more radically distinguishes popular spectacles—the football match, Punch and Judy, the circus, wrestling or even in some cases the cinema—from bourgeois spectacles, than the form of the participation of the public." For the former, whistles, shouts, pitch invasions are characteristic, for the latter the gestures are distant, heavily ritualized—applause, obligatory but discontinuous and punctual cries of enthusiasm—"author, author" or "encore." . . . A certain distance, Bourdieu argues, has been central in this bourgeois economy of the body: a distance between "reflexion" and corporeal participation.[4]

After the performance finished, the "pitch invasion" by the two punks was drowned by the ritualized applause of the audience. Whether this "invasion" was by design or genuinely spontaneous,[5] I have not been able to discover, but this hardly matters for my argument. If it was deliberate, then it is a credit to Clark that as he becomes incorporated, he constantly shatters the new institutional frame within which he is placed. Deliberate or not, it forcefully revealed the conventions governing spectatorship and the representation of the body, the parameters of acceptable bodily involvement within different class cultures.

This anecdote can serve as a metaphor for the operation of "The Young Ones" (TYO hereafter),[6] a show that builds its comedy, first and foremost, on the bourgeois space and structure of the situation comedy, a space that is then invaded by the "visceral hyperbole"[7] of slapstick, "vulgar" humor. Two problems immediately emerge from this analogy. First, with television, the space of the performance can never literally be invaded. We should not fall prey, however, to a shallow media determinism and suggest that television is, as a result of its spatial inaccessibility, an innately bourgeois medium. The "distance" characteristic of bourgeois spectacle is reconstituted in most situation comedy by the denial of the "fourth look," the direct gaze of character/performer to viewer. Thus direct address works to break down this separation, for example, in Rick's digression on earwax in the episode "Cash":

> Shot 1 (MS, Rick addressing Mike and Vivian): I'm so hungry I could eat my own earwax.
>
> Shot 2 (MCU, Rick addressing camera): And we all know how horrid that tastes, right, kids?

Furthermore, within the diegesis social spaces are constructed that manifest the same drama of corporeality and "reflection." In most sit coms, space is divided into two regions: "inside," the space of stability, usually the home or work, and "outside," the region from which threats to the "inside" emerge.[8] "Space" here is both literal and figurative; the literal space of the home, which represents the ideological "space" of a particular set of values. For example, in "The Dick Van Dyke Show," the stability of Rob and Laura Petrie's marriage is usually threatened by an external agency or institution—for example, an artist's studio, where Rob is exposed to the sensual excesses and "loose" sexual mores of abstract expressionism. TYO, as we will see, continually inverts this binary relationship within the diegesis.[9]

The second problem emerging from the analogy between TYO and Clark's performance is that the opposition on which it is founded, between "bourgeois" and "proletarian" spectacle, is perhaps overly schematic. Class itself is articulated in many different ways (accent, dress, eating habits) and differently within apparently similar societies (accent is a far more significant index of class in Britain than in the United States); and the determinations of class intersect with many others (race, gender, age, region, education). Therefore, a binary schematization seems unduly crude. However, the complex warp and weft of determinations, the proliferation of "invisible" subcultures, does not preclude the evolution of institutionalized forms around broader, clearer oppositions. Certainly the work that has been done on the traditions of twentieth-century comedy suggests that there are two basic modes that correspond closely to Bourdieu's two categories of spectacle. Henry Jenkins terms these two modes the "anarchistic" and the "literary-theatrical," and sets out their distinguishing traits as follows:[10]

Anarchistic	Literary-Theatrical
Stemming from vaudeville, oral tradition	Rooted in nineteenth-century naturalistic drama, literary tradition
Performer dominates character	Character dominates performer
Stereotypes	Individuation, psychological
Spontaneous interaction, reflexivity	Illusionistic, adherence to script
Physicality, sexual candor	Understated verbal humor
Corporeality	Reflection

Jenkins calls for greater historical specificity when dealing with modes of comedy, since the heuristic value of such a table of formal oppositions is attenuated without examination of those historical moments when the categories bleed into one another. My aim is to demonstrate how these two modes interact in TYO, within the social and televisual context of the 1980s. The continuing existence of the two traditions, and the validity of the distinction, can be observed in the contrast between, on the one hand, Benny Hill, Paul Hogan, and Les Dawson, and on the other, "The Good Life," "Yes, Minister," and "Butterflies."[11]

The humor of TYO, I have suggested, lies in its evocation of the bourgeois space of the sit com, which is inflated to tumescent proportions, then inverted and punctured. From this perspective, the structure of TYO is very different from that of "Monty Python's Flying Circus." For all the manifest similarities between the two shows, "Monty Python" had a discrete structure, a series of loosely connected sketches. Though "Monty Python" makes many references to other TV shows and genres, there is no underlying genre, as there is in TYO, on which the parody is constructed. The continuity of the sit com parody is repeatedly fragmented by discrete sketches, but it does constitute a trampoline, an area off which all the other aspects of the show bounce and collide.[12]

There are (at least) four aspects of the show where it simultaneously draws upon and distends the conventions of the sitcom:

1. The organization of setting and space
2. Narrative form
3. Spectatorial address
4. Style of performance.

Initially I want to expand upon each of these aspects, then attempt to explore their intermeshing in a particular sequence.

SETTING AND SPACE

In his structural analysis of the sit com, Mick Eaton suggests that there is a "third model" in addition to the prevalent situations of the "home" and "work," a model that partakes of both— "Doctor in the House" and "Rising Damp" are his examples. The situation usually concerns a group connected outside of their work space, though the family is only tangential—part of the "outside." TYO clearly refers to this model. I would modify Eaton's analysis by suggesting that the family, in this model, is displaced onto the group of characters, so that they play familial roles. In TYO, Rick constantly attempts to fulfill the role of the disciplinary parent over the irresponsible children (Mike, Neil, Vivian). Eaton writes:

The ideology held by the institution of television as a machine for the production of meaning is that the family is a sufficiently stable situation, settled enough to be able to bear repetition and to deal with the onslaughts of the outside in a recognizable, characteristic way.[13]

In TYO, the difference between the "inside" and the "outside" is questioned by the fluidity of the boundaries between the two. The only "stability" here is that of relentless inversion. The show's structure effects a double inversion. First, it is a sit com that deals with the anti-familial, with that which is typically excluded or marginalized in the sit com—youth. Thus, when Neil asks Mike to buy some toilet cleaner in "Sick," the others react in horror at such a bourgeois, familial gesture: "No way was Cliff Richard sitting on a clean toilet when he wrote 'Wired for Sound'!"[14] The "inside" of this series, then, is the "outside" of most.

This initial inversion is then taken a step further, in that the "outside" in TYO—middle-class, familial life—is shown to be no less grotesque and anarchic than the "inside." Thus, in "Sick," when one of Neil's snot missiles hits the middle-aged/class man in the ear, he retaliates with a brick, and takes great relish not only in smashing a window but also in hitting the woman (whom he believes responsible for the snot) on the head with a second brick—much as Vivian thrives on pummeling Rick and Neil. This double inversion is present throughout the series, but it comes to the fore in "Sick," with a riot developing as a result of the original snot-brick exchange.

The riot is brought into the house ("inside") via Brian Damage, and even Mr. and Mrs. Pie (Neil's parents), champions and agents of "nice" sit coms like "The Good Life" (TGL), are drawn into the riotous spirit as Mrs. Pie smashes a piece of furniture in protest at its shoddiness. The boundaries and difference between the "inside" and "outside" are at every moment subverted and questioned, in contrast with the pattern of controlled destabilization and restoration of the two regions in the conventional sit com.[15]

NARRATIVE FORM

The disruption of this pattern is also related to the narrative form of TYO. In a typical sit com each episode has a basically linear structure. That is, an event will disrupt the stable situation (which effectively exists only in the time between shows), and the narrative will plot the progress and delay of the characters in their attempts to reestablish stability. Every event will feed into this central narrative line, though there may be one or two subplots that run from show to show and have little to do with the particular narrative of any given episode. TYO stretches the tolerance of any sense of continuity to the breaking point, though it always institutes a specific problem/disruption at the beginning of each episode and periodically loops back to it. There are a number of regular, discrete features that disrupt narrative continuity—for example, Alexei Sayle's asides and the subliminal images.

Another device is the evolution of a separate, parallel narrative out of a minor detail in the main proairetic line. In "Cash," for example, Neil believes that a "poltergoost" is responsible for the disappearance of household goods. In fact, Vivian has been stealing them to burn for heat. In a realist narrative, the "poltergoost" line of action would be closed off after Neil had been enlightened. In "Cash," however, two ghosts emerge shortly after Neil has been informed, arguing about the authorship of Shakespeare's plays. We follow the ghosts as they pass through the wall into another house. In this house a woman is watching television, and the action moves to the program she is watching, a mock safety message involving a cricket bat, an overripe tomato, a meringue, and a plastic-wrap packet of mashed banana and jam. After this, the narrative moves back to the main characters as Vivian comes to the window of the woman's house to borrow a cup of sugar. Thus, the metaphor of the "loop" seems appropriate in describing this type of narrative movement.[16]

There are many smaller examples of these narrative non sequiturs; at the beginning of "Sick," for example, Mike interrupts the main line of action three times, each time attempting to ask what a large, uncooked fish is doing in his bed. The mystery is never answered: he can barely pose the question logically. The "fish" does not even return as a motif in a different context. It is, therefore, an utterly discrete narrative segment.

The flouting of narrative continuity and the subordination of character to performer are central features of the anarchistic comedy, that stem from the sketch structure of vaudeville and music hall. But these are also features of the historical and contemporary avant-garde[17]—the play with linearity, between author and character, and character and performer. To what degree can we see these features as deriving from the vaudeville tradition or from avant-gardism? Need we pose the question in this either-or manner? Part of the problem in moving toward an answer is the paucity of historical research on the connections between modernism and popular cultural forms, except in the obvious instance of Brecht. Faced with the problem of disentangling avant-garde from popular practices, the largely textual approach I am taking in this chapter reaches an impasse. The opening anecdote suggests that the mode of reception may be the crucial factor. As long as the audience remained unified in its aesthetic attitude, its detached "reflection," it was unthreatened by the potential offensiveness of Clark's performance. This potential was released only when the punks collapsed the aesthetic distance between stage and orchestra seats, bringing the transgressions of the performance (freedom with the body, sexual ambiguity) that much closer to the social life of the audience.

SPECTATORIAL ADDRESS

A third aspect of the sit com that TYO lays bare and caricatures is its mode of address. John Hartley has argued that in an effort to deal with the massive diversity of actual television audiences, television (and the television industry) has constructed an imaginary, childlike spectator:

> TV is a paedocratic regime; that is, the audience is imagined as having child-like qualities and attributes, TV addresses its audience as children, and is characterized by child-like pre-occupations and actions.[18]

We have already seen an example of TYO's exposure of this mode of address in Rick's earwax aside (". . . right, kids?"); it is constantly present in the bombastic overacting. It may be objected that TYO is targeted at a different audience than the middle-class sit coms with which I am comparing it—specifically, at the youth market. Certain features of the show, like the song section, are directed at this audience; but other aspects of the show, like the literary and political references, are directed at older audiences—college students and yuppies. Furthermore, Rick's mode of address is at about the level of a prepubescent spectator and is, therefore, just as incongruous and parodic in relation to any adolescent as to an adult audience.[19]

As with the (de)construction of spatial boundaries, the parody of sit-com address operates in TYO not merely through caricatural distension but also through inversion. The characters are utterly protean; while one moment they may behave like children, the next they may produce a sophisticated and articulate political comment. At any point a character may slip from an idiom of (archaic) adolescent scatology ("poo-face") to the dry register of the academic, as in Vivian's outburst against TGL:

> VIVIAN (ripping through TGL credits): No, no, no, we're not watching the bloody "Good Life!" Bloody, bloody, bloody! I hate it! It's so bloody nice! Felicity "Treacle" Kendal, and Richard "Sugar-Flavored Snob" Briars! . . . (unclear) . . . They're nothing but a pair of reactionary stereotypes, confirming the myth that everyone in England is a lovable, middle-class eccentric, and I hate them![20]

STYLE OF PERFORMANCE

Earlier I referred to the acting style of TYO as "bombastic." My use of the term indicates how reified the discourse of naturalism is, how it functions as a hidden evaluative criterion: "bombastic" in relation to naturalistic acting conventions. There are a number of more suggestive ways of describing the style of performance: "grandiloquent," in the sense that Barthes talks of the overstated gestures of wrestling;[21] "pantomimic" or "clownlike," conjuring up the excessive "oh, no, he didn't/oh, yes, he did" exchange between audience and performer in the circus, as in this exchange among Rick, Neil, and Vivian at the beginning of "Sick:"

NEIL: Vivian, will you shut up, you're giving me tunnel vision!

RICK: Stop shouting, Neil!

NEIL: Stop shouting yourself!

RICK: I am not shouting!

NEIL: Yes, you are!

RICK: I bloody well am not! If you want to hear shouting, matey, this is it! Eaear! Eaear!

VIVIAN: It's funny, but being ill makes me lose my usual tolerant and easygoing approach to communal living (throws Molotov cocktail into Rick's room).

Alongside this pantomimic "grandiloquence" exists a phatic hyperbole in which we see the inflation of bourgeois niceties to nonsensical proportions—for instance, in Damage/Sayle's line in "Sick": "This has gone on far too seriously long enough by half!"

My concern thus far has been to demonstrate how TYO invokes and undermines the codes and conventions of the sit com as the basis of its comedy.[22] Through a more detailed analysis of a particular segment, I now propose to analyze the interweaving of these devices and to explore more fully the relation in TYO between the "anarchic" and "literary-theatrical" modes, both of which inform the show. At the core of my discussion will be the representation and treatment of the body, the fundamental site of contestation between the two comic regimes.[23] The segment I want to concentrate on is again from the episode "Sick," from the entrance of Vivian's mother to the beginning of the parody of TGL. First, a brief description.

Vivian's (punk) mother enters the living room, telling "the boys" that someone has impaled a head on their fence. She claims to have brought Vivian a present; in fact she has brought him an empty bottle of vodka, and she exits (having pinched Vivian's testicles for being sexist) with the memorable line "Up yours, ugly." The criminal, Damage, makes his demands and lines the boys up against a wall. Part of the ceiling collapses as a result. Neil starts to wail, not at the threat of death but at the impending visit of his parents. The boys rush to clean the house (in fast motion); Damage polishes his gun. Vivian finds three witches in the corridor; they pronounce him Thane of Corridor, Outside Toilet, and the Little Gravelly Patch Next to the Garden Shed. Vivian responds that the idea of his taking over the house by murdering the others "would make a great play." Neil's parents arrive and complain about Neil's involvement in a show like TYO, urging him to appear in a "nice" sit com like . . . "Grange Hill." After a parodic "excerpt" from the latter, Mr. Pie realizes his mistake—he had meant TGL. The credit sequence for the latter show begins, until Vivian leaps through it, refusing to be subjected to such a tasteful show. Rick and Vivian argue about Felicity Kendal. Vivian complains that the police are too "nice" in such shows; a cop enters and smashes a chair on Rick. Mrs. Pie avers, "None of this would ever have happened if you were making a nice show . . . ." The image fades, and the next sequence shows the young ones in their garden, taking on "the good life"—self-sufficiency—and "the timeless wonder of the English countryside."

I have chosen this episode and this sequence because of the explicitness with which it satirizes the conventions of the literary, realist comedy as exemplified by TGL. All comedy transgresses social conventions and codes, but the limits of transgression are set generically. To put it another way, in comedy a certain play with social conventions is permissible—indeed, necessary—but this "playground" is delimited by the dictates of "good taste."

TGL deals with an upper-middle-class couple who decide to surrender their corporate life-styles and attempt self-sufficiency by turning their garden into a small farm. This involves their regular engagement with soil, manure, and animal placentas. The show revolves around the oppositions between the "earthy" Tom and Barbara and their tactophobe neighbors, Margo and Jerry; the "inside" is the pastoral dream of Tom/Barbara, threatened by the demands of the bureaucratic "outside," the clean-shaven corporate world of Margo/Jerry. Within the context of the bourgeois, literary regime of comedy, the show is quite radical, in that it confronts the alienation of the corporate life-style, and reveals a neurotic and repressive attitude toward bodily functions. That it is, however, still firmly within that regime is revealed by TYO's parody:

VIVIAN: Did you see that episode where the pig was going to have a baby? Now that was quite a promising idea. But it was all done so bloody nicely! We didn't see anything!

Just as the discussion in "Panorama" expresses a diversity of views that are nevertheless held within the discourse of parliamentary democracy,[24] so TGL transgresses the conventional treatment of the body to a generically and socially defined degree. Interestingly, TGL finally reveals its position within the larger frame of bourgeois comedy in the episode in which Tom/Barbara are robbed. Finally, we see, they are united ideologically with Margo/Jerry through their common belief in the right of ownership and the sacrosanct nature of private property (not to mention monogamy). Their dream of "the good life" is founded on the nest egg of corporate capital.[25]

Neil's parents are, of course, explicit representatives of the bourgeois values embodied in the literary comic regime. That, at least, is their dominant function, figured immediately in Mrs. Pie's ritualized, distanced kiss into the air in front of Neil, and in her subsequent revulsion at the smell of Vivian. I have already indicated that this characterization is at one point inverted. This play on what constitutes a mother is prefigured by the incident with Vivian's mother. She is initially depicted as everything a mother should not be—sexually explicit, and cruel to her son. She then claims that her mission to the house is to function as a mother should—to nurture her ailing son. This image is set up only to be undermined, as we have seen—"Up yours, ugly!" Thus, the mothers of both Vivian and Neil undergo a series of transmutations that in fact mirror each other:

Vivian's Mother	Neil's Mother
Bad (dress, last present for son when 2 yrs old)	Good (concerned for son's health)
Good (bearing present for son)	Bad (smashes up furniture)
Bad (twisting testes; false present)	Good (encourages son to defend father)

This sequence of inversion upon inversion is suggestive of the mutating, anarchic quality of the show as a whole.

Nowhere is this more apparent than in the segment currently under scrutiny. Neil's parents enter and complain about his involvement with unwholesome types, who turn out to be the cast and crew of TYO. Thus, the fictional Neil is confused with the performer Nigel Planer. Such reflexivity is characteristic of the anarchic comic regime. It is pursued here through the smashing of the chair, the weakness of which is revealed (by Mike) to be a necessity for the next scene, in which it is to be broken on Rick. A little further on, a policeman enters, in direct response to Vivian's complaint that the police are unrealistically depicted in TGL. He then smashes a (false) real chair on Rick, informing him that he would not have done so had he (Rick) been Felicity Kendal. Through this labyrinth of reflexivity, as paradoxical as an Escher drawing, questions of realism and representation are raised, and the relativity of social "truth" is posed. Most significantly, though, this reflexivity is imbricated with all those other elements of the anarchistic regime—most notably the "grandiloquence" of the acting style and the coprophilia. It is this interweaving with those other elements that marks off TYO's reflexivity from the self-consciousness of the literary avant-garde, which tends to be far more cerebral.[26]

The physicality of TYO barely needs documenting—spots, snot, farting, belching are constantly foregrounded. We have seen how snot—rather than any particular character—is the initial motor of the narrative in "Sick."[27] The shit-encrusted toilet eats the brush and belches; Vivian practices acupuncture on Neil with six-inch nails, hammering them, among other places, into his buttocks. Farting carries an even greater importance in "Cash"; so pervasive is the presence of gas that it virtually subordinates the characters. In this episode, Vivian becomes "pregnant"; he is in fact suffering from severe flatulence, incubating a massive fart. It is in conjunctions such as this that the subversive potential of carnival is at its greatest, collapsing the Christian spirituality of conception with the profanity and materiality of gas, not to mention the inversion of sexuality. An immaculate conception indeed!

The body fixation functions in "Sick" to expose the transgressions of bodily expression in TGL as rather slight. This is emphasized in the next segment of the show, in which Vivian "plants" a row of cabbages (six cabbages nailed to a board) while Neil scatters seed—still vacuum packed. In depicting the bucolic dream of TGL as the exercise of Habitat horticulture, "Sick" reveals it to be no more than a myth produced by capital (cf. the plowman's lunch).

At this point, the name of Mikhail Bakhtin becomes unavoidable, but I do not want to employ his notion of the carnivalesque unreservedly. There is, as Colin Mercer has pointed out, a danger in an unthinking transposition of "Carnival" across several centuries (not to mention, in Marxist terms, a major shift in the mode of production, from feudalism to capitalism):

In the body politic popular culture and its modes of reception have been located somewhere below the belt. One response to this, and a mistaken one, is to "go for the vulgar," to sing the glories of an essential and corporeal popular art over the "bourgeois" religions of quiet appreciation and distance or, in some cases, to sing the glories of carnival, citing Bakhtin as they go.[28]

So while Bakhtin is clearly useful in an analysis of TYO, my intention is to consider how the carnival form (as it has been abstracted from Bakhtin's historical study) operates and is modified in the particular textual system and historical context of TYO.

Two elements of Bakhtin's theory of the carnival are salient to my analysis. First, the clash between a classical, literary discourse and a vernacular, oral one. This can be observed linguistically in the shifts from intellectual erudition to regional, working-class vernacular. We have already seen this in Rick and Vivian, but it is most apparent in Alexei Sayle, the fifth member of the group, who appears as a different character each week. In "Sick," as Brian Damage, he slips from sublumpen inarticulateness to intellectual fluency within seconds. In his "asides" as Alexei Sayle, the two discourses are "spoken" simultaneously, the vernacular carried in the scouse accent, the bourgeois, political erudition carried in the content of the jokes:

It's been a terrible blow to my life looking like Mussolini, you know, 'specially when I was a kid. I was about seven, down at the youth club, you know, dancing away like, you know, it was in the sixties, and I was doin' the twist. This girl comes up to me and says, "'Ere, are you Mussolini? I said, um, um yeah, yeah. She said, "I thought you was dead." I said no, it was just me day off. So she pulls me across the dance floor and butted me in the face. I said, what's that for? She said, "That's for the invasion of Crete."

This discursive tension is also manifested in the clash between the two comic regimes: the bodily ("below the belt") humor of the anarchistic, and the verbal humor of the literary-theatrical. As I suggested above, Vivian's "gas pregnancy" is a classic instance of this aspect of the carnivalesque.

The second element of "carnival" relevant to TYO is the "material bodily principle," the obsession with the materiality of the body and, more particularly, with the protuberances and orifices of the body. For Bakhtin, the "carnival" was a means of neutralizing human "cosmic fear" by linking it materially to the environment, rather than aggravating this fear to the point of complete alienation, as, he argues, Christianity did:

The struggle against cosmic terror in all its forms and manifestations did not rely on abstract hope or on the eternal spirit, but on the material principle in man himself. Man assimilated the cosmic elements: earth, water, air, and fire; he discovered them and became vividly conscious of them in his own body. . . . We must here stress that it was in the material acts and eliminations of the body—eating, drinking, defecation, sexual life—that man found and retraced within himself . . . all the cosmic matter and its manifestations, and was thus able to assimilate them. . . . Cosmic terror is the heritage of man's impotence in the presence of nature. Folk culture did not know this fear and overcame it through laughter. . . . Official culture, on the contrary, often used and even cultivated this fear in order to humiliate and oppress man.[29]

It is notable, in this respect, that Mike is (quantitatively) the least important of the four, as he is physically the smoothest of the characters, possessing neither Rick's spots, Neil's hair, nor Vivian's embossed body (spots, studs, safety pins). John Fiske[30] has applied this element of the carnivalesque to contemporary professional wrestling, suggesting that the "excessive materiality" of the "material bodily principle" functions as a release from subjectivity—that is, as a celebration of the materiality of events before they are inserted into discourses (discourses that, by and large, have been employed to cultivate "cosmic fear"). While this is a persuasive account of wrestling, the "material bodily principle" works quite differently in TYO, precisely because the show incorporates the two (class-differentiated) regimes of humor. Wrestling is comparatively univocal. The two regimes in TYO are interwoven in a particular way, characterized by the following excerpt from the beginning of "Sick":

(Vivian is taking money from Rick's "purse.")

RICK: Thief! Thief!

NEIL: Thieves rush in, where angels fear to tread.

RICK: No it's fools, Neil, fools.

NEIL: Thieves rush in where fools fear to tread.

RICK: Andy Williams said that.

VIVIAN: Alexander Pope.

RICK: Oh, well, you're a little snob, aren't you, Vivian?

VIVIAN: Wimp. Pervert. Nobend.

RICK: What repartee! Sticks and stones may break my bones . . . .

VIVIAN: That's the first sensible thing you've said all day. (Vivian hits Rick on the head with a large plank of wood.)

The pattern here, in which Rick is physically punished for his (often incorrect) literary allusions (Pope) and affected vocabulary (repartee) is repeated time and again. Later in the same show,

Damage hits him for making an allusion to "Dr. Kildare."[31] At these moments, the anarchic regime literally launches itself upon the more "refined" literary sensibility. The "bodily principle" thus takes on a specific signification in opposition to the literary-theatrical regime: it signifies tastelessness, baseness, and vulgarity. Within wrestling there is, structurally, no other regime against which it is pitted.[32] From a bourgeois perspective, the "bodily principle" is a chief characteristic of the working class, and is precisely what is meant by the derogations "vulgar" and "tasteless."[33]

I have attempted to specify the way in which different voices (social discourses and comic regimes) are elaborated in a particular text. As Colin Mercer suggests, such a project of specification is crucial if we are to move on from the crude schematization that theory generates, and to recognize the complexity of specific cultural products:

> In his autobiography, Roland Barthes remembers the films of Chaplin where, he confesses, "he found a kind of delight in this art at once so popular and so intricate: it was a composite art, looping together several tastes, several languages. Such artists provoke a complete kind of joy, for they afford the image of a culture that is at once differential and collective: plural. This image then functions as the third term, the subversive term of the opposition in which we are imprisoned: mass culture or high culture."
>
> . . . A critical cultural theory and practice needs more insistently to recognize this complexity and pluralism, the multivocality of contemporary cultural forms. . . . Part of the pleasure which Barthes is hinting at here consists in the fact that these "different languages" do, indeed, hang together persuasively. But not just randomly . . . . We would still have to pose questions of the mechanisms by which these "voices" hang together in this way and not that.[34]

Moving on from this, and as a conclusion to this chapter, I want to consider the pleasures that the particular "looping" of TYO offers, how its pleasures can be distinguished from those offered by the purely anarchistic and the purely literary-theatrical.

Most discussions of pleasure seem to spring from a basic opposition in Freudian theory between passivity ("the principle of constancy") and activity, between instinctual, presocial drives and social restraints. Though pleasure would seem to rely on some movement between the two poles, it is ultimately to be found in the inert, passive state.[35] This is taken to its ultimate in the idea of Thanatos, the death instinct, neatly summed up as follows:

> The idea is that the Nervous System wants to eliminate sensations in order to remain at rest. In short, you desire something in order to stop wanting it, like scratching an itch. Follow this to its extreme and the best way to get rid of feelings is to shuffle off this mortal coil altogether.[36]

In the work of Barthes, the underlying opposition is carried through, although moved onto an entirely social terrain: *plaisir* vs. *jouissance. Plaisir*, the pole of inertia, is now conceived of as a return to comforting, familiar ideological codes. If a nonsocial, nonideological aspect remains, then it is displaced onto the other pole, where *jouissance* is defined as a wrenching out of—or, rather, a falling in between—all codes, into an asocial limbo both terrifying and purifying.[37]

While in the 1970s and early 1980s most cultural theorists placed an emphasis on the *plaisir* terminal, the "commodity fix" notion of pleasure, in which pleasure is conceived of as confirmatory and subjugating, the ground seems to have shifted substantially. Some commentators, such as John Fiske, now argue that pleasure always involves some form of resistance to (rather than complicity with) the ideological codes offered by any given cultural product.[38] My aim here is to approach a definition of the type of pleasure TYO offers, at least to a middle-class, intellectual audience. My definition operates squarely within the opposition described above, although it prioritizes the play between the poles as the source of pleasure. Furthermore, it stays firmly within the social; neither presocial inertia nor postsocial otherness seems to catch the pulse of this type of pleasure.

Nevertheless, Barthes again is useful. In "Myth Today" he describes "inoculation" as one of the rhetorical figures of myth:

One immunizes the contents of the collective imagination by means of a small inoculation of acknowledged evil; one thus protects it against the risk of a generalized subversion.[39]

This, I would like to suggest, is an excellent description for the operation of the literary comic regime. The pleasure offered by such a regime is ultimately complicit, that is, we take pleasure in temporary disruptions caused by conventionalized transgressions.

Am I now going to celebrate the daring subversiveness of TYO, avatars of proletarian freedom? Like Rabelais, the coryphaeus of the people? Not quite. If the term "inoculation" can describe the operation of the literary comic regime, then I would like to suggest another medical metaphor for the play of pleasure and power in TYO: emesis. Refusing merely to flirt with the boundaries of the socially acceptable, the show embraces—indeed, gorges itself on—the bodily excesses of the anarchistic regime, to a nauseating degree—from the perspective of the refined, literary regime. In saying this, I am not suggesting that TYO represents the "destruction of pleasure as a radical weapon.''[40] Pleasure—or, rather, the ways in which we find pleasure—is always more complex, more cunning, than such puritanical polemics admit. Just as there is an intense pleasure in crying, so there is in vomiting up what has been repressed, the "poison" that the social body cannot accept but that never disappears from experience.[41]

We must radically modify notions of pleasure that take human expression at (literally) face value, seeing pleasure only in smiles and laughter, and pain only in grimaces and crying. While it may seem banal to state this, it is remarkable how such simplistic notions persist in critical theory, as well as in quantitative "media effects" work. The metaphor of emesis is felicitous in that it connects with Bakhtin's theory of the carnivalesque; in vomiting we momentarily connect ourselves with the material world in a most intimate manner. My emphasis, though, is on pleasure, and it is through the opposition of inoculation and emesis that we can start to break down the monolith "pleasure," to differentiate and perceive its particular forms and aspects.

NOTES

1. Clark attended the schools of the Scottish Ballet, the Royal Ballet, and the Ballet Rambert.

2. The dance described, *New Puritans*, was part of Clark's 1984 repertoire; it was not performed as part of the Edinburgh Festival show. It is, however, representative of Clark's style.

3. Louis Althusser, "The 'Piccolo Teatro': Bertolazzi and Brecht," *For Marx* (London: Verson, 1977), 149-150.

4. Colin Mercer, "Complicit Pleasures," in *Popular Culture and Social Relations*, ed. Tony Bennett, Colin Mercer, and Janet Woollacott (London: Open University Press, 1986), 59. "Reflection" refers to the mental attitude evoked by the artwork in the Kantian aesthetic tradition: a contemplative, disinterested state removed from the social. See Pierre Bourdieu, *Distinction: A Social Critique of the Judgment of Taste*, trans. Richard Nice (London: Routledge & Kegan Paul, 1986), esp. 485-500.

5. Through his earlier performances within "fringe" culture and his work with punk groups like The Fall, Clark has acquired a sizable punk following—a following that, apparently, does not feel alienated by his movement into the domain of official culture.

6. "The Young Ones," a BBC production, is currently broadcast in the United States on MTV on Sunday nights. The cast includes Rik Mayall as Rick, Christopher Ryan as Mike, Adrian (Ade) Edmondson as Vivian, Nigel Planer as Neil, and Alexei Sayle as the Landlord.

7. Mercer, "Complicit Pleasures," p. 60.

8. Mick Eaton, "Television Situation Comedy," in *Popular Television and Film*, ed. Tony Bennett, Susan Boyd-Bowman, Colin Mercer, and Janet Woollacott (London: British Film Institute/Open University Press, 1981), 26-52.

9. We could argue that television represents the complete reversal of bourgeois space, in that it is just one part of the space of the home, that it is surrounded and enveloped by this familiar space. This differs fundamentally from the design of the church and the theater (institutions that are, of course, historically connected), which rigidly demarcate the spaces of performer (actor, priest) and audience.

10. Henry Jenkins, "Toward a Critical History of the British Screen Comedy," unpublished seminar paper, and "'What Made Pistachio Nuts?': Anarchistic Comedy as a Cultural System," *Velvet Light Trap* (forthcoming). His sources are Orwell's essay on comedy, "Funny, not Vulgar," and his essay on postcards, "The Art of Donald McGill"; Marion Jordan's essay "Carry on . . . Follow That Stereotype," in *British Cinema History*, ed. J. Curran and Vincent Porter (London: Weidenfeld and Nicolson, 1983); and Michael Chanan, *The Dream That Kicks: The Prehistory and Early Years of Cinema in Britain* (London: Routledge & Kegan Paul, 1980).

11. My claims regarding the play with space in "The Young Ones" are made in the context of the contemporary, evolved sitcom form. The enjambment of vaudeville comic conventions with those of literary narrative was common in such early American sit coms as "The Burns and Allen Show," "The Goldbergs," and "The Adventures of Ozzie and Harriet," in which domestic space is "theatricalized." These shows, however, began before the sit com was an evolved, stable form, and the combination of divergent performance conventions takes on rather different significances in a contemporary context. For a fascinating discussion of early televisual form and spectatorship, see Lynn Spigel, "Installing the Television Set: Popular Discourses on Television and Domestic Space, 1948–1955," *Camera Obscura* , No. 16 (1988):11–46.

12. I am referring here to the structure of "Python's" television shows. The films bear more resemblance to TYO, in that they use a particular genre as a platform or "trampoline"—the biblical and Arthurian epics in "The Life of Brian" and "The Holy Grail," respectively.

My insistence on distinguishing the two shows derives from a sense that many offbeat comedy shows are unjustly lumped together under such buzzwords as "carnival" or "zany," as in this extract from John Hartley's essay "Invisible Fictions: Television Audiences and Regimes of Pleasure" (conference paper, 1985, p. 19):

. . . parodies and cross-genre hybrids . . . can seem not just disruptive but even subversive. This applies to those shows that combine social and political criticisms with parodies of TV forms, such as TW3, MONTY PYTHON, NOT THE NINE O'CLOCK NEWS, THE GILLIES REPORT, SPITTING IMAGE, THE YOUNG ONES; such shows virtually constitute a genre of their own now, the genre of zany comedy. [A later version of Hartley's paper is in this volume—Ed.]

Of course the shows have many common features, but each elaborates a different comic mode in a distinct way.

13. Eaton, "Television Situation Comedy," p. 36.

14. There is a double irony here in that whatever Cliff Richard represented in the 1950s, in the 1980s he is the epitome of sanitized, middle-of-the-road pop, with none of the literal filth of punk or the ideological filth of androgynous glam-rockers.

There have been a few sit coms that deal with youth outside of a familial context—"Please, Sir!" comes to mind. But these remain exceptional.

15. The controlled nature of this pattern of destabilization and restoration in the sit com is most clear in Eaton's diagrammatic representation (Eaton, "Television

Situation Comedy," p. 41). It would be difficult, if not disingenuous, to produce a similar diagramming of the movement between "inside" and "outside" spaces in TYO.

16. Another example of this parallel narrative is the love affair between the carrot and the banana in "Bored." Here, elements that are merely "realism operators" in realist narrative assume equal importance with the (displaced) central characters.

17. The avant-garde is, as such, the missing third term from both Bourdieu's and Jenkins's cultural dichotomies. Bourdieu makes some comment on the relation between the avant-garde and popular culture (*Distinction*, p. 294).

18. Hartley "Invisible Fictions."

19. The different broadcast contexts of the show in the United States and the United Kingdom relate to the different audience potentials I am disucssing here. In Britain, the show was typically screened in the evening on BBC2, the more "intellectual" of the two BBC channels, whereas in the United States the show is broadcast on MTV.

20. Richard Briars and Felicity Kendal play the leading roles (Tom and Barbara, respectively) on TGL.

21. Roland Barthes, "The World of Wrestling," *Mythologies*, trans. Annette Lavers (New York: Hill and Wang, 1972), 15-25.

22. Clearly, the technique is basically parody, but I want to specify the operation of this parody in the context of class-oriented forms and pleasures.

23. I am appropriating Harley's metaphor in order to emphasize that these modes are systems of rules that attempt to govern our responses and pleasures, a sense that is lost in the terms "tradition" and "mode."

24. "Panorama" is the BBC's main current-affairs debate show. It is analyzed in Stuart Hall, Ian Connell, and Linda Curtin, "The 'Unity' of Current Affairs Television" in *Popular Television and Film*, ed. Tony Bennett et al. (London: British Film Institute, 1981). 88-117.

25. In saying this, I don't mean to imply that all sit coms, at all times, interpellate the viewer in an entirely closed ideological system because they issue from the bourgeois, literary tradition. Such texts are potentially fractured and polysemic; the robbery in "The Good Life" is a case in point. I am concerned here with a distinction between comic regimes at a larger, possibly cruder, level.

26. See, for example, the work of Jorge Luis Borges, John Barth, Thomas Pynchon, Robert Coover, and Donald Barthelme. There are, of course, exceptions—for example, William S. Burroughs. Beyond literature, exceptions proliferate: Viennese body art and some American performance artists (Chris Burden, Vito Acconci) spring to mind. As I have already noted, there seems to be a limit to the explanatory force of a purely textual approach when distinguishing avant-garde and popular practices. Nevertheless, further work might fruitfully distinguish between liberation of the flesh (an open acknowledgment of the body, in the Bakhtinian sense) and mortification of the flesh (a punishment inflicted on the body for its very materiality; hence, an attempt to "spiritualize" it). My sense is that avant-garde body art relates more to the latter than to the former.

27. The ambiguity of the title "Sick" reinforces this sense of inversion—the characters are sick (ill), but sick (vomit, bodily excretions) is so pervasive that it virtually subordinates the characters. See my comment on farting in "Cash."

28. Mercer ("Complicit Pleasures," p. 60), referring to Mikhail Bakhtin, *Rabelais and His World*, trans. Helene Iswolsky (Bloomington: Indiana University Press, 1984). Although Bakhtin concludes with the claim that Rabelais's "work

sheds its light on the folk culture of humor belonging to other ages" (p. 474), elsewhere in the same work he is much more cautious (e.g., p. 321).

29. Bakhtin, *Rabelais and His World*, pp. 335-336, cited in John O. Thompson, *Complete and Utter Theory of the Grotesque* (London: British Film Institute, 1982), 43.

30. John Fiske, "Rock 'n' Roll Wrestling," paper delivered at the Society for Cinema Studies Conference, Montreal, May 1987.

31. A reference to the American hospital drama of the 1960s, "Dr. Kildare," a show that clearly emerges from the literary, rather than the vaudeville, performance tradition.

32. It could be argued that the conventions of wrestling work in opposition to those of sport (fair play, beauty of the human body), and that these conventions are structuring absences—present in their absence, so to speak. While this can be argued, I would maintain that the coequal textual, present presence of the literary and anarchic regimes constitutes a qualitatively different text, a different elaboration of voices.

33. See Bourdieu, *Distinction*, p. 486, for further ruminations on this matter. These different attitudes toward the body are, of course, socially derived. Farting, belching, and spitting are perfectly acceptable habits among the working class—indeed, they are often the object of competitiveness. But again we need to be wary of ignoring other determinations—these habits, within the working class, are more prevalent among men.

In this light, it is ironic that it is now a norm among contemporary Marxists to denigrate pre-Althusserian notions of ideology as "false consciousness" with the phrase "vulgar Marxism," employing an aspect of middle-class aesthetic snobbery as a rhetorical device in political theory.

34. Mercer, "Complicit Pleasures," p. 62. Barthes quote is from Roland Barthes, *Roland Barthes,* trans. Richard Howard (London: Macmillan, 1977), p. 54.

35. ". . . pleasure is in some way connected with the diminution, reduction or extinction of the amounts of stimulus prevailing in the mental apparatus . . . similarly unpleasure is connected with their increase." (Sigmund Freud, *Introductory Lectures on Psychoanalysis*, ed. James Strachey [London: Norton and Co., 1966], 356). Pleasure becomes detached from the satisfaction of instinctual needs, but other pleasures always echo and replay these initial pleasures. On this, see ibid., pp. 314–315.

36. David Zane Mairowitz, *Reich for Beginners* (London: Writers and Readers/Unwin, 1986), 54. For a more solemn definition, see Sigmund Freud, *Beyond the Pleasure Principle*, trans. and ed. James Strachey (New York: W. W. Norton, 1961), pp. 32–35.

37. ". . . what pleasure wants is the site of a loss, the seam, the cut, the deflation, the *dissolve* which seizes the subject in the midst of bliss." Roland Barthes, *The Pleasure of the Text*, trans. Richard Miller (New York: Hill and Wang, 1975), 7.

38. See, for example, John Fiske and John Watts, "Video Games: Inverted Pleasures," *Australian Journal of Cultural Studies* 3, no. 1 (1985):89–104.

39. Roland Barthes, "Myth Today," in his *Mythologies*, trans. Annette Lavers (New York: Hill & Wang, 1972), 150.

40. Laura Mulvey, "Visual Pleasure and Narrative Cinema," *Screen* 16, no. 3 (Autumn 1975):7.

41. I should stress that this is just one form of pleasure that TYO may offer to a particular audience—I am not attempting an exhaustive account of the show's pleasures. The youth audience may derive more pleasure from the breaking of

televisual codes, a level of understanding where they have a greater competence than many adults. They are less likely to derive the kind of pleasure I have attempted to describe, which hinges on the relation between physical humor and literary "subtlety." Gender would doubtless produce further differentiations of pleasure, although David Morley's ethnographic study indicates that men and women situated in the professional middle class (along with men and adolescents in general) enjoy the show for similar reasons, while housewives dislike the show: "The main point here seems to be that for women for whom maintaining domestic order is their primary responsibility and concern, comedy of this kind is seen as something of an insult, in so far as it is premised on the notion that domestic disorder is funny! . . . It is the women who have moved out of their traditional, feminine position who do not conform to this basic pattern of response." (David Morley, *Family Television: Cultural Power and Domestic Leisure* [London: Comedia, 1987], 170–171). It is partly on the basis of this evidence that I have assumed a relative homogeneity, in gender terms, when dealing with a middle-class, intellectual audience, and the type of pleasure it may derive from the show.

5

Collective Blindness and American Television

Robert J. Thompson

A funny thing happened on TV during the February "sweeps" in 1987. The producers of "L.A. Law" (NBC, 1986–) chose to begin the most important ratings period with a story about an armed robbery suspect being tried for stealing the valuable semen of a breeder's prize bull. The story was such an important part of the episode that it got top billing inthe *TV Guide* description. In one courtroom scene, we learned that the prize bull was now dead. On the evidence table sat the last remaining test tube filled with the precious seed, Black Barney's final issue. Then, in a clumsy moment, the tube was upset and sent careening across the courtroom. In *slow motion*, an effect usually reserved for especially violent or highly emotional scenes, we watched Barney's heritage splatter all over the jury.

Stories like this aren't uncommon on television anymore, but they were just a few years ago. The credit for bringing semen to television should go to the creator and executive producer of "L.A. Law," Steven Bochco. When he first introduced this material (and other scandalous substances) to TV on "Hill Street Blues" (NBC, 1981–1987), however, nobody seemed to notice.

Until its fall from grace, it was hard to find anyone with a bad word to say about "Hill Street Blues." Many saw the show and claimed that American television had finally come of age. To show its approval, the industry gave Emmies, the audience gave Nielsens, and the critics gave almost unanimously good reviews. While the show would later become a superannuated thorn in NBC's side (which the network finally plucked from its schedule at the end of the

1986–1987 season), when "Hill Street" was "in," it was outré. Back then, even in the universities, where commercial television is seldom taken very seriously, "Hill Street Blues" was being validated as a rare example of television "art." In 1984 the British Film Institute published a book including several essays on "Hill Street" that employed a style and rigor usually reserved for analyses of literature or "the cinema."[1]

With all this praise, attention, and analysis, though, one striking feature of the show didn't get written or talked about much: "Hill Street Blues" veritably oozed with filth. Lots of people had, of course, noticed the gritty appearance of the show, and Todd Gitlin acknowledged and described its "make it look messy" approach in his book *Inside Prime Time*.[2] But few had much to say about the show's high density of references (both verbal and visual) to garbage, dirt, feces, urine, flatulence, vomit, saliva, sweat, pus, nasal and vaginal discharges, and semen. It was almost as if a collective blindness had caused this body of details to go unnoticed.

Over the years, I have taught television criticism at the high school, undergraduate, graduate, and adult education levels. Although most of the members of my classes have been dedicated students of television and regular viewers of "Hill Street Blues," most of them had not noticed this seething feature of the show. They registered a good deal of surprise when examples were presented to them. The students had seen most of the episodes from which the examples were taken, but had not noticed the examples as part of a complex and ongoing presentation of scatological material.

One of the remarkable things about "Hill Street Bues" was the frequency with which this material was presented. Each episode used to begin with an "overture" of about five minutes, which always included the morning roll call and preceded the opening theme music and credits. In one episode, this section began with a shot of one of the cops at roll call drawing attention to the state of his digestion by dropping seltzer into a glass of water. Directly after this, one of the regular characters was seen groaning because of the large boil on his buttocks. Still less than four minutes into the show, and still before the opening credits, Howard Hunter, the head of the precinct Emergency Action Team, suggested to the captain, Frank Furillo, a solution to the developing problem of police patronization of prostitutes. When Furillo failed to catch his indirect reference to masturbation, Howard responded, "Judas Priest, man, how to you spell relief?" As Frank walked away, Howard found what he believed to be apple juice in the station's community refrigerator. He asked to whom it belonged and, when no one replied, he took and drank. Spitting it out and claiming that it was rancid, he decided that it "must've fermented." Immediately following Howard's eucharist, Lt. Henry Goldblume opened the refrigerator, then shouted that someone had taken his bottle and that he was due at the urologist in an hour.

In short, within the first six minutes of the show, a time traditionally used on television as an attention getter to hold the audience through the credits and the first set of commercials, references to indigestion, infection, masturbation, the buttocks, and urine were explicitly presented. And the opening of the show was just the beginning. Before the second act of the same episode, the afflicted officer and his partner had an extended dialogue about his boil ("Why don't you get that fella on your tushy reamed? This is a hospital, you savin' it or something?"), the gonorrhea infection of a recently killed cop was discussed ("We're gonna be burying some very dirty blue underwear tomorrow"), and Fay Furillo, the captain's ex-wife, was vomited upon by a drunk as she was paying a visit to the station ("My best pair of boots was just saluted by one of your wine stewards!").

The writers and producers of "Hill Street" carefully exaggerated the number of opportunities that would arise in which bodily fluids and emissions could be presented. Take sweat, for example. The "Hill Street" station was nearly always a place in which to sweat. Often the city experienced a heat wave that lasted for three consecutive episodes. Everyone was sweating profusely. These same conditions were reintroduced later in the season, *in the middle of winter*. In one such episode, it was freezing cold outside. Inside, however, the furnace was malfunctioning and the station became extraordinarily hot. Once again, sweaty bodies populated the screen.

Even the ongoing stories in "Hill Street" were frequently characterized by scatological themes. Throughout the course of the series, for example, Howard Hunter was dealt a surprisingly urine-rich fate: he was urinated on by the governor's dog and later by his own puppy; one of his few romantic interests, a nurse, ran off with a urologist; and, as already mentioned, he drank the specimen of his colleague. Fay Furillo also was cast in an ongoing series of scatological contexts. Burglars entered her home and defecated on her rug ("They didn't only take things. They left something. On the living room rug"), vagrants vomited on her, men (on several occasions) and a woman (on one occasion) exposed themselves in front of her.

Furthermore, many episodes included substantial story lines that featured bodily emissions. One such story concerned the delivery of chop suey to all of the employees at the station. Before long, there were lines at the rest rooms and references to diarrhea, vomiting, and peristalsis. In another episode, a man in a filthy tenement had somehow gotten his head stuck between the wall and the toilet bowl, and the bathroom was filled with police trying to release him. This visual oxymoron—the wrong end of the body was near the bowl—recurred through half the show. A more recent example concerned the semiregular appearance of the obscenely and allegorically named prostitute Lotta Gue. In case anyone missed the joke, Lotta was constantly correcting the officers on the pronunciation of her name, "goo." But the most elaborated of these ongoing stories was the one about Officer Bobby Hill's already mentioned buttocks boil. Its development from "too early to lance" to "an eruption the size of a Texas ruby red grapefruit" was followed through three consecutive episodes as a major story line.

The above examples are, of course, only a very small sampling of the strong presence of bodily emissions in "Hill Street Blues." And when it became a big ratings success, the show's style proved to be as fecund as it was fecal. Other shows wishing to adopt the "Hill Street" formula also adopted its scatological fetish, seeing the possibility that there was gold in that thar filth. While still producing "Hill Street," Steven Bochco developed the short-lived baseball drama "Bay City Blues." One of the major ongoing stories in this series concerned the bed-wetting problem of the team's star hitter, and the show's staff was in a constant battle with network censors for the right to show bare-bottomed men in the locker-room scenes. What's more, the pitching coach offered a thesaurus of bodily emissions that could take the place of saliva for use on spitballs. "St. Elsewhere" (conceived by NBC as "'Hill Street Blues' in a hospital")[3] also continued the tradition, with a vengeance. The first image every week in the opening credits included a large pile of garbage bags stacked in front of the hospital. By the end of the episode this garbage, metaphorically at least, had been liberated and spread all over the halls of St. Eligius in a celebration of the fluids of the human body.

Why was it that scatology was not only given such a prominent position in "Hill Street Blues" but also was being used by other shows wishing to imitate the success of "Hill Street"? One reason was artistic. Among other things, this material functioned as a striking metaphor for the urban chaos featured as the underlying theme of the show—using the leaking, farting, puking human body to represent the equally unhealthy body politic. Apart from connecting the organismic body and the body politic, the refuse and filth of "Hill Street" richly elaborated the metaphoric structures of the show.

A poignant example of this was seen in an episode from the third season entitled "Trial by Fury." Here defilement, pollution, and taboo reached their highest levels yet when a nun was raped, murdered, and mutilated in a church. Later, having committed a legal atrocity in order to expedite the wheels of justice, Furillo went off to his own church to confess. Before his car pulled up to the church, however, a street cleaning vehicle swept slowly past the building. Within the context of the whole show, this served to emphasize the hopelessness and futility of trying to control the urban environment. A nun had been killed, the public had erupted into violent vigilante mobs, and order had been violated on every level, but all the city could do was send Sisyphus to clean the surface of the streets.

The refuse and scatology of "Hill Street" can therefore be artistically justified, but it's also likely that this feature of the show was included as a device to earn higher ratings. After all, much of the material we have been talking about is sensational, shocking, and, most of all, sexual. There's no question that the use of such material in pursuit of ratings success had many precedents in commercial television. The situation comedy "Three's Company" was perhaps the most notorious.

Unlike "Hill Street Blues," however, "Three's Company" stands as one of TV's classic whipping boys. While it was a major ratings success, one would be hard pressed to find many critics who would defend the show. One of the principal charges brought against "Three's Company" concerned its heavy use of the double entendre. Both critics and the PTA pointed out what gratuitous filth and obscenity lay just beneath the thin verbal disguise of most of the dialogue in the show. "Three's Company" was cited as a prime example of the critically disclaimed genre "T&A TV," a genre Fred Silverman developed to bring high ratings to ABC's programs through the frequent presentation of "tits and ass" on shows like "Charlie's Angels" and "The Love Boat."

For all its critical praise, however, "Hill Street Blues" owed a lot to the T&A tradition. For example, in one episode a teenager from a girls' school (who had been trying to seduce Officer J. D. LaRue for some time) left J. D., after some suggestive flirting, with the parting words, "Don't have too hard of a day." In another episode, Henry Goldblume was watching a beautiful woman expose her tightly skirted buttocks as she bent over in search of her contact lens. Overhearing someone ask, "Is it soft?" (referring to the lens), Henry mused to himself, "No, not at all." Since the woman's body looked quite soft, Henry was presumably referring to a part of his own body. Shortly after he was married, Officer Renko, in yet another episode, returned to the station with a broken nose and announced, "I've hurt my proboscis," to which Sergeant Yablonski replied, "Your honker don't look so good either."

Critically acclaimed sister show "St. Elsewhere" once again followed the lead of "Hill Street" with sexual word games that were even more risqué. In the first season, for example, resident doctor Wayne Fiscus got stuck in an elevator with another resident, nymphomaniac Cathy Martin. She proceeded to face Dr. Fiscus and get down upon her knees, clearly preparing to perform fellatio. Later, the elevator began to move again and when the doors opened to a waiting crowd, Cathy exited as though nothing had happened. Wayne, however, was left in the elevator to zip his pants, and as he did so, he announced to the entering passengers, "Going down."

These fairly overt references to the states of male erections (which are quite characteristic of both "Hill Street Blues" and "St. Elsewhere") make the double entendres in "Three's Company" seem quite flaccid in comparison. Yet the principal audience for these shows is educated, young, urban dwellers—an audience so desirable to advertisers that these programs can usually command the same rates for commercial spots as shows that have considerably higher ratings but do not have the same audience makeup. Many of the members of this audience consider themselves above and outside the "mass audience" of other television programs. Why, then, was this comparatively select audience being appealed to with some of the same techniques used in "Three's Company"?

Maybe it was the sheer pleasure of "getting" the joke. Network standards and rules block a good deal of material from appearing on the air. Until very recently, the bolder the producer, the more bowdlerizing the network response to his or her work. In slipping forbidden bits and pieces past the network censors, the producers and writers of "Hill Street" archly devised many creative, funny, and rascally ways to disguise some pretty filthy material. Having himself published an essay on the subject,[4] the show's former executive producer, Steven Bochco, was aware of the limitations of network censorship and managed to use them to his creative advantage. "Hill

Street" (and later "St. Elsewhere") went much further than other shows in its presentation and disguising of forbidden material.

Some of these carnal riddles are complex enough that one does feel a certain sense of pride in not having missed them. In an episode of "St. Elsewhere," for example, Dr. Craig was dictating his novel, the part about the "youngest girl in the Lingus family, Constance." To get the joke, one has first to become suspicious of the name "Lingus," then to move the names together, "Constance Lingus," then to convert the first name to its diminutive, "Connie Lingus," and finally, to have an SAT verbal score high enough to know what "cunnilingus" means. A sophomoric joke, yes, but a fairly complex linguistic game to be playing while watching TV. Perhaps the upscale audience was finding some smug satisfaction in believing that they, as educated and worldly individuals, were the only ones "getting it"—the only ones understanding these dirty secrets.

The interesting point is that not much of anything, good or bad, was being said about these secrets. My students at Northwestern University were clearly more upscale, educated, and urban than most television viewers, and they weren't "getting it." Television had been kept so clean for so long by stringent self-censorship policies that most of my students were conditioned to a certain mode of viewing and interpreting. The double entendre of "Three's Company" was one thing, but "Lotta Gue" couldn't *possibly* be a deliberate attempt to talk about vaginal secretions on American prime-time television. The conditioning was so complete, in fact, that most people I knew didn't have to dismiss the joke as impossible because they had never spotted it as a joke in the first place. It was especially interesting to watch a group of high school students (with whom, in normal discourse, you can't even say "I'm coming" without eliciting snide, knowing chuckles) as they let pass such potential laughs without response. They laughed at "Three's Company," which alluded to sexual acts, but often sat straight-faced through "Hill Street," which alluded to the specific fluids involved in those acts. This is not to say that every viewer missed every allusion. But viewers didn't seem to be cognizant of the fact that the program was completely saturated with bodily fluids and emissions.

For four decades, the people on TV have been presented as the cleanest people in the world. Consider the language that has been used to describe what is acceptable on television. No "dirty" movies are allowed. Theatrical movies that do appear must be "cleaned up" for TV. Even more striking is the commercials' celebration of the immaculate, from "scrubbing bubbles" to "breath deodorants."

Today's classrooms hold students of television, and they know that they can raise their hands only if they're Sure. But instead of being shocked by the uniqueness of the violation of this televisual tradition of cleanliness by "Hill Street," the violation, for many people, used to disappear under the conditioned conviction that dirty things cannot be shown on TV.

This unseen nature of the scatology in "Hill Street" might be further illuminated by looking at one of the basic differences that have traditionally separated television from the movies. Movies are eager to exhibit forbidden material, and we are eager to watch the exhibitions. Besides Cinemascope and 3-D, sex was one of the important ways in which the movie industry attempted to lure the living-room-bound TV viewer back into the theater. At a theater, we anxiously accept the "dirty" material we know is not allowed on TV. The aforementioned high school students laughed at all of the off-color double entendres when they saw "Porky's." It was an R-rated film that was *supposed* to contain such material; therefore they saw it. When the film was over, however, one left the grit and nudity for the next group of viewers just as one left the empty popcorn containers on the sticky theater floor. But "Hill Street Blues" is a television show, not a movie, and the blindness to its scatology that many experienced seemed to indicate a fundamentally different set of expectations between the televisual and the cinematic. TV is in the home, and home is a place where cleanliness is supposed to be maintained and respected. Many people can still remember their grammar school teacher's interrogative, "You wouldn't put your feet up on the furniture in your home, would you?"

The people on American TV are no longer, as they once were, the "cleanest people in the world." Burglars defecate on the floor indoors, urine is drunk from a bottle, and prostitutes bear names that reveal their vaginal states. When "Hill Street" presented all this material, however, most Americans didn't seem to notice. Most seemed to feel that commercial television was, as it always had been, a safe, clean, domestic medium, and they saw there only what they were expecting to see.

But the jig is up. Or, rather, the scatological tune that Steven Bochco was once fiddling alone is now the one everyone's dancing to. Dr. Ruth says "penis" and "vibrator" and "lubrication" on "The Tonight Show" without batting an eyelash. Even if condom commercials were never allowed on the air, the word "condom" was heard on TV during the height of the controversy over the airing of those commercials by many more people than will ever have occasion to use one. And as more and more people get cable and VCR machines, forbidden material originally intended for the theater is now readily available for viewing in the living room.

With the appearance of "L.A. Law," Bochco's latest TV series, viewers have had no other choice than to shed their collective blindness to televised scatology. When he launched a vial filled with bull semen, Bochco escalated his war against television expurgation: this was a hard scene to relegate to the subconscious in the conditioned conviction that television couldn't present stories about litigants crying over spilled sperm. There it was, in slow motion. With a deregulator in the White House and television censorship loosening up, Bochco no longer needs to work as hard to sneak his taboos past the network.

Some will probably argue, however, that the more Bochco is allowed to get away with, the more his dirty talk has become not much more than just that. Because they are now less disguised, some say his scatological symbols have grown tired and formulaic, now owing more to the Beastie Boys than to Rabelais. While any show that helps its audience see more deeply and clearly should be congratulated, as the metaphoric function of bodily emissions in shows like "Hill Street Blues" gives way to the broad fraternity humor of shows like "L.A. Law," television scatology's golden age seems to be passing.

NOTES

1. Jane Feuer, Paul Kerr, and Tise Vahimagi, eds., *MTM: Quality Television* (London: British Film Institute, 1984).

2. Todd Gitlin, *Inside Prime Time* (New York: Pantheon, 1983).

3. Michele Brustin, "St. Elsewhere: Creative Changes Through Re-examination," paper presented at the Third International Conference on Television Drama, Michigan State University, East Lansing, May 20, 1983. (Ms. Brustin delivered this paper when she was a vice-president for drama development at NBC.)

4. Steven Bochco, "The Censorship Game," in *TV Book*, ed. Judy Fireman (New York: Workman, 1977), pp. 54–56.

6

"He's Everything You're Not . . .": A Semiological Analysis of "Cheers"

Arthur Asa Berger

The basic question that semiology (or semiotics or structuralism) asks of a television program or film or advertisement—or any "text"—is this: How do people understand what's going on? How do people derive meaning from a text? How do they know how to interpret facial expressions, body movements, clothes the characters wear, kinds of shots, the scenery, correctly? How is meaning generated and conveyed?

A hint comes from Jonathan Culler, who write in *Structuralist Poetics*:

The notion that linguistics might be useful in studying other cultural phenomena is based on two fundamental insights: first, that social and cultural phenomena are not simply material objects or events but objects and events with meaning, and hence signs; and second, that they do not have essences but are defined by a network of relations.[1]

Meaning, Culler tells us, stems from considering phenomena as signs and from looking at the relationships among these signs. These two notions are at the heart of the semiological enterprise. In this semiological analysis of the pilot episode of "Cheers,"[2] we will be considering the text as a collection or system of signs. We will define signs in the Saussurean manner as a combination of a sound and an image (signifier) and a concept or understanding (signified).

The problem of meaning arises from the fact that the relation between the signifier and the signified is arbitrary and conventional, so signs can mean anything. And, as Umberto Eco points out, they can lie. A signifier (such as a gesture) can mean different things to different people, depending upon their social class, cultural level, location, and other factors. Since the relation between signifier and signified is arbitrary, we must discover the codes that explain the signs, that help us interpret the signifiers. In addition, we must look for important relationships (other than that of signifier and signified) found in texts that help us understand cultural phenomena.

Here again Saussure is useful. He writes in his *Course in General Linguistics*, "[C]oncepts are purely differential and defined not by their positive content but negatively by their relations with the other terms of the system. Their most precise characteristic is in being what the others are not."[3] Nothing means anything in itself, and everything (as far as concepts are concerned) is dependent on relationships. The most important relationship is that of polar or binary opposition; binary oppositions are the fundamental way in which the human mind finds meaning. This notion has been adapted by Claude Lévi-Strauss[4] into a means of looking at texts such as myths and Greek tragedies—and, by extension here, "Cheers." In essence we search for the hidden set of oppositions that inform a text and thus generate meaning. This meaning is not necessarily recognized by people but is there nevertheless, and can be elicited by the semiologist.

SIGNS

The title of the series, "Cheers," tells us something. It suggests happiness, good spirits (in this case literally as well as figuratively), and companionship. "Cheers" is a toast we make when drinking with others, so there is an element of conviviality and sociability involved. In this series, which takes place in a bar named Cheers, we thus find ourselves with expectations about what might transpire. We expect something pleasant . . . and we are not disappointed.

Boston

The bar itself is a sign system. It is not drab or shabby, like a working-class bar, nor is it a fancy, trendy bar. It seems to be a neighborhood bar that caters mainly to middle-class people. The bar and the row of liquor bottles are primary signifiers of what might be called "barness." And the bar is in Boston, which gives it a certain flavor and gives us certain understandings because of the way Boston is perceived. Boston has an identity due, in part, to its being on the east coast and closely identified with English culture, the revolutionary period, and Harvard University. Bostonians are perceived as somewhat effete and a bit snobbish—though this is reserved for upper-class, aristocratic (Protestant) types and certainly not for the Irish working-class types one finds there. The fact that this series takes place in Boston, I would suggest, prepares us for all kinds of characters—eccentrics, snobs, weirdos, con artists.

Blondness

One of the most important signs in the text is the color of Diane Chambers's hair. She's a blond, and blondness is a sign of considerable richness and meaning. America is a country where "gentlemen prefer blonds," and blond hair coloring is the most popular color sold. But what does blondness signify?

For some women blond hair color is a means of escaping (or attempting to escape) their ethnic identity, or, in some cases, their age. It is used to cover gray hair. But there are other aspects that are much more important. Some of these are pointed out by Charles Winick in his book *The New People*:

[F]or a substantial number of women, the attraction of blondeness is less an opportunity to have more fun than the communication of a withdrawal of emotion, a lack of passion. One reason for Marilyn Monroe's enormous popularity was that she was less a tempestuous temptress than a non-threatening child. The innocence conveyed by blonde hair is also suggested by the 70 percent of baby dolls whose hair is blonde.

D. H. Lawrence pointed out that blonde women in American novels are often cool and unobtainable, while the dark woman represents passion. Fictional blondes also tend to be vindictive and frigid.[5]

This innocence of the blond is appealing to men because blonds, not being experienced, could not be very judgmental about men's sexual performances—if, that is, things ever get to that stage. Thus, when Sumner calls Diane a "child," there is more significance to the term than we might imagine.

The book that Diane attempts to read and her numerous allusions to and quotations from great literary figures are signs of her (and Sumner's) status as intellectuals. And the lack of a "proper" response (awe, respect) by Sam and his friends is an indication of their status as nonintellectuals. They are more interested in the Boston Patriots than in John Donne, in linebackers than in literature.

Names

Let us move on to something a bit more speculative—an examination of the names of the characters to see whether we can find anything of interest and significance. Another name for Diane (Diana) in mythology is Artemis, a virgin huntress associated with the moon. Thus she is well named, for her basic role in the series is that of an object of sexual desire, a "child"/woman who becomes embroiled in a battle of the sexes with the hero, Sam Malone. (I will not comment on the fact that her last name, Chambers, suggests a room—especially a bedroom, my dictionary tells me.)

Sam's name does not tell us much, though we might make something of the fact that we can find an "alone" in Malone and it is his status as a male with no ties that facilitates the battle with Diane. Carla Tortelli is another matter; in her name we find "tort," which is a description of her argumentative personality. She is an injured party (her husband left her with four children) and bitter about it. Even Sumner Sloane's name is interesting, for he is, in effect, "on loan" to Diane from his ex-wife Barbara. She takes him back when the time is appropriate. Norm, the fat beer drinker, is a perfect everyman figure and well named; he is a representation of the typical American bar patron, drinking the beverage of the common man. "Coach" is a different matter; his name is used ironically. He is not a guide and teacher but, instead, an absent-minded and somewhat daffy character who cannot remember his own name and is always confused.

I cannot argue that the names of the characters were deliberately chosen for their semiological significance, but it is interesting (and maybe more than purely coincidental) that the characters have the names they do. The writers of the series are educated and bring in many names from "elite culture," such as Kierkegaard and Nietzsche[6] (to show that Diane is an intellectual). It wouldn't be too much of a stretch of the imagination to assume that there was some conscious thought about the names of the characters.

CODES

If the relationship between signifier and signified is arbitrary, we must have rules for interpreting things, and these rules are what we call codes. Codes tell us what signs mean. What complicates matters, as I suggested earlier, is that different groups and subgroups have different codes in certain cases and there is, at times, code confusion between a creator or user of a sign and an interpreter or receiver of a sign. Thus we have the problem of what Umberto Eco calls "aberrant decoding." He writes in his essay "Towards a Semiotic Inquiry into the Television Message": "Codes and sub-codes are applied to the message in the light of a general framework of cultural references, which constitutes the receiver's patrimony of knowledge; his ideological, ethical, religious standpoints, his psychological attitudes, his tastes, his value systems, etc."[7] Codes are connected to culture and social class to a great degree, which means that people who watch "Cheers" may not always "get" everything the writers have put into the show. Or some people, at least.

In the same light, the characters themselves do not understand one another all the time; this is a source of the humor in numerous cases. Let me suggest that humor, in general, is connected to code confusion and violation. The difference between what one expects (knowing the code) and what one gets (due to code confusion and violation) generates laughter. We are dealing with a form of incongruity or perhaps, to be more accurate, an explanation of incongruity. The situation is very complicated, for we find the characters in "Cheers" do not understand one another and the audience of "Cheers" does not understand everything that goes on in the episode. Nevertheless, the audience probably gets a lot of the humor—or large enough audiences do—for the series to be successful.

Let's consider the codes of "Cheers" in some detail. First, we know we are watching a comedy and thus are prepared to laugh, to give everything a nonserious, humorous interpretation. Therefore we watch the program with certain expectations that color the way we interpret the events in the episode and relate to the characters. Since it is a comedy, we also expect to see eccentric types who play off against one another; we are prepared for the zanies, weirdos, and others who are found in comedies and who often represent "types" rather than being three-dimensional characters.

In this episode of "Cheers" much of the humor comes from misunderstandings and misinterpretations made by the various characters, though there are also some "nonresponses." These two forms of code violation or aberrant decoding come from the different social and cultural backgrounds of the characters. Diane and Sumner are highly educated, middle-class types, whereas the rest of the characters are working class and presumably less educated.

Thus, when Carla talks about putting her husband through school, Diane assumes "school" means a university, not a television repair academy. And when Coach talks about "working six years on his novel," Diane asks, increduously, whether he's writing a novel. She discovers, instead, that he's reading one. Cultural and class differences are at the root of these misunderstandings. The same can be said of the scene where Diane has answered the phone and is talking to a woman with whom Sam has presumably spent the night. He doesn't want to talk to the woman and his mouth is full of food, so he tries to indicate to Diane that she should tell the woman he's gone for a haircut. Instead Diane says, "He's taking a mime class." She may be intelligent, but she doesn't have much common sense. The same thing can be said about Sumner, who leaves his young fiancé in order to retrieve a ring from his ex-wife.

We find a case of "nonresponse" in the scene where Sumner Sloan has just introduced himself and informed Sam that he is "professor of world literature at Boston University." Instead of being awed, Sam says nothing; he refuses to "validate" Sumner, a response that university professors and students to whom I have shown the program find hilarious. Sam's nonresponse is viewed as a proper one because Sumner is so pompous and deserves, we feel, to be deflated. Sumner has violated the egalitarian code that is so important in American culture and has set himself up for his punishment.

Below I list some codes and violations found in the episode so we can see how important this phenomenon is.

Code	Violation
Common sense	Diane and the "mime" scene
Propriety	Diane, as waitress, sits with patrons
Egalitarianism	Sam's nonresponse to Sumner's identification of himself
Loyalty	Sumner jilts Diane
Law	Kid tries to get a drink with false identification
Self-awareness	Coach doesn't know his own name
Logic	Alcoholic owns a bar
Normalcy	Eccentric types found in "Cheers"

This list indicates the importance of code confusion and violation in the text. In order for viewers to understand this text fully, they must be able to recognize the violations of the codes, which means they must be able to interpret facial expressions and other signs, understand motivations, and assess characters. That is, viewers must bring a great deal of knowledge to the text; and the more they know, the more they will understand. "Cheers" must be seen as a figure to be interpreted against the ground of American culture and society; and culture, from our perspective, is a collection of codes and sub-codes. When we watch "Cheers," we are, semiologically speaking, decoding a text . . . whether we know it or not.

OPPOSITIONS

Bipolar oppositions, we have learned, are a basic means by which we find meaning; this is because nothing has meaning in itself. It is the network of relationships that is crucial to the generation of meaning. What I have written deals with concepts, but it also may be used to understand characters in a text. Let's look at some oppositions between various characters in "Cheers": Diane and Carla, Sam Malone and Sumner Sloane, and Diane and Sam.

Diane	Carla
Tall	Short
Blond	Dark hair
Single (to be married)	Was married (now single)
Cool/reserved	Hot/bitchy
Middle class	Working class
WASP	Ethnic
Innocent	Experienced
(Schoolmarm)	(Bargirl)

We can see that these two characters are opposites in many important respects. The same can be said for Sam Malone and Sumner Sloane.

Sam Malone	Sumner Sloane
Tall	Short
Young	Old
Jock	Egghead
Modest	Pompous
Regular guy	Goof
Common sense	Intelligence
The world	The academy
Hires Diane	Abandons Diane

Sumner's character is, in a sense, defined by how different he is from Sam. Diane has said, in an important line spoken to Sam, that Sumner is "everything you're not." And this is quite true. Sumner is an intellectual, but he lacks common sense and morality—he abandons Diane after being "mesmerized" by his former wife, Barbara. He is a highly stereotyped figure: academics are conventionally seen as intelligent but unworldly, lacking common sense and often lacking decency. Sam has no problem in immediately sizing Sumner up as a "goof." This polarity between the intelligent but impractical and unworldly scholar and the uneducated but naturally "wise" common man has deep roots in American culture, and can be found in the early 1800s in our idealization of the various "nature's noblemen" we identified with. It is connected to ideas we had about ourselves and the way we contrasted ourselves with Europeans.

In essence, we saw ourselves as innocent, wise, egalitarian, individualistic characters living in a classless society in a state of nature, and contrasted this with Europeans, whom we saw as guilt-ridden, trained conformists living in a hierarchically organized society dominated by institutions such as the church and nobility. Sam is shown as a classic American "regular guy" figure, and Sumner is portrayed as a European-like character. The fact that he is a professor of world literature suggests his lack of Americanness and that he has, somehow, been tainted.

Finally, let us move to the central opposition between characters in this text and the opposition that is to be crucial in the series—the differences between Diane Chambers and Sam Malone.

Diane Chambers	Sam Malone
Female	Male
Blond	Dark hair
Middle class	Working class
Education	Common sense
Vulnerable	Worldly
Beauty	Beast (magnificent pagan)
Worker	Boss
Useless	Handy

One of the common themes in the series is to be the "battle" (of the sexes) between Sam and Diane. They are attracted to each other but refuse to admit it; they cannot fall in love and get married lest the series become a "domestic comedy," so they spend their time flirting, becoming involved in ridiculous situations from which they extricate themselves with great difficulty. That obviously is their fate. We do not know this when we see the pilot, but we can presume this will be the case from our knowledge of the genre and the logic of the situation.

In addition to the oppositions that exist among characters, there is a central set of oppositions in the text that is worth considering. These oppositions involve characters but have broader implications.

Youth	**Adulthood**
Kid who can't drink	Grown-ups who can drink
Young teaching assistant	Old(er) professor
Working Class	**Middle Class**
Workers, patrons	Sumner Sloane, Diane Chambers
The Future	**The Past**
The marriage	Ex-baseball player
Grad student	Ex-wife of Sumner
Con Artists	**Marks**
The kid	Sam
Sumner's ex-wife	Sumner
Inside	**Outside**
The bar	The outside world
Regulars	Strangers, aliens
The Beauty	**The Beast**
Diane	Sam

These oppositions are of central importance in the episode—and in the whole series. It is the "battle of the sexes," "the battle of the classes," and a whole series of other confrontations that generate not only dramatic interest and tension, but also humor, because the possibilities for misunderstanding and misinterpretation, are enormous.

There is another kind of opposition worth mentioning here: that between the main characters, who will appear in each episode, and the various characters, such as Sumner Sloane, who will be seen in only one episode. As we watch the series, we will get to know the main characters, and the series will function as a kind of "ground" that will help us interpret what these characters do and understand them better. They will have a different "status" than the characters who appear for an episode and then disappear. These characters will remain more stereotyped and one-dimensional; we will understand them because they will be "types," with conventional signs and codes. With each episode the main characters, even though they may be stereotyped, will become more real because we will know more of their history.

Thus the characters in a television program/series that lasts a long time become, so to speak, a part of us; their history merges with our lives. And the situations in which they become involved take on a significance for the regular viewer that they do not have for the casual viewer. This leads, I suggest, to an inevitable humanization and rounding of the characters, especially in a medium like television, where facial expressions and other signifying systems reveal character tellingly. It might be argued that regular viewers of a series like "Cheers" see more in a given episode than casual viewers do, though in the pilot episode I'm discussing, all viewers start on an equal footing.

From a semiological perspective, stereotyping involves the use of conventional and easily understood signifiers and codes . . . and easily perceived oppositions. This instant decoding is necessary because television programs don't have a great deal of time to develop characters, and must rely on commonly understood attitudes about types of people and their motivations. Stereotyping may also be connected to the inability of some audiences to decode more complex characterizations.

A SYNTAGMATIC ANALYSIS OF "CHEERS"

I would like to turn, now, to an analysis that uses the ideas of Vladimir Propp and suggests that in many respects "Cheers" is a "modernized" fairy tale. In his *Morphology of the Folk Tale* Propp argued that tales can be analyzed in terms of a number of functions that are found in all tales. Each of these functions, he said, is to be understood as "an act of a character defined from the point of view of its significance for the course of the action." In his analysis of a number of Russian tales, Propp elicited some 31 functions that were the basic components of all the tales. These functions, which might also be called something like "narratemes" (building blocks found in all stories), can be applied to forms other than fairy tales. Alan Dundes writes in his introduction to *Morphology of the Folk Tale*:

Propp's analysis should be useful in analyzing the structure of literary forms (such as novels and plays), comic strips, motion picture and television plots, and the like. In understanding the interrelationship between folklore and literature, and between folklore and the mass media, the emphasis has hitherto been principally upon content. Propp's *Morphology* suggests that there can be structural borrowings as well as content borrowings.[8]

The table below offers a morphological analysis (and a synopsis) of the pilot episode of "Cheers." I have had to modify things somewhat and take some liberties with Propp, but I don't think I stretch things too far.

Proppian Sign	Proppian Function	Event in Cheers
α	Initial situation	Sam, Diane, Sumner introduced
β^1	Absentation	Sumner leaves bar to get ring
γ^2	Interdiction (inverted)	Sumner tells Diane to stay in bar
θ^1	Victim submits to deception	Sumner goes to ex-wife Barbara's place; Diane lets him go
A^{11}	Villainy	Barbara "casts a spell" on Sumner
a^1	Lack	Diane "lacks" Sumner; waits
B^4	Mediation (misfortune is made known)	Diane discovers Sumner has gone to Bahamas with Barbara
$\uparrow$	Heroine "leaves home"	Diane cannot return to Boston University
E^2	Heroine's reaction to action of a future donor	Diane tells Sam she doesn't talk with bartenders
F^9	Magic agent	Various characters sympathize with Diane
K^{10}	Initial misfortune or lack is liquidated	Sam offers Diane a job at his bar
T^3	Transfiguration: heroine given a new appearance	Diane becomes waitress, wears uniform
$w°$	Heroine "married"	Diane starts a relationship with Sam

Each function, I should point out, can have a number of different variations or subcategories, which explains the numbers found after the symbols. The "formula" for the "Cheers" episode is

$$\alpha \ \beta^1 \ \gamma^2 \ \theta^1 \ A^{11} \ a^1 \ B^4 \ \uparrow \ E^2 \ F^9 \ K^{10} \ T^3 \ w°.$$

This formula is, I might add, a highly simplified version of what might be done. But this analysis does give a good idea of the kind of thing that can be done when Propp is applied to a text, and shows that Propp's functions can be applied to narrative texts other than folk tales.

It is obvious that there are many folktale/fairy-tale elements in this episode, and it does not strain credulity too far to suggest that it is, though highly camouflaged and modernized, a fairy tale. (I would argue, in the same manner, that there are fairy-tale elements in many of our important modern story forms: science fiction, detective stories, westerns). There is a good reason for this. Fairy tales play an important role in our development as children and, it might be asserted, in our adult lives as well. As Bruno Bettelheim wrote in *The Uses of Enchantment*:

Through the centuries (if not millennia) during which, in their retelling, fairy tales became ever more refined, they came to convey at the same time overt and covert meanings—came to speak simultaneously to all levels of the human personality, communicating in a manner which reaches the uneducated mind of the child as well as that of the sophisticated adult. Applying the psychoanalytic model of the human personality, fairy tales carry important messages to the conscious, the preconscious, and the unconscious mind, on whatever level each is functioning at the time. By dealing with universal human problems, particularly those which preoccupy the child's mind, these stories speak to his budding ego and encourage its development, while at the same time relieving preconscious and unconscious pressures. As the stories unfold, they give conscious credence and body to id pressures and show ways to satisfy these that are in line with ego and superego requirements.[9]

To suggest, then, that there are fairy-tale elements in "Cheers" is not to diminish its significance but to do just the opposite. If "Cheers" is a kind of adult fairy tale, so much the better for it. (There may be a connection between Propp's functions and psychoanalytic phenomena that would explain why the fairy tale, even in its modern versions, plays such an important role for us.)

The pilot episode involves Diane's initiation into a different world, into the "real" world of working-class people who drink in bars. She has several moments of recognition—when she finds out that she has been jilted and when she realizes what kind of work she is suited for. She is a beauty who finds herself with a "beast" (magnificent pagan), a "princess" who finds herself with an innkeeper in a quasi-medieval city, Boston. The princess has been ditched by her would-be prince; this kind of thing happens all the time in fairy tales.

"Cheers" has proven to be one of the most successful television programs of recent years, and is still being produced, even though the inimitable star of the show, Shelley Long, left it after the 1986–1987 season. Her descent from English classes to the working classes lasted many years and provided a great deal of first-class comedy. (Comparative literature professors from Boston University—and perhaps other universities—may not have been amused.)

CONCLUSION

A semiotic analysis of a text such as "Cheers" focuses on how meaning is generated and conveyed, and thus on such matters as signs and codes, polar oppositions, and sequential structures. The text functions as a figure against the ground of culture, and the figure reflects (though not always in perfectly accurate ways) the ground, just as the ground helps interpret the figure. A text such as "Cheers" is extremely complex and could yield a semiological analysis of great length. The lighting, the pacing, the dialogue, the costuming, the blocking, the facial expressions of the characters, the music, the sound—all lend themselves to semiological analysis because they all function as signs (and, in particular, signifiers).

I have offered a semiological quick study of "Cheers" in an attempt to show how a semiological or semiotic analysis of this text might be done. There's plenty of room at the bar for others.

NOTES

1. Jonathan Culler, *Structuralist Poetics: Structuralism, Linguistics and the Study of Literature* (Ithaca, NY: Cornell University Press, 1975), 4.

2. The first episode of "Cheers" aired on September 30, 1982, on NBC and was 30 minutes in length. The cast was Shelley Long as Diane Chambers, Ted Danson as Sam Malone, Rhea Perlman as Carla Tortelli, John Retzenberg as Cliff, George Wendt as Norm, and Nicholas Colosante as Coach.

3. Ferdinand de Saussure, *Course in General Linguistics* (New York: McGraw-Hill, 1966), 117.

4. Claude Lévi-Strauss, *Structural Anthropology* (Garden City, NY: Doubleday, 1967).

5. Charles Winick, *The New People: Desexualization in American Life* (New York: Pegasus, 1968), 169.

6. Mentioned in later episodes.

7. Umberto Eco, "Towards a Semiotic Inquiry into the Television Message," *Working Papers in Cultural Studies* 3 (Autumn 1972):115.

8. Alan Dundes, "Introduction," in Vladimir Propp, *Morphology of the Folk Tale*, 2nd ed. (Austin: University of Texas Press, 1973), xiv–xv.

9. Bruno Bettelheim, *The Uses of Enchantment* (New York: Knopf, 1976), 5–6.

7

And Justice for All: The Messages Behind "Real" Courtroom Dramas

Wende Vyborney Dumble

Featuring real people in exciting situations has long been a favorite strategy of television writers and producers. Game shows, from "Cash and Carry" to "Wheel of Fortune," have offered housewives and blue-collar workers a chance at wealth. Talent shows from "Doorway to Fame" to "Star Search" have held out the prospect of stardom to the boy and girl next door. Novelty programs from "This Is Your Life" to "Candid Camera" have focused on the reactions of individuals to unexpected events. Other programs—"Campus Hoopla," "American Bandstand," "Real People"—have shown how real people amuse themselves.[1] All of these programs are based on a common appeal: average Americans having more fun, handling more adventures, gaining more wealth, or enjoying more fame than the genuine average American viewer.

Adventure, wealth, fame, and even fun are luxuries to the average person; they are thus cloaked in the mystery of the familiar yet unknown. Mystery breeds guilt, which has only two possible outlets. That which produces guilt may become a target of identification, or it may be victimized.[2] "Reality programming" is based on the former strategy. By linking ordinary people with extraordinary situations, the extraordinary is made ordinary. Wealth, fame, adventure, and fun are less mysterious when "real people" are seen enjoying them.

The material in this chapter is based on the following programs: "The People's Court" (broadcast on KOVR February 3, 5, 11, 12, 13, 16, 17, 18, 1987); "Superior Court" (broadcast on KOVR February 3, 5, 11, 12, 13, 16, 17, 18, 1987); and "Divorce Court" (broadcast on KOVR March 3, 4, 10, 12, 13, 14, 1987).

The purpose of reality programming is to make personal and accessible the mysterious influences that pervade our lives.

Among these influences is the law. "We are surrounded by law. There is virtually nothing we do that doesn't have a legal element, whether it's buying or selling, living or dying, marrying or divorcing, breathing or polluting."³ The law is one of the ultimate mysteries of modern life. While it deals with issues of life, death, property, and the pursuit of happiness, it is hidden in thick tomes filled with fine print, and it can be interpreted only by acolytes whose three years of rigorous training entitle them to charge enormous fees for their services. By the triple barrier of knowledge, tribulation, and expense, "the law" is removed from the common man.

It is unsurprising, then, that one of the oldest and most persistent types of reality programming, second only to the game show, is the proto-trial.⁴ Proto-trial programs are set in courtrooms and consist of real trials acted or reenacted with varying degrees of spontaneity. The grandfather of modern programs like "The People's Court" is "Famous Jury Trials," which began on radio in 1936 and aired on television from 1949 to 1952. It featured reenactments of trials, with a real jury making the decision. It was followed by "The Black Robe" (1949–1950), "Justice" (1954–1956), "Traffic Court" (1958–1959),⁵ "Divorce Court" (1957–1962), "The Verdict Is Yours" (1957–1969), and "Day in Court" (1958–1965).⁶ The predominant modern programs are "The People's Court," "Divorce Court," and "Superior Court."⁷

Despite some minor variations in format, these programs all present a common central idea: justice is accessible and comprehensible to the common citizen. It is the purpose of this analysis to explore the strategies used in modern programs to present this idea. Three themes shared by "The People's Court," "Divorce Court," and "Superior Court" will be examined: the tension between reality and drama, the trial as person-to-person combat, and the mutability of good and evil.

ANALYSIS

Reality Versus Drama

All three programs make some overt claim of depicting a real trial and do, to some extent, support that claim. A genuine, if retired, judge presides over each court. "People's Court" also uses real plaintiffs and defendants with a genuine case pending—and without a script. "Divorce Court" uses real lawyers and limits the amount of action scripted, while "Superior Court" is entirely acted and scripted. All three also claim to draw from and modify cases that have appeared in the California courts, in statements ranging from the mild "inspired by cases and issues in the California family courts" of "Divorce Court" to the "What you are witnessing is real" of "People's Court." All three programs downplay the effects of casting and editing; these appear on the screen briefly, in fine print, among the closing credits. The message is clear: this is justice in action.

These programs are, of necessity, bound by some dramatic form. That a program should have a structure is a given: it has a time limit and a certain number of commercial breaks within which writers, producers, and editors must work. But form, from a Burkean perspective, is that structure which develops and satisfies expectations in the audience.[8] A genuine trial has its own rituals of filing forms, clarifying procedural issues, selecting a jury, swearing in witnesses, waiting for a decision, all of which allow justice to move forward at a stately pace dictated by conventional form: that form which "involves to some degree the appeal of form *as form*."[9] But the conventional form of a trial often causes it to drag on for days, weeks, or months. To fit the gist of a trial into less than 30 minutes, the conventional form must be severely compressed, yet enough must remain so that the result is clearly a trial. Even "People's Court," which boasts of its spontaneity in its advertisements, is severely edited. During one case that filled approximately 15 minutes of air time, Judge Wapner reminded parties that they must limit their presentation to two hours. The loss through editing may, therefore, be as great as seven-eighths of the available material.

A prolonged analysis of the resulting dramatic form would be far less revealing than an exploration of the changes that producers and writers choose to make in the conventional form of the trial: what they include and what they omit. The proto-trial is not merely a drama; it exists in tension with reality. The decision to portray certain aspects is a decision not to show others.[10] As such, it can profoundly affect the messages sent by the program. Two decisions are central: the content of the cases and the extent of judicial procedure shown.

The cases to be tried are chosen to appeal to basic human emotions. Both "People's Court" and "Divorce Court" are based entirely on this choice. The former offers only the petty battles of the man next door and the merchant around the corner—battles that involve people like the typical viewer. The latter offers the death throes of a central societal institution, fueled by the emotions of love, hate, and jealousy. Divorce, like difficulties with friends and merchants, is experienced or feared by most Americans. On both programs the situations are occasionally bizarre (riding home from the prom in a hearse; contending over unmentionable—but mentioned—sexual practices), but the essence of these programs is personal and immediate.

"Superior Court" has, by nature, a wider range of cases available. And certainly the claims that appear are various and sensational: negligence leading to suicide, assault on a minority family, fraudulent impersonation of Burt Reynolds, murder on the high seas, an adolescent petitioning to be permitted an abortion. Yet a qualitative pattern emerges. As coproducer Stu Billett explains, "We will be doing shows about divorce, criminal law, 'deep pocket' insurance cases—things people can get involved in. We're not going to have things like AT&T suing the U.S. government."[11] Again, the personal and immediate are chosen.

The elimination of tedious and lengthy procedural concerns is a dramatic device to make justice seem accessible. Dramatically, it makes sense to introduce main characters and move directly to the action. The entire program can thus be devoted to developing the relationships among the characters in order to ascertain the truth about the case. This emphasis on characters has the additional benefit of increasing audience identification with the characters.

In reality, much of the progress to justice occurs outside the courtroom. In trying a case under civil procedure, there are determinations of jurisdiction, notices to defendants, pleadings, discovery, and choice of a judge or jury trial, all of which can be argued, replied to, and motioned against.[12] These are never referred to beyond Judge Wapner's automatic "I have read your complaint" at the beginning of every session of "People's Court."

In addition, television trials are consistently decided on substantive rather than procedural issues. That is, the statute of limitations and other regulations concerning who may sue whom for what, when, and where are not at issue. Decisions are based solely on guilt or on major constitutional issues. The sole exception is the rare case on "People's Court" in which the wrong party is being sued—surely the simplest form of procedural error.

Finally, the posttrial process of appeals and subsequent actions is generally ignored. On "Divorce Court," subsequent suits to alter child support, alimony, and custody arrangements are possible, but they are not mentioned unless a specific decision involves a waiting period for further decisions on specific issues. "Superior Court" admits that appeals occur but minimizes their impact. After the decision, a typed paragraph is superimposed over the bustling courtroom. Read by a solemn voice, it briefly details who served what time, what appeals occurred, and what the final outcome was. A process of years is effectively reduced to a few seconds.

Through these three alterations in courtroom procedure, much of the mystery of the legal system is dispelled by simple omission. Justice as dramatized is accessible because it is entirely a question of fundamental human issues.

The Trial as Combat

Proto-trial programs share a time slot and a general mood with their cousins, the game show and the talent show. These programs appeal to the archetype of good pitted against evil in a battle for treasure. This link may decrease the mystery surrounding the courtroom by mitigating the solemnity of what occurs within, but the battle in court is nonetheless much more serious. "Evil" is rooted not in bad luck, ignorance, or lack of talent but in guilt of murder, physical abuse, adultery, fraud, breach of contract, and so on. And although game shows and proto-trials both offer cash prizes, the stakes of the former are as often refrigerators and brand new cars, while the stakes of the latter include revenge, freedom, and even life itself. The presence of "real" people in the archetypal conflict places the mystery of the trial into a comprehensible human context.

The combat motif is established immediately within each program. On "People's Court," the plaintiff enters the courtroom while "reporter" Doug Llewellyn details his or her identity, claims, and the prize, all of which are also printed on the screen. The same procedure is followed for the defendant. Then, while a message touting the reality of the program runs up the lower half of the screen, the plaintiff and defendant are shown side by side. This introduction resembles nothing so much as the stereotypical beginning of a boxing match: "In this corner . . . ." "Divorce Court" opens with a brief description of the parties and their claims, and "Superior Court" begins with the respective opening statements of the lawyers, following which the salient facts are repeated in voice-over. In all three cases, it is unmistakably clear that X is about to verbally battle Y for prize Z.

This is hardly an unreasonable way to present an adversarial system of justice; indeed, the procedure of beginning with the opening statements of the lawyers is essentially identical to how a genuine trial proceeds once the jury has been selected. A more indicative example is how the combat motif is used to humanize and demystify the lawyers on "Superior Court."

It should first be noted that "Superior Court" is the most lawyer-oriented of the three programs. "People's Court," of course, uses no lawyers. "Divorce Court" uses real lawyers, some of whom appear frequently; but it seems that the Horace Rumpoles of Los Angeles are not moved to practice family law. "Divorce Court" lawyers are stolid to the point of anonymity, leaving the histrionics to their clients. When counsel approach the bench, it is usually time for a commercial.

On "Superior Court," when counsel approach the bench, it is time for the fireworks to begin. "Superior Court" lawyers are colorful recurring characters who exhibit a lively interest in winning the case. Thus "Superior Court" exploits an otherwise unrecognized opportunity for identification. While the witnesses can exhibit only limited complexity of personality because of time constraints, so much "private" conversation is scripted between lawyers and their clients, lawyers and other lawyers, and lawyers and the judge, as well as examination and cross-examination, that lawyers can be developed as individuals within and across episodes.

Were steely-eyed, sharp-witted hired gun Maddox West to be pitted against idealistic black public defender Olympia Hall, two versions of what a lawyer is would be presented and contrasted. Stated as an abstract problem, the juxtaposition would be of interest only to specialists in legal communication. Portrayed as combat between two developed characters, the juxtaposition presents a message about lawyers, and also provokes some small amount of thought about what a good lawyer is. Lawyers are portrayed not only as specialists in arcane matters but also as human beings motivated by easily comprehensible desires, such as greed or idealism. Demystifying the legal profession is a major step toward demystifying the legal system. While much of the mystery surrounding the system is generated by the conventional form of the system itself, previous media depictions of lawyers have contributed significantly. As Terry Fisher, coproducer of "L.A. Law," points out, "[In earlier legal shows] the lawyer was a saint who represented an underdog—who everyone else said was guilty—and he would always win in the end. Or else lawyers would be portrayed as unscrupulous."[13] While the unscrupulous lawyer is an excellent candidate for victimage, the saintly lawyer is only a moderately acceptable candidate for identification.

Because his motives are so much purer than those of the average viewer, these motivations become a further veil of mystery. Through the influence of classical and Christian mythology on American culture, the saintly lawyer may also be suitable for victimage. Justice is thus more accessible if the practitioners of justice are "real" people.

The Mutability of Good and Evil

The peculiarity of the proto-trial combat between good and evil is that good and evil are seldom known quantities at the outset. Instead, their respective qualities emerge during the course of the testimony. By the end, good and evil have presumably shown their true colors, and the audience is given confirmation or disconfirmation of their conclusions by the judge's ruling. How, then, are good and evil depicted? It is appropriate to examine the terms associated with characters who prove to be one or the other. By examining the associational clusters, one may find "what acts and images and personalities go with notions of heroism, villainy, consolation, despair, etc."[14]

The surprising answer is that there is no consistent portrayal of good or of evil. Even honesty and dishonesty are not sacred. The role grows out of the situation, not the character.

"People's Court," for example, has a common pairing of outraged customer versus outraged merchant: this is the scenario in 5 of the 11 cases viewed for this analysis. It is a powerful pairing, as most people have at some time felt an urge to take action against a merchant who provides shoddy wares or mediocre services. The outraged consumer is a strong potential hero role. Usually (four out of five times) the customer wins, even when the customer is sued by the merchant. However, lines such as these are heard in the decision and the subsequent interviews: "I don't want all furniture salesmen to get a bad name because of this incident," "*Most* limousine companies don't operate like that," and "I'm not ruling against you because you're a car wash owner. Most take reasonable precautions." This individual may be shifty-eyed, but the message is that the impression should not be generalized into a villainous archetype. In addition, Judge Wapner's regular scolding for immaturity reduces even the consumer-hero to less than heroic proportions. The winner may act out the fantasies of the audience, but he or she is not necessarily someone the audience should emulate.

For "Divorce Court," much the same holds true. The party who cries the most on the stand is not consistently the party who wins the larger award. Nor is a clean-cut appearance or an unblemished past any indicator of what facts will emerge.

For "Superior Court," it is more profitable to examine the lawyers, as they present the most developed characters. No one lawyer consistently wins or loses. And while none of them are always paragons, neither are any perpetually amoral. Maddox West, for instance, becomes hero-for-a-day by exposing the insurance fraud scheme practiced by attorney Ralph Bell, Bell's client, and a chiropractor's secretary. His performance on other cases, however, indicates more desire to earn the largest possible fee than concern for the underdog. By the same token, prosecutor Charles Wingate is often portrayed as obnoxiously zealous. But when an opposing counsel taunts that a search warrant was obtained without probable cause, Wingate laments, "Why is it that the cops are always wrong and the criminals always right?" For audience members who are distressed by newspaper reports of suspected criminals who "get off" on technicalities, this is a powerful appeal to sympathy for Wingate.

Beyond the mere indeterminacy of good and evil, hints to the audience that one character is good do not mean that good will triumph. In one episode of "Superior Court," a bigot accused of terrorizing a black family is shown plotting perjury. When his attorney removes himself from the case rather than allow that, the bigot tells her that he simply won't tell the next public defender that his alibi is fake. Sure enough, the epilogue states that he was found innocent when retried.

Does good triumph when a bookmaker is acquitted because the evidence against him was obtained by intruding on his privacy with an amplifying device?[15] Or when a pregnant teenager is allowed to seek an abortion? Or when blacks can be laid off in such numbers that affirmative action programs are dismantled, solely because of a "last hired-first fired" policy? In terms of finding heroes and villains, these are questions without clear answers. One viewer's triumph of good may be another viewer's triumph of evil, if these cases are viewed in terms of individual personalities and actions.

Good and evil are neither consistently portrayed nor consistently rewarded. The combat is deliberately muddied, and a message is sent that the legal system cannot be trusted to punish the guilty and reward the wronged. Most people would agree that this is a true message. Is it also a fatally negative one, destined to reduce identification?

As suggested earlier, there is no guarantee that the person the audience is rooting for will be rewarded by the judge. "Superior Court" habitually polls the audience in its studio gallery for its opinion prior to the decision. It is significant that the majority *always* concurs with the judge's decision. Despite the mutability of good and evil, despite the limitations of the legal system, the audience feels that the correct decision is the one mandated by law. This fortunate circumstance results from the attitude with which controversial cases are presented. When a difficult point of law is in question, the lawyers carefully lay out the legal grounds for their side, and those grounds held to be relevant are reinforced by the judge's statement of his decision. A legal consultant may even be called upon for further explanation at the end of the program. The essential message here is that the law is designed to have limitations and imperfections for the protection of all individuals. Loopholes that seem to harm society, such as probable cause, are actually protections for individual rights, such as privacy. Because the audience is shown how their personal rights are preserved by "loopholes," they can accept and identify with the idea that heroism and villainy are determined by objective, consistent law rather than by personal qualities.

IMPLICATIONS

Having explored the positive messages sent by "People's Court," "Divorce Court," and "Superior Court," it becomes necessary to evaluate how these messages compare with the reality of justice. The social reality formed by proto-trial programs does not exist in a vacuum. It is forever in tension with another social reality created by other mass media portrayals of the courts and by actual experiences in the courts.

The concept of social reality is based on the idea that "The terms in which the world is understood are social artifacts, products or historically situated interchanges among people."[16] The "true" nature of an artifact or institution is less inherent within it than linked to the general world view and experiences of the perceiving culture. This is not necessarily a solipsistic view; there are certainly incontrovertible characteristics of the justice system, notably the codified procedures that make trials possible. But equally important are the ways in which the system is predominantly perceived and evaluated. The persuasive impact of proto-trial programs can thus be understood only with reference to other available messages about the judicial system. Three implications emerge: that frustration with the system may result, that the social values of justice may be lost, and that viewers may be discouraged from using the justice system.

Frustration with the System

The proto-trial distorts the conventional form of the courtroom. This reinforces the comprehensibility and accessibility of the system by omitting much of the reality. Even with a lawyer as a guide through the procedural jungle, a litigant familiar with "Superior Court" or "Divorce Court" is likely to be frustrated by the gorges to be bridged before the actual trial. For the "People's Court" fan, even more frustrations lurk. In the course of 7 episodes (11 cases), Judge Wapner suggested only once that *all* plaintiffs should seek a lawyer's advice before proceeding to small claims court.

To the proto-trial fan who goes to trial, the contrast between the program and the reality is likely to increase the mystery of the judicial system: a process expected to be simple, brief, and familiar proves to be extremely lengthy, complex, and unfamiliar. A lawyer may be consulted, at the price of again increasing an aspect of the mystery. If the client should receive any hint of the complexities through which the lawyer moves, there may be two results. The lawyer may, thanks to his or her ability to understand the more than 1,000 rules of civil procedure, revert to a figure of mystery. Or the client, having internalized the idea that lawyers are human, may thereby lose faith in his or her lawyer's ability to see justice done. In either case, the techniques used to present the justice system as accessible are counterproductive.

It is noteworthy, however, that these effects should occur only in the instance that a viewer is a central participant in a trial. The significance of this distinction will become clear in light of the remaining implications.

Loss of Social Values

While the proto-trial programs encourage identification with individuals, they tend to ignore the societal stake in justice. This is particularly clear in the portrayal of trial as combat.

Although the adversarial system does use verbal combat to determine the truth, is determining a winner the true purpose of the judicial system? Is the intent of the law not also to protect the peace and prosperity of society as a whole? As Harvard professor of law Arthur Miller says, "Because the law seeks to draw a measure of harmony out of considerable discord in our society, its basic approach to any significant problem involves a compromise."[17] This is an attitude neglected by all three programs. Even the handling of constitutional issues on "Superior Court" is only a partial exception: the emphasis in these programs is on how the delicate balance protects the rights of *you*, the individual audience member. In general, while neither party may win the entire award sought, the final words of the judge are "Decision for . . . ." Then the camera contrasts the joy of the winner with the despair of the loser. While the combat motif has a deep appeal for the audience, and thus promotes identification with the agents of justice, it downplays the role of the community in the quest for justice.

Furthermore, the community is never the overt source of justice. There is never a jury on the modern programs, only a judge. Removing the instrument of participatory democracy can only be deleterious to community involvement in justice.

There is no inherent reason why there should be *no* juries in any of these trials. If the other procedures of the court can be shortened to fit the time slot, so can the procedures surrounding the jury. All that need be done is omit jury selection and let deliberation take place during the final commercial break. Something of the sort must have been done on "Famous Jury Trials." Even if "People's Court" and "Divorce Court" are to be considered immune to a demand for a jury trial because of their limitations in content, the decision to produce programs with such limitations must be taken into account and the value of showing personal, immediate plights weighed against the absence of the jury.

There is no excuse for the perpetual lack of a jury on "Superior Court." Defendants in criminal cases are entitled to a jury trial. Further, the civil cases shown are largely torts: negligence, wrongful death, breach of contract, misrepresentation, and so forth. In many states, including California, a jury trial has been held to be a right in such cases.[18] True, the right to a jury trial may be waived, but this is not advised in cases where there is a strong appeal to sympathy[19]—the sort of case endemic to "Superior Court."

Relying on a judge unaccompanied by a jury to produce justice sends a potentially dangerous message. If acceptable results can be reached without a jury and no arguments for a jury are ever presented, why should the audience continue to believe that juries are necessary in real trials?

There are already powerful arguments against the jury system. One current area of controversy is whether juries should be used in complex antitrust cases—cases like *AT&T* v. *United States*, which "Superior Court" producers believe to be incomprehensible to the average person. One alternative is the inquisitorial system, exemplified by Judge Wapner's active role in "People's Court" trials. Economist Gordon Tullock argues that such a system prevents one party from having an unfair advantage due to greater resources.[20] Since many people believe that the current system favors the rich over the poor,[21] this is a potentially persuasive argument. Tullock admits that "the possibility of the undermotivation of judges is a real problem," but he extends this problem to the adversarial system as well.[22] And with judges like Burns of "Superior Court," Keane of "Divorce Court," and Wapner of "People's Court," what audience member will feel worry about undermotivation? They clearly are highly motivated and competent.

Tullock further worries that juries are undermotivated. Given encouragement from proto-trial programs to place faith in the wisdom of the judge, why should the average viewer be motivated to serve as a juror? Jury duty is already an inconvenience to most people. Even the entertainment value of being a juror is severely decreased if the same entertainment can be obtained without losing a day's work, hiring a sitter, or fighting for a parking space downtown. In a practical sense, motivation to serve is reduced by these programs, while, in an intellectual sense, the audience is gently shifted toward favoring anti-jury arguments it hears elsewhere. It could be argued that these programs, by making the courtroom an interesting place, motivate the audience to be jurors, but, as with the audience member who becomes a litigant, the contrast between illusion and reality can only serve to make the reality more mysterious and frustrating, thus increasing the persuasiveness of anti-jury messages.

Legal scholars find this message alarming. Philip Corboy, chair of the American Bar Association Section of Litigation states, "The jury is not a luxury we can no longer afford. To the contrary, it is a necessity that we cannot afford to lose."[23] In addition, "If citizens feel the system of civil justice belongs to them and is administered by them, respect for the system will be enhanced."[24] This is the sense the audience is losing, and the price may be the loss of the jury system. Identification with individual combatants is seemingly effective in increasing identification, but it is identification with characters. The audience is not encouraged to accept its proper role in the justice system: that of the society that makes justice possible.

Use of the Justice System

Despite the ostensibly positive messages presented about the justice system and the identification encouraged with its participants, these programs may actually discourage viewers from using the justice system. In two senses, as discussed above, this is a curse. Viewers who believe they understand the system because of "People's Court," "Divorce Court," and "Superior Court" may become frustrated after their first experience and feel greater guilt in future confrontations with the law. Viewers may also lose interest in serving on juries and in participating in the societal aspects of law. In another sense, however, this discouragement may be a blessing. The tone of the programs provides a subtle message that going to court is not a necessary action for reasonable people.

At first viewing, this seems impossible. Most episodes of "People's Court" close with Doug Llewellyn admonishing the audience to "Take 'em to court!" Trials are brief and exciting. Certainly Judge Wapner and Judge Keane sometimes exhibit a low opinion of the litigants, but this is scant antidote for the glamor and excitement of "Superior Court."

Or is it? Social psychologists are divided into two general points of view on the effect of programming and other influences that tend to cause people to rehearse activities in their minds. One line of argument suggests that rehearsal-viewing has a cathartic effect: identifying with a character who performs the desired act is equivalent to performing the desired act oneself. The desire to act is thus decreased significantly.[25]

The other, more frequently supported line of argument says that rehearsal-viewing encourages performance of the desired act by making the act acceptable.[26] If the characters with whom the audience is able to identify were presented only in a favorable light, the audience's desire to sue would probably be increased. Two factors mitigate this effect. First, the audience is not, as has been shown, allowed to develop consistent hero figures. The rewards of litigation are uncertain and, while audience members can better identify with flawed characters, they are less motivated to emulate those flaws. Second, the low opinion of the litigants expressed by Judges Wapner and Keane should somewhat lessen identification with any characters by making their flaws salient. This lessening of identification serves as immunization against Llewellyn's message and as the final message of the proto-trial programs: the actions taken by the characters were satisfying, but they are not to be emulated. Not only does this message benefit the courts by working against unnecessary overcrowding; it also protects viewers from disappointment and guilt arising from the contrast between the social realities of the proto-trial programs and of the experience of a trial.

CONCLUSION

Most proto-trial programs share an educational purpose. As "People's Court" and "Superior Court" coproducer Stu Billett claims, "People really learn about the legal system by watching *People's Court*, and we want that to happen with this program [*Superior Court*] too."[27] Attorney Marc Zafferano offers confirmation: his firm uses "People's Court" to explain the legal system to clients who are nervous and confused about their upcoming trials.[28] But proto-trial programs teach attitudes as well as facts. Out of three common themes—drama versus reality, the trial as combat, and the mutability of good and evil—three interrelated messages emerge. The legal system deals with fundamental human issues. The trial involves a battle between human beings. And the system serves individual ends as best it can, at the price of some apparent unfairness. These three messages combine to create a social reality of the judicial system as accessible and comprehensible. There is a coherent pattern of mystery reduction through identification at the individual level.

When this positive social reality is compared with the alternative social reality obtainable from other common experiences, three disturbing implications emerge: (1) exposure to the reality of the legal system is likely to frustrate a viewer; (2) the lack of a jury and of other references to the societal value of justice may cause viewers to forget—or never learn—their first duty to the legal system; (3) these shows probably discourage litigation and actual use of the system, further removing the audience from the real courtroom.

Juxtaposition of these messages and their ultimate implications results in an overall conclusion about these programs. They provide a positive message that justice is accessible and comprehensible *so long as viewers are not participants in genuine trials*. The learning that takes place is essentially passive; the result is a positive view of the justice system and a largely realistic understanding of its limitations, without any incentive to participate. That any learning occurs at all is good: the facts and procedures depicted do provide a basis for further explanations, and a positive view of the system can only help build a more pleasant and secure social reality. But a passive citizenry is dangerous. By subtly encouraging a passive view of the citizen's role in the judicial system, these programs fall short of their pedagogical potential. While no 30-minute program can take the place of a law degree or even of a course on the legal system, a few unobtrusive alterations, such as use of a jury and an occasional reference to the procedural complexities preceding the trial, could significantly increase the realism and improve the message of these programs. Only when these changes have been made can what we are witnessing truly claim to be real.

NOTES

1. Tim Brooks and Earle Marsh, *The Complete Directory to Prime Time Network TV Shows: 1946–Present*, rev. ed. (New York: Ballantine, 1981), 136–137, 213, 757, 128.

2. Kenneth Burke, *Permanence and Change* (Los Altos, CA: Hermes, 1954), 277–282.

3. Arthur R. Miller, *Miller's Court* (Boston: Houghton Mifflin, 1982), 4.

4. The term "proto-trial" is chosen on the same rationale that has given the world terms like "proto-Attic" art. Although the proto-trial is certainly not an actual trial, the germ of the real thing can be seen.

5. Brooks and Marsh, *Complete Directory*, pp. 242, 91, 394–395, 776.

6. Alex McNeil, *Total Television: A Comprehensive Guide to Programming from 1948 to 1980* (New York: Penguin, 1980), 748, 190, 176.

7. Richard Zoglin, "Tell It to the Judges: Oyez! Oyez! Daytime TV Fills up Its Courtroom Docket," *Time*, November 24, 1986, pp. 90–91. A fourth program, "The Judge," was unavailable for viewing, but is expected to have a similar format.

8. Kenneth Burke, "Lexicon Rhetoricae," in his *Counter-Statement*, 2nd ed. (Los Altos, CA: Hermes, 1953), 126.

9. Ibid., 127, emphasis in original.

10. Michael A. DeSousa, "Symbolic Action and Pretended Insight: The Ayatollah Khomeini in U.S. Editorial Cartoons," in *Rhetorical Dimensions in Media: A Critical Casebook*, rev. ed., ed. Martin J. Medhurst and Thomas W. Benson (Dubuque, IA: Kendall/Hunt, 1984), 225.

11. Nancy Blodgett, "Stay Tuned: New TV Shows Have Law Themes," *American Bar Association Journal* 72, (August 1, 1986):25.

12. Maurice Rosenberg, Jack B. Weinstein, Hans Smit, and Harold L. Korn, *Elements of Civil Procedure: Cases and Materials*, 3rd ed. (Mineola, NY: Foundation, 1976).

13. Terry Fisher quoted in Blodgett, "Stay Tuned," p. 25.

14. Kenneth Burke, "The Philosophy of Literary Form," *The Philosophy of Literary Form*, 3rd ed. (Berkeley: University of California Press, 1973), 20.

15. This might be included in a broad definition of procedural decisions. There are two mitigating factors. First, the entire focus of the program was this issue: it was not a minor piece of procedure within another trial. Second, probable cause is not generally considered by lawyers to be a procedural issue.

16. Kenneth J. Gergen, "The Social Constructionist Movement in Modern Psychology," *American Psychologist* 40 (March 1985):267.

17. Miller, *Miller's Court*, p. 287.

18. Rosenberg et al., *Civil Procedure*, p. 849.

19. Robert E. Keeton, *Trial Tactics and Methods*, 2nd ed. (Boston: Little, Brown, 1973), 246–247.

20. Gordon Tullock, "On the Efficient Organization of Trials," *Kyklos* 28 (1975):51–59.

21. Miller, *Miller's Court*, p. 3.

22. Tullock, "Efficient Organization of Trials," p. 66.

23. Philip Corboy, "Chairman's Corner," *American Bar Association Journal* 66 (January 1, 1980):22.

24. Peter W. Culley, "Civil Juries," *Maine Law Review* 35 (1953):29.

25. Kenneth J. Gergen and Mary M. Gergen, *Social Psychology* (New York: Harcourt Brace Jovanovich, 1981), 301–303.

26. Ibid., pp. 286–293.

27. Jo Stu Billet quoted in Blodgett, "Stay Tuned," p. 25.

28. Marc Zafferano, conversation with author, Atherton, CA, March 6, 1987.

III
CRITICAL STUDIES OF NONFICTION TELEVISION

8

The Ratings "Sweeps" and How They Make News

Meg Moritz

If advertising is the primary selling tool for today's mass-produced media products, then promotion must be a very close second. In the marketing of records, books, films, and prime time television programs, to take the best examples, promotion has become a vital method for reaching the American consumer.

U.S. News and World Report offered a four-page examination of this phenomenon in a 1983 article titled "In Today's Marketplace, It's Hype, Hype, Hype." To illustrate the point, the writer cited promotional gimmicks such as the 20-city talk show, tours routinely set up by publishers for their authors, the $3–10 million budgets commonly used to advertise and promote Hollywood films through guest appearances by stars, and the free and widespread delivery of video clips to TV reviewers.[1]

Since they have ready access to free air time, television promoters have become masters of hype. A case in point: during the 1982 Super Bowl telecast, Mr. T launched his career and his prime time TV series by making three separate appearances in which he delivered a brief but effective promotional message. The bouncer-turned-actor told the audience: "Listen up. The A Team is looking for a few bad men. If you think you're tough enough, see us right after the Superbowl."[2]

The power of television promotions is that they build their own momentum through a cross-fertilization of images carried out by the very media structure they seek to penetrate. Thus we see Mr. T on the Super Bowl telecast and then perhaps on the "Today Show." Soon his growing celebrity status leads to articles in *People* and *Time*.

Then there's a Saturday morning Mr. T cartoon show, followed up with Mr. T tee shirts and lunch pails. It's a process that has been proven effective and is routinely used not only to promote television entertainment shows but also to promote television news shows. It is this use of promotional material that will be examined in this chapter.

Though news promotions take place year round, they are most intense during the ratings sweeps, the month-long periods in November, July, February, and May during which audience ratings are taken in local markets across the country. Since the ratings generated during these months set the advertising rates for all the other months, local stations and networks alike are careful to program and promote their best material during sweep months. Networks, for example, typically air their blockbuster programs during the ratings sweeps. Expensive miniseries such as "Peter the Great," "Wings of Eagles," and "North and South" are designed to run in sweeps, as are major made-for-TV movies such as *The Burning Bed* and *An Early Frost*. And along with the programs come intense and expensive promotional campaigns to get the shows and their stars mentioned in magazines and newspaper television supplements, on radio, and, of course, on the television stations that will air the programs.

The object of all this is to generate higher ratings, and thus higher commercial revenue. At the local station level, a major portion of that revenue is earned by news programs. This situation results in a dilemma that pits journalistic codes and values against commercial considerations. And commercial considerations seem to be winning. News, according to journalistic traditions in the United States, is not supposed to be determined by its audience appeal or by its popularity. In his study of television news, Gans described a process in which "editorial and business departments operate independently of each other. Business department officials would like to influence editorial decisions in order to increase audience size and attract advertisers, but they can only make proposals. Although some feel that journalists do not understand what the audience wants, they also know they cannot interfere."[3] A closer look at what goes on today at local stations during ratings sweeps throws that strict division into question.

Just as the networks hold their trump programming cards until ratings are being taken, so do local news departments stack their deck during the sweeps. While the networks offer their most elaborate entertainment fare, the locals offer a host of investigations and specials on everything from AIDS victims and ambulance breakdowns to radon gas in your basement. And it is heavily promoted in newspapers, on radio,—and of course, on television, both before and during the news shows.

In essence, the promotions promise the best local television journalism of the year. But the promise is often empty, and sweeps reports continually come in for heavy criticism as poor journalism, poor television, and poor attempts to entice the viewer. Speaking of the sweeps specials offered by all three Chicago network-owned stations, (ABC's WLS-TV, CBS's WBBM-TV, and NBC's WMAQ-TV), *Tribune* critic Steve Daley found them "undistinguished and repetitive. Traditionally sweeps stories run the gamut from the cynical to the insipid to the downright moronic. Sex and horrific illness are the hallmarks of any true sweeps period, as are blatant and unvarnished plugs for a station's own network entertainment programming."[4]

The purpose of this study is to look at the forces at work in local television news during the sweeps period in order to determine how and why news specials come into being, to evaluate whether the criticism aimed at sweeps news is accurate, and, if it is, to establish why, during a time when stations want to deliver their best, they frequently deliver some of their worst.

Many of the data are drawn from material aired by WMAQ-TV because the author worked there and has access to many of the people involved in formulating sweeps stories. Sweeps news is a phenomenon that has been identified at local news departments around the country. A description of how this phenomenon unfolds at one of the biggest local news operations in the country may shed light on how it functions at other stations.

HOW SWEEPS FUNCTION

Before the 1960s, radio and television ratings were sampled at various times throughout the year. The system enabled ratings companies to spread their work loads out more or less evenly over the calendar year. But in the 1960s, the American Research Bureau (now Arbitron Ratings Co.) introduced its concept of "sweeping" all local markets during the same time period twice a year. As rating techniques became more sophisticated and as the dollar stakes became greater, stations and buyers demanded uniform samplings that would permit year-to-year as well as market-to-market comparisons. *Electronic Media* explained the rationale thus: "With the sweeps, agency buyers had audience data on every market during a common, comparable four-week period. This eliminated seasonal and program variations in planning spot buys of network affiliates."[5]

Today, Both Arbitron and Nielsen Media Research conduct ratings sweeps four times a year. In September 1987, Nielsen monitored 2,100 homes nationwide with its new people meters. The number of people meters in any particular area roughly reflects the number of households in that area. Chicago, for example, has 3.4 percent of the TV households in the country; it also has 3.4 percent of the Nielsen people meters. In addition, Nielsen monitors local viewing in 15 of the nation's top markets with its older TV meters (roughly 500 in the Chicago market). All meters are linked via telephone line directly to Nielsen computers that record viewing data automatically.[6] During sweeps, Nielsen also mails out several hundred diaries to randomly selected households. Each member of the household is asked to record viewing choices for a week. The information gives Nielsen more detailed data on who in the household—male or female, young or old—is watching what program. Television critic Gordon Walek pointed out how detailed the ratings information can be. "Meters also provide some demographic information in that Nielsen knows the size of the family, its income level and profession. But the diaries offer more specific information, such as whether the man of the house is watching *Miami Vice*, which he usually does, or the woman of the house is watching *Falcon Crest*."[7]

Once they became established, sweeps were quickly identified as being critical to advertising rates year round, and thus to total station revenues. Affiliates learned to play the ratings game to their economic advantage. If a local station was affiliated with a network whose prime time ratings were low, the station could opt to drop the network lineup and substitute proven successes. Movie classics such as *Casablanca* were trotted out to boost the audience size. When sweeps were over, the local station would reinstate the network rundown.

Since a network's audience strength comes from viewership at the local level, pressure built to deliver winning programs during sweeps so that affiliates would stay with the network offerings. The response has been an ever increasing network effort to outdo the competition. Major audience draws are held for sweeps months in almost every case. One of the rare exceptions, NBC's "Andy of Mayberry" anniversary show, caused affiliates to complain so bitterly that programming chief Brandon Tartikoff offered a public apology. "I know you were upset that 'Mayberry' ran in April," he said. "We are doing a sequel that will run during sweeps."[8] At the same time, he went on record for more made-for-TV movies, such as the very successful *The Burning Bed, An Early Frost, Adam,* and *Unnatural Causes*, that would be aired during sweeps. Further he pointed out that the network was holding some original scripts from hit shows for May sweeps. Thus, reruns of "St. Elsewhere" might appear in April, but original scripts would be unveiled in May.

To go along with their lineup of specials, the networks created massive promotional campaigns aimed at increasing audience size, the ultimate determinant of revenue. Edward Jay Epstein explained the cost-benefits ratio thus:

Regardless of the size of the audience, network costs are essentially fixed, and affiliates receive a set amount of compensation per hour from the network no matter how much the network is able to sell the time for; therefore, revenues and profits can be increased through gaining a higher Nielsen rating. . . . Networks have a very powerful incentive to maximize their audience, or at least their Nielsen ratings, since it involves no real diminishing returns.[9]

Local stations face a similar economic reality. The importance of their standings during sweeps is hard to overestimate. A winning sweeps "book" can be cause for champagne and roses in executive offices; a losing "book" can cause heads to roll. But whether ratings are up or down at any station, one thing is clear: they are very carefully watched. At WMAQ-TV, for example, a memo goes to every employee at the end of the ratings period. It is signed by the general manager of the station and gives various data compiled from Nielsen and Arbitron about station performance. Typically, the memo includes a cover letter urging even greater success the next time around. An employee memo issued after the November 1985 sweeps offers a typical example: "Our growth in 1985 came as the result of all our efforts and we should all feel very proud. What we cannot be, however, at this pivotal time is content, as our greatest challenges are still ahead of us."[10]

At the local level, ratings successes hinge on the performance of news shows. The critical question for the local station during sweeps is how to take advantage of the audiences generated by the programs and promotions created by the networks in an effort to help affiliates build audiences. Epstein explained, "Network executives and advertisers believe that a significant portion of the audience for any program is 'inherited' from the preceding program. In this 'audience-flow' theory, the audience is viewed as a river that continues to flow until it is somehow diverted."[11]

Success in the sweeps at local stations can be demonstrated in a number of ways: one is by beating the competition; another is by holding the network audience lead-in or, better yet, increasing it. This is the goal of station executives during sweeps.

NEWS SPECIALS IN SWEEPS

To achieve that goal, local stations have followed the lead of the networks, offering a host of special reports as a regular part of the news and then promoting them heavily throughout the market. A variety of institutional forces impact on how those reports are selected, produced, and promoted; in many instances it seems clear that journalistic considerations play only a minor part in the process.

One of the more obvious techniques in selecting topics for news specials might be termed piggybacking. This begins with the network lead-in as the general subject for the report. Some examples: NBC unveils "Peter the Great," an extravagant miniseries, and WMAQ-TV does companion pieces every night on the Russian community in Chicago; NBC does a three-hour special on its sixtieth anniversary, and WMAQ-TV looks back at its first anchorman. The attraction of these kinds of news specials lies in their promotional value. Every time the network promotes its special, the local station can piggyback its news spin-off promo. In print, the same kind of double package is used, the network footing the bill for a large ad while the local station tacks on a smaller one promoting its product.

The results of this kind of piggybacking of stories and promotions can leave a lot to be desired. On the level of promotion alone, the network is at a considerable advantage. NBC's television promotions for "Peter the Great" were highly polished, packed with slick images, and every bit the equal of a Hollywood movie trailer. The local WMAQ-TV promotions on the Russian community in Chicago, shot with a single camera and a news crew, could not deliver the same stylish look. When the two promos played back to back, as they typically did during the series, the local effort looked particularly weak. On the level of content, the weakness was evident as well, at least in part the result of having to spread the limited material over the entire run of the miniseries.

Some story topics are tied to hit shows and attempt to take advantage of a particular segment of the audience. This was the case with the three-part series on "Miami Vice" done at WMAQ-TV during the November 1985 sweeps. Station research done by Frank N. Magid Associates had indicated that those 18–35 years old who tuned in heavily to "Miami Vice" were not staying to watch the 10 PM news. "They were not going to other stations for news or even to 'Mash' reruns," according to the station's manager of news advertising, Greg Stephan.[12] They were simply tuning out.

The "Miami Vice" series was an experiment, an attempt to see if the demographically desirable 18–35 segment could be carried over into news with heavy promotion of a series in which they presumably would have some interest. The experiment worked from the promotional standpoint. "We went from a 22 share to 27 or 28 and we gained a full ratings point," Stephan said.[13] Over the course of a year that increase could generate about $800,000 in added revenue for the station.[14]

From a journalistic standpoint, however, the series had numerous problems. Unlike the network, the local news department does not hire new producers, writers, and talent for its sweeps specials. These specials are produced during the regular workday with the regular complement of reporters and producers. Some overtime may be incurred, but it is frequently kept to a minimum. The emphasis is on expedience. At least that was the case with the news series on "Miami Vice."

No reporter was dispatched to Miami. No interviews with the show's principals were conducted. All the videotape for the series, with the exception of some Chicago street scenes and an interview with a local critic, came from the NBC station in Washington, D.C., which had just completed a five-part series on the show. Every sound cut with the show's stars and with its creators was therefore predetermined before a script was attempted. This certainly is the reverse of the normal journalistic process.

The series was slickly produced and relied heavily on music and footage from "Miami Vice," so it looked good. Its promise of an inside view of "Vice" was not delivered, however, and the pieces essentially repeated information that had appeared in several print stories about the show.

Cost considerations and promotional value were the overriding reasons for a two-part series in the May 1986 sweeps on foreign television commercials. The series consisted of TV ads from British and French channels and one interview shot in Chicago. The ads were supplied by the NBC station in Los Angeles, which had done a longer series on the same subject, and by some international advertising firms. The Chicago series was edited in one day.[15]

Some sweeps specials are designed to showcase a particular talent and at the same time give the promotion department a hot topic to work with. A three-part series on relationships in the 1980s done during the February 1986 sweeps is a case in point. The idea came from the station's general manager, Dick Lobo, who apparently had seen a similar story in *Time* and thought it had potential for a series of featured reports on the 10 PM news. He suggested reporter Marlene McClinton as the talent, apparently because she was young, female, attractive, and black, all desirable qualities from a promotional standpoint.[16]

"The story proposal was made specifically for Marlene, but she didn't go for it because it was too lightweight and she considered it inconsistent with her desire to build a reputation as a hard news type,"[17] according to series producer Len Aronson.

Aronson was brought in to work on the project with McClinton. His job was not only to work with her on the series but also to convince her to participate in the project. From the start, their approaches to the series were at odds. "The scope of the project was never clearly defined" by the people who came up with the series idea.[18] Aronson wanted to focus on people, while McClinton preferred to concentrate on statistics and hard data.

The series was keyed to Valentine's Day, the first part airing on February 12, the second the next day, and the final one on Valentine's Day. The promotion department brought in an advertising agency to work up a campaign, but the content of the series was still not formulated. "Promotions," Aronson recalled, "was breathing down our necks the whole time."[19] Finally, reporter and producer agreed that the three parts would explore the following: (1) why it's hard to meet people in the 1980s; (2) where people go to meet partners in the 1980s; (3) how to keep a relationship together in the 1980s.

As the deadline for the series approached, it became clear that not enough material was on hand to sustain one, much less three, strong sweeps specials. "We decided we didn't have the time, the inclination, or the clear sense of purpose to deal with the subject in a totally serious way."[20]

In an attempt to strengthen the visual appeal of the series, Aronson gathered music videos and movie clips, which were then combined with some local footage, a few "expert" interviews, and some statistics. The content of the series was noticeably weak. Part 1 revealed that it's hard to meet people because of television: "Many of us are spending too much time in front of the tube." Other obstacles included "the changing roles of women in the work place, the increasing fear of incurable sexually transmitted diseases, and the natural fear of rejection."[21]

Part 2 told us that the place to meet a partner in the 1980s is a health club. "The health industry knows it has captured the bodies of the health-conscious. It also wants to capture their hearts." If that doesn't do the trick, there are always video-mating services, the laundromat, the library, introductions through friends, and ads in the personal columns of newspapers.[22]

Part 3, airing on Valentine's Day, took a decidedly commercial tack. "Gems, gifts, flowers, candies, cookies, and cards help serve as the cement that binds both would-be and established lovers."[23]

Teases, like the series itself, were crafted out of the stockpile of music videos and movie clips. Again, the visual appeal was the primary concern. One suggestion for a promotion prior to the news show carrying the series illustrates the point:

Our relationships sweeps tease shows the scene from *Raiders of the Lost Ark* where a frightened woman is terrorized by a mad Nazi with a redhot branding iron. We thought an appropriate line under this might be something to the effect of: "Do you remember your first flame? Are you looking for that perfect partner? Marlene McClinton looks at relationships of the '80s in a special series called *Maybe This Time*, tonight at 10."[24]

After the series aired, the executive producer of the show that aired it said it was a disservice to viewers and shouldn't have run. Others, including one newspaper columnist, agreed. The consensus in the newsroom was summed up by one staffer's comment: "Maybe next time." Aronson was not happy with the final product, and McClinton took the unusual step of mentioning the names of the producer, crew, and editor on the air, saying privately that she was not about to take the heat for the series alone.

THE PROCESS AT WORK

Clearly, a number of forces are at work that impact on the selection and production of sweeps news specials. Journalistic values, cost considerations, promotional appeal, and public service can all play a part. Any one of these can become the critical factor in any given instance. But overall, the creation of the largest audience appears to be the primary concern.

Selecting subjects for sweeps is an ongoing process that typically involves a brainstorming session with the station's top management, including the news director and the head of advertising and promotion. Participants come armed with a schedule of all major network programs, provided by New York to all local stations about two months before the programs air. "We knew virtually everything about May by mid-March," according to the promotion department.[25]

Working from that programming list, the management team generates a list of news specials. For WMAQ-TV, it covers virtually every 10 PM newscast during the ratings sweep. One of the mainstays of the selection process is the piggyback approach seen in "Peter the Great" and its news companion pieces, "Born in the U.S.S.R." When these assignments are made, it is rare that any prior research has been done to determine the journalistic validity of the suggested stories. It is simply assumed that a reporter will find an interesting story (or four interesting stories if the assignment is for four parts).

Clearly the objective is to maintain audience flow from the network to the local news show. The process is not unique to WMAQ-TV or to news promotions, but it does apply. This planned flow, as Raymond Williams described it in *Television: Technology and Cultural Form*, is "intensified in conditions of competition":

It is evident that what now is called "an evening's viewing" is in some ways planned, by providers and then by viewers, *as a whole*; that it is in any event planned in discernible sequences which in this sense override particular programme units. Whenever there is competition between television channels, this becomes a matter of conscious concern . . . the flow effect is sufficiently widespread to be a major element in programming policy.[26]

Not all sweeps specials are tied to network shows. Some are generated directly from the news department and are justified by their journalistic content. A special done on the 10-year anniversary of the withdrawal from Vietnam is one example. But even here, the promotional value of the piece is recognized and exploited. Other special reports are selected to promote the news department itself and the "stars" of its shows. In the May 1986 sweeps, for example, weatherman John Coleman did a five-part series on vacation spots within a day's drive of Chicago. The reports were all delivered live, via the station's new satellite news gathering (SNG) truck.

The promotion manager explained, "This was a case of interesting content combined with being a showcase for one of the show's stars, and a chance to promote the station's SNG truck, since we're the first ones in the market to have it."[27]

The importance of a story's promotional value can be seen in any station's promotion budget. At WMAQ-TV, the promotion department's budget doubled from 1984 to 1986, increasing to approximately $8 million annually. Sixty-five percent of that money is spent during the three sweeps months considered most crucial to setting advertising rates. (July sweeps are not taken into account because summer reruns do not reflect the schedule for the rest of the year.)

The May sweeps set advertising rates for six months, until the November sweeps are taken. Consequently, an all-out effort is made to promote material in May. At WMAQ-TV, print ads are either purchased or obtained through trade-outs in *TV Guide*, local newspaper supplements, and daily newspaper listings pages. In 1986, 19 radio stations carried 30-second spots promoting the top news stories of the day and the sweep special for the 10 PM show. These were followed immediately by another 30-second spot teasing the 9 PM prime time show leading into the news. The cost in cash and trade-outs was about $40,000 a day.

Most promotional spots that air on WMAQ-TV are done in-house. (The relationships tease cited earlier is an example.) When a promotion calls for unusual special effects to increase its audience draw, it will be done at a production house. The "Miami Vice" promotions, for example, were done out of house, and a single spot cost $8,000—more than the cost of the piece itself.[28]

Sensational story topics are always good candidates for promotional material. In a notorious incident in 1967, WBBM-TV advertised a special report on a Northwestern University pot party that was staged for their cameras. The incident touched off a congressional investigation, and while this kind of blatant staging may still be "quite rare,"[29] other techniques to provide provocative news content during sweeps have evolved. Investigations are launched and conducted with an eye on the sweeps. In May 1986, for example, WMAQ-TV aired its series on radon in homes around the state. The investigation included the largest radon sampling ever done in Illinois and required considerable long-term planning. From the start, it was targeted as a sweeps series.

But even without sensational content, promotion becomes a critical ingredient during sweeps. Stephan explains the goal of these pieces: "You can always make a 30-second spot interesting—even if the piece itself is not—because you tease. You promise apple pie a la mode. What you don't say is it could be very average-tasting pie and ice cream."[30]

It's a case of what Robert Stam calls news imitating commercials, "by advertising itself, its news teams and upcoming news specials."[31] This tease system operates every day, not just during sweeps. But during sweeps, it is usually the sweeps specials that are promoted, even if other material in the news show would provide more significant information. On the evening of the NBC sixtieth-anniversary show, for example, a look back at WMAQ-TV news, the piggyback news report, was promoted at the end of the 6 PM news: "I'm Ron Magers. Tonight at 10, on the sixtieth anniversary of NBC, we'll take a look back at the people who pioneered the great tradition of television news in Chicago."[32]

It was similarly promoted before the NBC special, during the special, and just before the 10 PM news: "Next on Channel 5 . . . our special report opens the door to the past, with memories of Chicago's television pioneers." In both commercial breaks preceding the report, other teases promised "a special look back at the way things used to be" and, finally, "When we come back, a look at how it used to be done by the people who gave television news its traditions."[33]

For Stam, it is an instance of the news cultivating "the pleasing aspect of fiction . . . deploying what Barthes calls 'hermeneutic' teasers, pieces of partial information designed to stimulate interest."[34] And as is inherently the case with piggyback news specials, these teases also promote the network shows that gave them their impetus. Stam notes, "Both commercials and the news fit into generic moulds thrown up by the cinematic and televisual intertext, and this intertext is not intrinsically or invariably naturalistic but often, surprisingly, self-referential and reflexive. Far from being hermetically sealed off from one another, there is constant circulation between the programs."[35]

Cost considerations are another critical aspect of sweeps stories. Since the staff is not expanded to produce these extras, any assignment of reporter and crew to a special report reduces the staff available to cover news of the day. The news department was so strapped for staff when February 1986 sweeps pieces were being done that changes were mandated so the situation would not be repeated.

News Director Dick Reingold issued a memo promising to "schedule at least 9 reporters on the day shift as a minimum and to shoot no more than two 'hold for release' pieces at the same time."[36] The executive producer in charge of news specials announced that fewer five-part series would be assigned for sweeps; instead, the emphasis would be on one- and two-part pieces that would require less crew and production time. Producer Len Aronson, a veteran of several sweeps periods, likened the move to changing your restaurant from haute cuisine to a deli counter. "You offer the customers more variety, but not really a substantial meal."[37]

The promotion department welcomed the move, seeing it as an opportunity to "get more bang for the buck." Stephan described the advantages thus: "There are more topics, therefore there's more to tease. When you compel a reporter to come up with three parts, you can water down the final product. One piece might carry more punch, and strain on the news department (resulting from longer series) is always a consideration."[38]

WHAT THE PROCESS REVEALS

The process by which news specials are produced during ratings periods at local stations is a complex one that can operate differently in different circumstances. Yet some generalizations seem justified, and they reveal television news in its worst light.

Promotion Value Outweighs News Value

News specials are chosen for their promotional appeal. In some instances, this translates into selecting or creating the story with the greatest visual appeal. Like much of television news in general, specials are the result of "highly arbitrary choices even among those items that promise the most visual excitement and drama, while those stories that may be more important in terms of their long-term significance but have little visual, dramatic impact" may never be approached.[39] Sweeps specials heighten the tendency of television news to "give disproportionate coverage to events, or aspects of events, which are spectacular and spectacularly filmed."[40] Certainly the "Miami Vice" series was based on the use of the splendid visuals available in the show itself; a spin-off special on "Wings of Eagles" permitted the rebroadcast of the most dramatic moments of the Iranian hostage crisis.

In some instances, promotional value is derived from having reporters "star" in specials, demonstrating what Stam calls their "suave objectivity," their "forged articulateness," their "authoritative rationality."[41] And throughout, they give voice to "the ersatz communication of a global village which is overwhelmingly white, male and corporate."[42] Thus we see Marlene McClinton informing us that the "cement" that binds relationships is available to any consumer with enough cash to buy "gems, gifts, flowers, candies, cookies, and cards." We see reports telling us what a special, important, innovative program "Miami Vice" is. And we are reminded that this is the station that gave television news its finest traditions. All this from sweeps specials.

News Specials Are Primarily Designed to Build Ratings

News specials during sweeps result from an interlocking process between networks and local stations that is designed for one purpose: to attract the largest possible audience. To that end, the networks provide both programming and promotion.

NBC's Steve Sohmer is credited with developing the "Be There" and subsequent "Let's All Be There" campaigns that accompanied a turnaround in the ratings. Not only was Brandon Tartikoff able to promise affiliated stations "distinctive, competitive, commercial" prime time shows, he was able to assure them those shows would be promoted properly. "It only gets more exciting when you think who we've got promoting these shows like no one else can. Mr. Be There himself—Steve Sohmer."[43]

Sohmer promised Be There tee-shirts and balloons, "along with a complete package of on-air promos with 'windows' for their [the stations'] own messages and daily feeds from the network with teasers for the evening news." As Christensen and Stauth recount, "'News promotion,' Sohmer told them (the affiliates), 'will be our number one priority.'" That suited the affiliates fine, because their local news shows' ratings were crucial to the stations' finances.[44]

Since that promise was made in 1983, little seems to have changed. Speaking in April 1986 at a seminar on the future of local news, NBC's vice-president of editorial and production services, Tom Wolzein, indicated the network's continued willingness to help its local stations crate a strong, competitive news product. *Broadcasting* reported:

Overall, he [Wolzein] said, it remains in the networks' interest to help their affiliates attract large, local news audiences. . . . that commitment has been demonstrated through the network's expanding use of a six-transponder satellite distribution system and an increase of internal news feeds to as many as 50 stories per day.[45]

In an effort to boost news show ratings on the then fifth-place "Channel 5 News at 6," the NBC network took the unusual step in 1986 of enlisting its top news star to deliver teases. The system had Tom Brokaw taping a tease every day in New York for the 6 PM news. The copy was written in Chicago. At the close of the 4:30

newscast, approximately 5:28 PM, the Brokaw tape is played. He urges the audience to stay tuned not only for the local news at 6 but also for Brokaw's own network news program at 5:30. TV critic Steve Daley calls it the "try anything" mode of operation.[46]

That seems to sum up the approach to news specials that operates during sweeps. Institutional forces converge to come up with story topics that will carry the lead-in audience over to news. Added to that is the pressure to come up with promotional campaigns that may require a four- or five-week lead time. For both producers and reporters, to say nothing of viewers, it can be a frustrating endeavor. As producer Aronson notes, "They come up with ideas from *Time* and other magazines. There is no thought to what people in this community really care about. They're not attuned to that. They are Yuppie-oriented. And then promotions locks you into something you may not even want to do."[47]

NOTES

1. Alvin P. Sanoff, "In Today's Market, It's Hype, Hype, Hype," *U.S. News and World Report*, December 5, 1983, pp. 51–54.

2. Ibid., p. 52.

3. Herbert J. Gans, *Deciding What's News* (New York: Pantheon, 1979), 214.

4. Steve Daley, "Local Sweeps-Month Pap Belongs Under a Rug," *Chicago Tribune*, February 11, 1986, sec. 5, p. 5.

5. Mal Beville, "Sweeps Have Become a Costly Network Game," *Electronic Media*, April 14, 1986, p. 29.

6. Telephone interview with Terri Luke, Nielsen Media Research, Northbrook, IL, October 5, 1987.

7. Gordon Walek, "A Portrait of the Nielsens: How So Few Viewers Control Network TV," *The Daily Herald* (Arlington Heights, IL), May 29, 1986, sec. 2, p. 5.

8. Satellite teleconference given by Brandon Tartikoff, originating from NBC studios in Burbank, CA, April 22, 1986. Teleconference was downlinked in 15 cities so that media critics could participate in the news conference.

9. Edward Jay Epstein, *News from Nowhere* (New York: Vintage Books, 1973), 83.

10. Dick Lobo and Allan Horlick, "November '85 Sweeps," NBC memo, December 30, 1985.

11. Epstein, *News from Nowhere*, p. 93.

12. Interview with Greg Stephan, manager of news advertising, WMAQ-TV, May 12, 1986.

13. Ibid.

14. Ibid.

15. Interview with Len Aronson, a news producer at WMAQ-TV, May 10, 1986.

16. Ibid.

17. Ibid.

18. Ibid.

19. Ibid.

20. Ibid.

21. Excerpt from "Maybe This Time," WMAQ-TV report, aired February 12, 1986.

22. Excerpt from "Maybe This Time," WMAQ-TV report, aired February 13, 1986.

23. Excerpt from "Maybe This Time," WMAQ-TV report, aired February 14, 1986.

24. Internal memo, WMAQ-TV, February 12, 1986.

25. Stephan interview.

26. Raymond Williams, *Television: Technology and Cultural Form* (New York: Schocken Books, 1974), 91, 93.

27. Stephan interview.

28. Ibid.

29. Epstein, *News from Nowhere*, p. 99.

30. Stephan interview.

31. Robert Stam, "Television News and Its Spectator," in *Regarding Television*, ed. E. Ann Kaplan (Frederick, MD: University Publications of America, 1983), 36.

32. Excerpt from WMAQ-TV programming, May 12, 1986.

33. Ibid.

34. Stam, "Television News," p. 32.

35. Ibid., p. 36.

36. Dick Reingold, WMAQ-TV memo, May 23, 1986.

37. Aronson interview.

38. Stephan interview.

39. Martin Esslin, *The Age of Television* (San Francisco: W. H. Freeman, 1982), 59.

40. Paul H. Weaver, "Newspaper News and Television News," in *Television as a Social Force*, ed. Douglass Cater and Richard Adler (New York: Praeger, 1975), 16.

41. Stam, "Television News," p. 29.

42. Ibid., p. 39.

43. Brandon Tartikoff, quoted in Mark Christensen and Cameron Stauth, *The Sweeps* (Toronto: Bantam Books, 1984), 187.

44. Ibid.

45. "Local TV News: Nipping at the Heels of the Networks," *Broadcasting*, May 5, 1986, p. 76.

46. Steve Daley, "Channel 7 Likely to Sweep Evening News Ratings," *Chicago Tribune*, May 29, 1986, sec. 5, p. 4.

47. Aronson interview.

9
The Graphication and Personification of Television News
Herbert Zettl

If you were to compare your local newscast ten years ago with the one today, you would probably find precious little difference in content. People are still starving in Africa and other parts of the world, the Middle East is still in a mess, we continue to play Russian roulette in the area of arms control and atomic energy, and some of our fellow human beings go on murdering others in defiance of basic ethics, respect for life, and supreme law. But when we take a closer look at how the news is presented, we will witness a startling difference. While the earlier newscasts basically showed the newscaster, with the narrative illustrated by film clips, videotape, and chromakey inserts, today's news presentations are often quite similar to the razzle-dazzle of video games. Computer-generated graphics pop on the screen to give us headlines, field reporters and their stories are sqeezoomed in and out over the news anchor's shoulder, and fancy lettering repeats what we have heard the newscaster tell us. Through the magic of digital video, live scenes are frozen into still images and peeled off page by page, as though we were flipping through a magazine.

We may be tempted to write off such visual extravaganzas as mere attention-getting devices, or perhaps as a rather expensive gimmick prompted by the manufacturers of DVE (digital video effects) equipment, who invented such devices oblivious of use, and who now like to sell their goods and find some satisfaction in seeing their technical creations applied, however frivolously. But this would be quite short-sighted. By looking just slightly closer than the ordinary viewer at the various effects and their repeated use in news presentations, we will readily discover several new aesthetic phenomena and processes that beg for explanation.

For example, when we put a line and the name across a field reporter, squeeze an upcoming news event into a small frame within the television screen and have it hover over the anchor person's shoulder, or freeze an event image to simulate a magazine photo, then peel it off and make it tumble through the television screen space like a wind-blown autumn leaf, what will the viewer consciously or subconsciously perceive? Will such visual acrobatics facilitate or inhibit objective reporting? Could it be that such visual effects provide codes and subcodes that make us perceive the news stories or the news presenters in specific, perhaps intentional, ways?

It is the purpose of this chapter to answer, however tentatively, some of these questions.

THE PROBLEM

Specifically, the problem is (1) to analyze some of the special effects commonly used in news presentations; (2) to isolate the major nonverbal codes; and (3) to interpret them within the field of media aesthetics. This study does not concern itself with such major aesthetic variables as lighting, camera positions and movement, or sound.

ANALYSIS APPROACH

While the producers of television news in the United States are at least as concerned with the general "look" of the news (the news set, the type and number of visuals presented) and the personality of the news presenters as with the actual news content, most published studies concentrate on what, rather than how, news is presented. True to the tradition of literary criticism, we seem to feel much more comfortable discussing the type of news stories selected and how these stories influence the audience's perception of today's world[1] than with how the stories are displayed on the television screen. The few studies that are primarily concerned with presentation techniques rarely go beyond a mere description of what is being done[2] or how the presentation techniques differ among the various networks.[3] One of the findings in the diligent and admirable Schneider study reveals that "CBS uses lettering and generic graphics more than ABC or NBC, and ABC uses the live-on-scene technique more than the other two networks."[4] But exactly what nonverbal codes are transmitted by the lettering? How do we perceive graphics that are squeezed in a box over the news anchor's shoulder? Is there perhaps a difference in how we perceive the news people operating in the regular news set and those appearing in the "box"?

The method of the present study follows the rather difficult "soft approach" to research,[5] a looking at the obvious to discover the not-so-obvious. By careful and repeated observation of special effects in local and network television news, I tried to isolate significant aesthetic phenomena and processes, describe and classify them, and finally suggest ways in which the various nonverbal codes might influence our perception of news presentations.

For the initial analysis phase of news presentations, I used the major criteria I developed in *Sight Sound Motion: Applied Media Aesthetics*,[6] such as field of view (relative closeness of shots), selected graphic forces, the articulation of two- and three-dimensional space, and the motion within the frame.

The second analysis phase was a more careful look at the specific space manipulations within the two-dimensional field, especially those of DVE, and their relationship to the traditional simulated three-dimensional television space. The specific focus was on the meaning and possible aesthetic consequences of a secondary frame within the television screen, and on the display of written material on the television screen.

The third analysis phase is ongoing. It deals with establishing a reliable index that may facilitate the use of statistics in accepting or refuting various hypotheses. I realize that the application of statistics in the area of media aesthetics is quite difficult, not necessarily because the aesthetic factors and their effects are so subjective and elusive, but because our available measuring devices are not always sensitive enough to detect minute aesthetic differences.[7] This does not mean, however, that we therefore should eschew the idea of measurement in production research altogether. We need to work simultaneously on refining our aesthetic measuring tools and on delineating with great care just what it is we want to measure. This study is concerned with the latter.

BASIC OBSERVATIONS

Three basic observations are reported in this chapter: (1) the graphication of the television image, that is, the deliberate attempt to render the television image two-dimensional and graphiclike; (2)

first- and second-order spaces and their use in news presentations; and (3) the personification of the news anchor. All these terms will be defined and explained in detail later in the chapter.

GRAPHICATION TAXONOMY

Let us now take a closer look at some of the more prominent uses of DVE in news. These effects consist almost exclusively of various forms of lettering, stripes, and narrow bands that cut across pictures; secondary frames within the television screen; and computer-generated graphic images that move about the screen while undergoing topological changes. The main characteristic of all these digitally generated or manipulated images is their two-dimensional graphic appearance, not unlike those of the illustrations and captions in a magazine page. This tendency to render television images deliberately graphiclike I call graphication. Even realistic, camera-generated scenes can be readily "graphicated."

Although there are innumerable electronic effects possible, we can group the more commonly used graphication devices quite readily into eight categories: (1) straight lettering via character generator; (2) lettering combined with visual images; (3) an actual scene (static or in motion) with keyed-in lines and lettering; (4) persons with keyed-in lines and lettering; (5) a secondary frame that contains a static scene, with or without additional lettering; (6) a secondary frame that contains a scene in motion, with or without additional lettering; (7) a static computer-generated image that simulates three-dimensional space; and (8) an image (usually contained in the secondary frame) that changes its position on the television screen and undergoes structural (solarization, mosaic effect) and/or topological changes (expanding, contracting, or twisting). (See Figures 9.1–9.8).

AESTHETIC ANALYSIS

This part of the study deals with the major aesthetic factors and principal communication functions of graphication in news presentations.

Secondary Frame

The most widely used secondary frame is the "box" keyed over the news anchor's shoulder. Sometimes a large actual television set is used as the secondary frame. The large chromakey area with which the

Figure 9.1
Straight Lettering via Character Generator

Figure 9.2
Lettering Combined with Visual Images

Figure 9.3
Actual Scene with Keyed-in Lines and Lettering

Figure 9.4
Person with Keyed-in Lines and Lettering

Figure 9.5
Secondary Frame Containing Static Scene

Figure 9.6
Secondary Frame Containing Scene in Motion

Figure 9.7
Simulated Three-D Space

Figure 9.8
Topological and Position Change of Secondary Frame

anchor person interacts is still another widely used secondary frame. Occasionally we see a thin border in the shape of a television screen keyed over the full-screen television image, with parts of the scene bleeding through this secondary frame to the edges of the actual television screen. All these secondary frames are self-contained areas that, very much like framed pictures, become part of the total news scene on our television set (Figure 9.9).

In contrast with the usual three-dimensional "pyramidal" television space[8] generated by the camera lens (Figure 9.10), the secondary frame is always perceived as two-dimensional, very much like a picture in a magazine. The major aesthetic elements that contribute to this two-dimensionality are the picture borders, drop shadows, figure ground, and topological changes.

Picture Border

These secondary frames are purposely rendered picture like, that is, the secondary picture area is framed as though it were an actual photograph or a framed picture that is suspended somewhere in the television space or glued into a photo album. Most commonly, the picture area is clearly defined by a computer-generated border. Some of the borders are simply white or colored lines that delineate the secondary frame; others simulate actual picture frames (Figure 9.11). Sometimes the scene within the secondary area protrudes through the top of the frame (Figure 9.12). Because this effect simulates graphics we see in magazines, the abstracting graphication effect is stronger.

Drop Shadow

The electronically generated drop shadow at the side of and below the picture frame looks like a real cast shadow that falls onto a second, larger vertical plane (Figure 9.13).

Figure Ground

Whenever we see a clearly defined, smaller area within a larger field, we automatically perceive the smaller area as the figure that lies on top of the ground.[9] The ground, which seems to continue behind the figure, provides a relatively stable background for the less stable figure (Figure 9.14). The most widely used secondary

Figure 9.9
Secondary Frame in News Set

Figure 9.10
Normal Pyramidal 3-D Television Space

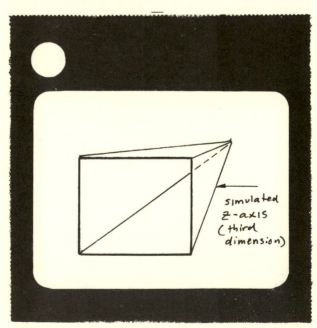

Figure 9.11
Simulated Picture Frame Around Secondary Space

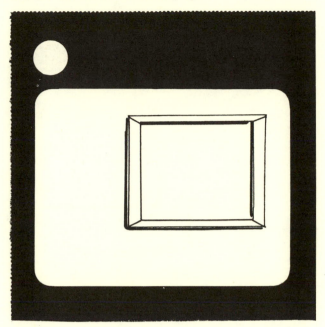

Figure 9.12
Protrusion of Secondary Frame

Figure 9.13
Simulated Drop Shadow on Secondary Frame

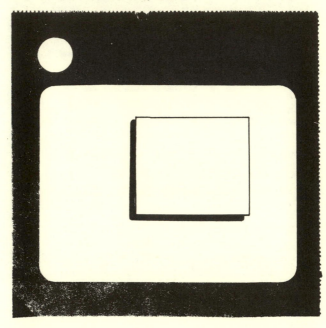

Figure 9.14
Figure-Ground Phenomenon

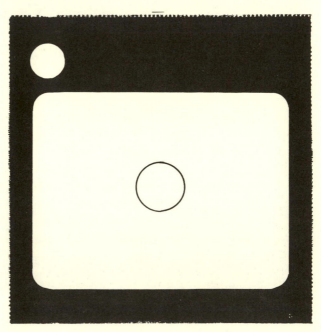

frame, the box insert that hovers over the news anchor's shoulder, is readily identified as the figure, and the out-of-focus news set as the common ground (Figure 9.15). Perceptually, the box seems to hang between the news anchor and the back of the news set. The secondary frame and the drop shadow make it clearly stand out from the background (see Figure 9.9).

Figure-Ground Reversal

Sometimes we experience a figure-ground reversal in which the area surrounding the secondary frame is seen as the figure and the secondary frame as a "window," a hole through which we can peek into another scene unfolding immediately behind it. Such a figure-ground reversal is most likely to occur when the secondary frame has neither special borders nor drop shadow, and especially when the scene behind the window is in motion (Figure 9.16). Such a window effect is highly graphicated, and does not make us perceive ordinary pyramidal television space. We still imagine, however unconsciously, another vertical picture plane, a "superground" lying behind the scene. After all, even the most meticulously executed linear perspective in a Renaissance painting does not make us perceive the picture space going through the wall on which it hangs.

Letters and stripes that are keyed over a scene also prompt the figure-ground perception. Like the letters on this page, letters on the television screen are inevitably seen as the figure, and the images behind the letters as the ground. This figure-ground relationship persists even if the ground happens to be a static or a moving three-dimensional scene. The letters or stripes seem to press the "three dimensional" television-mediated scene into a decisively two-dimensional submission. Much like the velvet ropes in banks, movie houses, and restaurants that keep us in line, the graphic stripes and letters keep the background scene in place and prevent it from pushing itself into the foreground (see Figures 9.3 and 9.4).

People are not immune to becoming graphicated through stripes and letters. Regardless of whether they appear in a studio or a field setting, the graphic lines and letters inevitably relegate them to background space (see Figure 9.4).

Topological and Structural Changes

Sometimes the graphicated images seem to consist of a stack of favorite photos that are peeled off one by one. While the individual

Figure 9.15
Figure-Ground Effect of Box in News Set

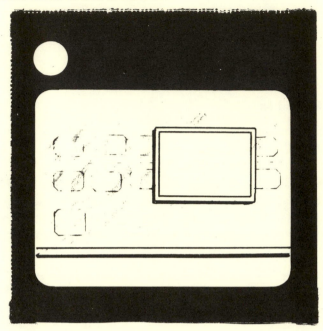

Figure 9.16
Figure-Ground Reversal with Scene in Motion

pictures that peel off are undoubtedly two-dimensional, the photo stack itself claims no third dimension. What happens perceptually is that the three-dimensional pyramidal space of the normal television scene is shrunk into a truncated Euclidean space with a highly limited z-axis.[10] All we have now is a series of two-dimensional frontal planes, one lying immediately behind the other, very much like a stack of photos or the pages of a thin magazine (Figures 9.17 and 9.18).

Other topological and position changes seem to make the graphicated image (such as the box frame over the news anchor's shoulder) tumble or fly like a magic carpet toward the horizon of the pyramidal television space. Mosaic and solarization effects are equally powerful graphication methods; they, too, contribute to the picturelike abstraction of the normal television image. Obviously, such topological and structural manipulations contribute greatly to the graphication process, rendering the graphicated images picturelike.

Graphication Paradoxes

Occasionally the use of DVE in television news plays tricks on our perceptual habits and expectations. For example, when the camera operator does not allow enough room for the placement of the secondary frame, the box will overlap part of the news anchor and appear to be in front of him or her. This Escher-like switch is quite startling, because we had assumed all along that the box was hanging *behind* the newscaster. We are equally surprised when the field reporter in the box looks over his shoulder, referring to the traffic jam behind him. While the scene in the box clearly shows a foreground, middle ground, and background, we do not assume any actual z-axis space (third dimension) in a heavily graphicated, picturelike box. The field reporter seems to be staring at the real background, the out-of-focus back of the news set.

But as soon as we have learned to graphicate an actual scene, we try, in the true spirit of Homo sapiens, to make the two-dimensional graphs three-dimensional again. Despite the three-dimensional rendering of the graph, we are very much aware of the basic two-dimensional character of the picture, just as we are when looking at a graph in a magazine (Figure 9.19).

At this point we might ask ourselves what the underlying purpose of such graphication is, and whether and how if at all such graphication techniques enhance the news. Are they merely a gimmick that

Figure 9.17
Truncated Euclidean Space

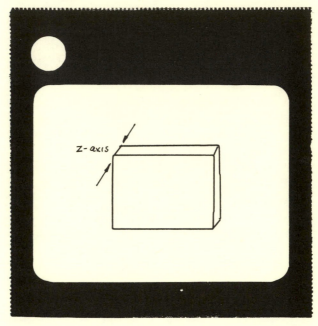

Figure 9.18
Picture Stack Illusion

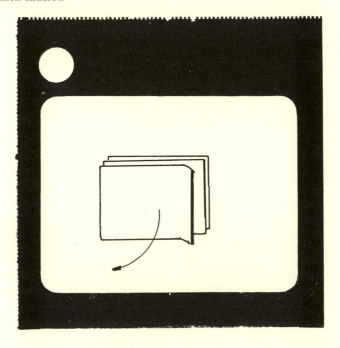

Figure 9.19
Three-Dimensional Graph

might, at best, keep us from switching channels? Or do they represent significant nonverbal codes that serve a variety of important communication functions that make us perceive the news images and the news people in a specific way?

COMMUNICATION FUNCTIONS OF GRAPHICATION

Despite the fun and creative potential of manipulating images through DVE, the electronic wizardry of graphication could not prevail if it did not fulfill important communication functions. Even without the benefit of a careful semiotic analysis, we can quite readily identify four major communication functions: (1) informational, (2) status conferral, (3) metalinguistic, and (4) aesthetic.

Informational Function

The informational function of graphication is to supply us with additional data. The words on the screen give us information we did not have before, or reinforce other visual and aural images. At best, iconic images such as a freeze frame of a car accident in the box above the news anchor's shoulder tell us in a flash what the story is about; at the least, they serve illustrative functions.

Status Conferral Function

We seem to put a special trust in the printed word, regardless of whether it appears in the Code of Hammurabi, the Talmud, the Bible, the Constitution of the United States, or the local newspaper. Once ideas appear in print, they attain a ring of truth, no matter how tentative they might originally have been.[11] In this age of accountability, a written record is valued much more than even the most sincere oral statement. Writing memoranda after an oral agreement has become a routine administrative practice.

Similarly, we back up important oral statements by having them appear in print on the television screen. We might interpret this practice as a necessary communication redundancy, an attempt to combat entropy and to assure information accuracy. But I think that the underlying and probably more important function of print on television is that it confers status on the message.[12] Although the printed word on television is just as transient and evanescent as the spoken word, we still attach more permanence, and therefore more communication value, to the former.

Metalinguistic Function

Graphication can become a code that provides the framework for the interpretation of the information we see and hear. The written code not only supports the verbal one, but often dictates what we ought to see and how we are supposed to see it. For example, if the graphication in the box shows a typical midwestern farm with the word "crisis" printed over it, we tend to interpret the accompanying story within the mental set of "crisis," regardless of what the story is actually about. This is nothing new. Similar effects were reported in 1953 by Tannenbaum,[13] who found that newspaper headlines had a significant effect on how the story was interpreted. Digitally created graphic symbols can fulfill similarly reflexive interpretation functions. For example, the digitally created graphic of a smoking gun signals a murder story, or the flame a disastrous fire.

Such graphication devices can lead to rather dubious interpretations. If, for instance, we key into the box over the news anchor's shoulder the digitally generated graphic of a smoking gun and the word "murder," we not only provide a prelude for the upcoming news story but also, if not primarily, a perceptual if not conceptual framework within which to interpret the story.[14] The casual viewer is likely to be seduced into confusing the picture of the suspect with the actual murderer, and probably into interpreting the total news story within the paradigm of the graphicated murder image. The power and the danger of such graphication techniques lie not only in the instantaneousness of such communication but also, and especially, in its intensity and permanence. While we tend to forget the various factual details of an audio-visual presentation over a period of time, we readily maintain and recall the opinion formed during the original presentation. This "sleeper effect," as Hovland called it when he conducted such experiments in the 1940s,[15] seems to function in today's television news presentations as well. We are much more apt to remember, and especially recall, the graphicated symbol than the more detailed story as told by the news anchor.[16]

Aesthetic Function

One of the most important functions of graphication is the division of television space into two separate and distinct parts: (1) the graphicated space, which we perceive as "picture" space; and (2) the normal television space, which we perceive as three-dimensional space. I would like to call the normal television space "first-order space," and the graphicated space "second-order space." The rest of this study is devoted to how we perceive and how we are affected by these two types of video space.

FIRST- AND SECOND-ORDER SPACE IN NEWS PRESENTATIONS

In its simplest configuration, the anchor person on the news set occupies first-order space; the box that is keyed over his or her shoulder, or the large television screen or chromakey area in the news set, represents second-order space (see Figure 9.9).

Throughout the discussion on graphication and its aesthetic characteristics, I emphasized the picturelike quality of the graphicated image in contrast with three-dimensional images in nongraphicated first-order television space. The various graphication devices applied to second-order space images are carefully designed to make us perceive pictures on television, a purposely abstracted form of reality. The picture frame that delineates second-order space is one of the major factors in this graphication process.

Much like a frame around a painting or photograph, the frame around the second-order box has a certain abstracting function. Arnheim's observations concerning picture frames are equally valid when speaking of borders around second-order television space. He writes:

The frame indicates that the viewer is asked to look at what he sees in the picture not as part of the world in which he lives and acts, but as a statement about the world—a representation of the viewer's world. This implies that the matter seen in a picture is not to be taken as part of the world's inventory but as a carrier of symbolic meaning.[17]

People who operate in second-order space are not immune to this abstraction process. For example, by showing the field reporter in a tightly framed box insert, we create a certain aesthetic distance, if not alienation, between the person appearing in this second-order space and the viewer that is very much in line with the Russian formalists' idea of *ostranenie,* or Bertold Brecht's *Verfremdungseffekte* (alienation effects).[18] When coupled with other graphication devices, such as lines and names keyed over the second-order image, we are constantly reminded that we are watching pictures of an event, rather than the event itself.

The graphication of second-order space is so strong that we perceive an event to be in second-order space even if the second-order image temporarily occupies the entire screen area. For example, if a field reporter appears first in a box insert and is then squeezoomed out to a full-frame image, we still perceive him or her as occupying second-order space, as long as he or she does not occupy the total screen area for a prolonged period of time. But even then, we can readily remind the viewer of second-order space by periodically graphicating the image through lines and/or letters (such as name titles or whether the event is live or not) over the field reporter (see Figure 9.4).

As a direct consequence of the second-order graphication and abstraction process, the nongraphicated images in first-order space take on more and more the reality character of the world in which we actually live. While second-order space emphasizes the difference between signifier and signified, first-order space muddles this difference and makes the viewer transpose (however uncritically) the television-represented world to a new—or, rather, different—reality experience. Second-order space acts as a necessary catalyst for this unique metaphoric process in which, to borrow a phrase from Fiske and Hartley, the real world is *displaced* rather than merely *displayed* in first-order space.[19] If first-order space is not juxtaposed with graphicated second-order space, we remain very much aware of the video space as defined by the borders of the television set, even if we as audience project images beyond the television screen. But this offscreen space in which we mentally complete the onscreen close-up figures is nevertheless closely tied to the onscreen space and the images displayed there.[20] As soon as first-order space is juxtaposed with a second-order space insert (such as the box over the anchor person's shoulder), however, we are perceptually quite willing to ignore the confines of the television set and to extend the scene into our actual living space. People operating in second-order space are, as George Linden would say, *in* space; those occupying first-order space, however, *inhabit* space. In contrast with the picturelike second-order space, first-order space has become "humanized."[21] The "matter" in first-order space has become part of the world's inventory.

PERSONIFICATION OF THE NEWS ANCHOR

Contrary to Tony Schwartz, who claims that people in television "have no corporeal form,"[22] this humanizing effect of first-order space, coupled with the customary intimate close-ups,[23] may cajole us into perceiving the anchor person, or anyone else operating in first-order space, as a real person rather than a television image, and into relating to the "first-order people" psychologically, if not socially, as extended family members or close friends one is used to having around the house. Persons in second-order space, however, are inevitably perceived as being *on* television. This incarnation process, giving the person in first-order space the flesh-and-blood qualities of a real person, I will call "personification."

I should emphasize again that it is not first-order space per se that contributes automatically to a personification of the news anchor. In the absence of second-order space, the personification of the news anchor is probably minimal. Indeed, if we graphicate this type of video space by keying the news anchor's name over the scene, very little, if any, personification is likely to occur (Figure 9.20).

As soon as we key in the box over the news anchor's shoulder, however, the personification process comes into play. The personification is further intensified by the anchor's interacting with the people in second-order space. For example, if the news anchor looks at and converses with the field reporter or guest in second-order space, we as viewers tend to associate with the anchor and to have the anchor share our viewing position. In effect, the anchor

Figure 9.20
Undue Graphication of News Anchor

and the audience watch the television event in second-order space together and from the same perspective. It is exactly the intended and calculated fragmentation, the separation of space, that leads to the personification of the news anchor, and not the illusion of shared space between the first-order and second-order people, as Jane Feuer erroneously concludes in her otherwise astute analysis of "Good Morning, America."[24] Indeed, "Good Morning, America" is an excellent example of the personification process through a deliberate split between nongraphicated first-order space and highly graphicated second-order space.

Charles Gibson operates in first-order space with its warm-colored, comfortable living room set that extends quite readily into the home viewing environment. No graphication is ever applied to this space. Most of his guests, including the newscaster, appear in a highly delineated second-order space, a television set he watches with us, the viewers. Even if during the interview the subjects in second-order space are occasionally allowed "out of the box" to oc-cupy the total screen area of the home television set, they are re-peatedly graphicated through name and location keys. And, as a constant reminder that we watch television *together* with Charles, the guests are periodically "put back into the box." The interview inevitably ends up with guests back in second-order space, when Gibson and we the viewers say good-bye to the guests on television. The close, personal relationship between Gibson and his viewers is, I think, to a large extent the direct result of his personification.

Because American television puts so much emphasis on the personality of the news anchors, we may well ask whether the ratings of newscasts may not be influenced to some extent by the degree of personification rather than by the actual content of news. Could there perhaps be some correlations between personification and ratings?

PERSONIFICATION INDEX

In order to correlate the degree of personification and the actual ratings for the newscasts, we need, first of all, a reliable personification index. Although my seminar members[25] and I established a tentative index some years ago (consisting of such variables as type, frequency, and duration of graphication of first-order space, type and color of scenery in first-order space, use and relative graphication of second-order space and frequency of direct communication between people in first-order space and people in second-order space), I am still in the process of refining the graphication and personification indexes and testing their reliability.

To see whether there are any possible connections between graphication and personification in news, we analyzed the same-day evening news on the three network affiliates in San Francisco—KGO (ABC), KPIX (CBS), and KRON-TV (NBC)—as to relative degrees of graphication and personification. I hasten to add that the graphication and personification indexes used at that time and their application were highly tentative; they were not subjected to the customary reliability tests. Nevertheless, the results were rather startling (see Tables 9.1 and 9.2).

As we can readily see, KPIX (CBS) has the highest degree of graphication of second-order space and the highest degree of personification of the news anchor. Interestingly, the Nielsen ratings for these newscasts show the same rank order as the personification ratings: KPIX, rating 14; KGO, rating 12, KRON-TV, rating 8. When we normalize the combined graphication and personification scores and compare them with the Nielsen rating figures, the correlation becomes even stronger (see Table 9.3).

Again, I would like to emphasize that the indexes for the graphication and personification and the resulting algorithms have not been tested sufficiently as to their validity and reliability. However, they were encouraging enough for us to pursue this type of analysis, to ask some more questions, and to establish some tentative hypotheses.

Table 9.1
Graphication Ratings

KRON-TV (NBC)	13
KGO (ABC)	12
KPIX (CBS)	14

The graphication index refers to second-order space graphication, and not to graphication in general. 20 = maximum second-order space graphication; 0 = minimum second-order space graphication.

For example, might not the "look" of a newscast determine its popularity more than its literal content? Could we perhaps predict with some reliability the relative popularity of newscasts simply by looking at them, ignoring to a large extent the literal news content—that is, what is being said? Could the newscast, in which we try to be more objective than in any other form of television genre, ironically be the most telling example of how the medium influences the message—a prophecy expressed by Marshall McLuhan in the 1960s?

Obviously these questions require a great deal more thinking and research before they can be answered with even a moderate degree of certainty.

SUMMARY AND CONCLUSION

In our analysis of the major special effects used in news presentations, we isolated a variety of devices that render the television image deliberately two-dimensional and graphiclike, similar to a magazine picture. This visual abstraction process I call "graphication." When juxtaposing the graphicated images, such as the box over the newscaster's shoulder, with the nongraphicated images in normal television space (the news anchor, set), we can distinguish between first-order space (the normal television space) and second-order space (the graphicated television space). Because the tightly framed, abstracted images in second-order space (such as the box) are perceived as pictures, we may under certain circumstances assign the first-order images (the news anchor's environment) greater "reality." This perceptual shift may well extend to the people operating in the different spaces. For example, the field reporter who appears in the highly graphicated box is definitely perceived as a person *on* television. Consequently, we may assign the news anchor in nongraphicated first-order space more corporeal qualities, a process I call "personification."

Table 9.2
Personification Ratings

KRON-TV (NBC)	4
KGO (ABC)	13
KPIX (CBS)	14

The numbers represent personification ratings for only five key personification indexes. The rating figures range from 0 to 20; 0 = lowest degree of personification, and 20 = highest degree of personification.

Table 9.3
Correlation of Personification/Graphication Scores and Nielsen Ratings

	Combined P + G Score	Nielsen Rating	Normalized P + G Score
KRON-TV (NBC)	17	8	8.0
KGO (ABC)	25	12	11.8
KPIX (CBS)	28	14	13.2

A normalized score means that the first column is brought to the same scale as the second column. This way, the comparison shows not only rank order but also the relative steps of ratings and the combined personification-graphication scores. For KRON-TV the P + G score (17) is normalized with the Nielsen rating (8) by dividing 17 by 8, which equals 2.125. All subsequent P + G scores are divided by 2.125 to normalize them with the rating figures.

Here are the tentative answers to the questions posed in this study: (1) Do the DVE enhance the news? Yes, if they provide additional information. No, if they operate as a delimiting paradigm, a schema, for the way the viewers are to interpret the news story. (2) Is there enough evidence to suggest that the popularity, and perhaps even the authority, of the anchor person is determined by video manipulation rather than by story content? A qualified yes. (3) Is the evidence for these assumptions conclusive? No, but it is sufficient to formulate four tentative hypotheses: (a) that the graphication of the television image fulfills important informational, status conferral, metalinguistic, and aesthetic functions; (b) that graphication renders the television image two-dimensional and graphiclike, very much like a picture in a magazine; (c) that the juxtaposition of highly graphicated second-order space with nongraphicated first-order space renders the latter more "real" than the former; and (d) that people operating in nongraphicated first-order space are more readily "personified," that is, appear more "real" (if not "corporeal") than people in second-order space.

NOTES

1. See Herbert Gans, *Deciding What's News* (New York: Pantheon, 1979); W. Lance Bennet, *News: The Politics of Illusion* (New York: Longman, 1983); Maxwell McCombs (ed.), *Setting the Agenda for Agenda-Setting Research: An Assessment of the Priority Ideas and Problems* (Buck Hill Falls, PA: American Association of Public Opinion Research, 1979).

2. George Comstock, *Television in America* (Beverly Hills, CA: Sage, 1980).

3. Frederick P. Schneider, "The Substance and Structure of Network Television News: An Analysis of Content Features, Format Features, and Formal Features," unpublished Ph.D. diss., Syracuse University, 1985.

4. Ibid., p. 190.

5. Chikio Hyaski, "Methodological Problems in Mass Communication Research," in *Studies in Broadcasting*, ed. H. Eguchi and K. Sata (Tokyo: Theoretical Research Center/The Radio and TV Culture Research Institute, NHK, 1973), 121–151.

6. Herbert Zettl, *Sight Sound Motion: Applied Media Aesthetics* (Belmont, CA: Wadsworth, 1973).

7. See Jon P. Baggaley, "Continual Response Measurement in TV Research," *Canadian Journal of Eductional Communication* 16 (1987); Hans Kepplinger and Wolfgang Donsbach, "The Influence of Camera Angles and Political Consistency of the Perception of a Party Speaker," in *Experimental Research in Televised Instruction*, vol. 5, ed. Jon Baggaley (Montreal: Concordia University, 1982); and Nikos Metallinos and Robert K. Tiemens, "Asymmetry of the Screen: The Effect of Left Versus Right Placement of Television Images," *Journal of Broadcasting* 21 (1977):21–33.

8. Rudolf Arnheim, *Art and Visual Perception*, new ed. (Berkeley: University of California Press, 1974), 287–294.

9. Kurt Koffka, *Principles of Gestalt Psychology* (New York: Harcourt, Brace and World, 1935), 177–210; Arnheim, *Art and Visual Perception*, pp. 227–239; Irvin Rock, *Perception* (New York: Scientific American Books, 1983).

10. Zettl, *Sight Sound Motion*, p. 175.

11. Paul F. Lazarsfeld and Robert K. Merton, "Mass Communication, Popular Taste and Organized Social Action," in *The Communication of Ideas*, ed. Lyman Bryson (New York: Institute for Social and Religious Studies, 1948), 95–118.

12. Ibid.

13. Percy H. Tannenbaum, "The Effect of Headlines on the Interpretation of News Stories," *Journalism Quarterly* 30 (1953):189–197.

14. See J. J. Roelofse, *Signs and Significance* (Johannesburg: McGraw-Hill, 1982), 58.

15. Carl I. Hovland, Arthur A. Lumsdaine, and Fred D. Sheffield, *Experiments on Mass Communication* (New York: John Wiley and Sons, 1949).

16. Olle Findahl, "The Effect of Visual Illustration upon Perception and Retention of News Programs," *Communications* 65 (1981):151–167.

17. Rudolf Arnheim, *The Power of the Center* (Berkeley: University of California Press, 1982), 52.

18. See Boris Uspensky, *A Poetics of Composition* (Berkeley: University of California Press, 1973); Theo Girshausen, "Reject It in Order to Possess It: On Heiner Müller and Bertold Brecht," trans. Peter Harris and Pia Kleber, *Modern Drama* 23 (1981):402–421; Arnheim, *The Power of the Center*.

19. John Fiske and John Hartley, *Reading Television* (London: Methuen, 1978), 48.

20. See Herbert Zettl, "Television Aesthetics," in *Understanding Television*, ed. Richard Adler (New York: Praeger, 1981), 121; Noël Burch, *Theory of Film Practice* (New York: Praeger, 1973), 17–31; Ned Rifkin, *Antonioni's Visual Language* (Ann Arbor, MI: UMI Research Press, 1982), 86.

21. George W. Linden, *Reflections on the Screen* (Belmont, CA: Wadsworth, 1970), 23–24.

22. Tony Schwartz, *Media: The Second God* (Garden City, NY: Anchor Books, 1983), 4.

23. In the past few years, the customary medium close-up of the news anchor has become tighter and tighter, and can now be called a big close-up. Because news in the United States is highly personalized, the "objective" medium shot advocated by Jamieson and Campbell, which is still used on European television, has been replaced by the more intimate close-up shot. See Kathleen H. Jamieson and Karlyn K. Campbell, *The Interplay of Influence* (Belmont, CA: Wadsworth, 1983), 46.

24. Jane Feuer, "The Concept of Live Television: Ontology as Ideology," in *Regarding Television*, ed. E. Ann Kaplan (Frederick, MD: University Publications of America, 1983), 12–22.

25. The students in my 1984 Seminar in Experimental Production contributed liberally to the graphication and personification indexes, and to the analysis of the three San Francisco newscasts.

10

Representations of Race in Network News Coverage of South Africa

Wendy Kozol

During the 1970s and 1980s, South Africa's stagnating economy intensified tensions between the white minority government and the black majority, periodically leading to outbreaks of violence. Amid this atmosphere of crisis and political pressure, in the early 1980s the government began to implement social reforms.[1] In 1984, South Africa altered its constitution, establishing separate parliamentary houses for whites, coloreds, and Asians. This and other reforms, however, have not seriously modified the present structure of apartheid. Conservatives have continually resisted change, frequently criticizing President P. W. Botha's National Party for "giving too much away." Responding to both conservative pressures and increased resistance activities, the government imposed a state of emergency in 1986 that produced another wave of repression and violence. In the midst of this social instability, on May 6, 1987, South Africa held its first election since 1981. Pressure from the right affected Botha's campaign strategy, whose central theme was the necessity for security to counter the threat of violent anarchy. Botha continually emphasized the government's military superiority in an appeal to right-wing voters. This strategy proved to be successful, since the National Party regained several seats it had lost to liberals in the previous election. More significantly, conservative politicians gained enough votes to become the main opposition party, indicating strong electoral support among white South Africans for the system of apartheid.

As was the case with violent incidents in the black townships of Sharpeville in 1960 and Soweto in 1976, these racial confrontations received extensive news coverage on American network television.[2]

Concern in the United States over racial conflicts in South Africa developed concomitantly with the American civil rights movement.[3] In particular, the rise of ethnic and black consciousness movements in the United States has increased many Americans' sensitivity to Third World peoples' efforts at independence from Western domination.

An equally important factor in the media's continued coverage of South African struggles is the fascination of American television news with social upheaval and violence. Because of the limited time devoted to international news, production factors like narrative coherence and availability of film or video footage determine what eventually becomes the "news" each night. Violent protest is a primary component of the news because it is visibly dramatic and easily explainable. Violence, therefore, also determines and limits our understanding of international developments.

Conflicts that occur in regions within the sphere of American self-interest have special appeal, and are more likely to be broadcast. Events in South Africa are vitally important to the United States because of heavy U.S. economic involvement and because of U.S. dependence on South African mineral resources.[4] In addition to governmental and economic concerns, problems between blacks and whites in South Africa resonate with the American public's historical memory of their own racial tensions. Domestic political agitation, which has grown more vocal and visible in the 1980s, has foregrounded these issues, and legitimized the news media's attention to South Africa. Protest by American demonstrators against the Reagan administration's policy of constructive engagement has become newsworthy, as has the movement urging U.S. corporations to divest themselves of their South African holdings. In 1986, American opposition to South Africa's policy of apartheid culminated in a congressional imposition of sanctions against South Africa. President Reagan's veto constrained this political action, indicating a decided ambivalence in U.S. attitudes toward South Africa.

The 1987 election in South Africa was a recent example of sustained examination of South African domestic events by American television networks. As reported on American television, South African politicians considered this whites-only election to be a crucial referendum on Botha's policy of slow reform. This study examines two U.S. TV networks' news coverage of South Africa during the period from April 27 to May 8, 1987, including coverage of the unrest prior to the May 6 election and the election itself. An

April 24 court ruling lifting censorship regulations made this an especially appropriate period to study because video footage was suddenly available after a period of restriction imposed by martial law. The networks studied were CBS and ABC. Previous studies have demonstrated that content of news programs is often remarkably similar from network to network,[5] and thus it is likely that NBC's coverage conforms fairly well to the following descriptions. Be that as it may, my observations apply to two of the most powerful and important news outlets in the United States, viewed regularly by millions of Americans.

Tuchman argues that the television news format provides a frame through which news content is selected, interpreted, and presented.[6] Far from being an objective medium that reflects reality, television constructs a particular way of looking at the world. This process of constructing a world view has profound implications when it involves representations of international events. As Altheide argues, "Coverage of foreign affairs is especially important since the viewing audience is less likely to have direct experience with life and issues in these societies and are therefore less able to assess the validity of the messages they receive."[7] Case studies such as this one offer an opportunity to understand how this structuring process works and what impact it has on our perceptions of other nations.

Many scholars dismiss the importance of film or videotape footage in television news, claiming such material is merely illustrative.[8] Filmed or taped footage, however, is an essential component of television news. Visual images modify and/or reinforce verbal texts. Adams points out that while scholars have always acknowledged that television is a visual medium, few have analyzed the content and meaning of this imagery.[9] Most studies of television news film or tape analyze how much audiences recall visual material but fail to consider what information is being conveyed. This analysis will concentrate on how visual messages encode and, in turn, reinforce prevalent cultural attitudes and values. Network news representations of South Africa rely on both conventions of news coverage and broader cultural codes. As semiotic analyses have shown, visual codes are not autonomously determined in news practices but derive from and interact with larger cultural discourses.[10]

In many ways news coverage of South Africa conforms to characteristic features of international news formats by focusing on violence and dramatic events. Depictions of race add a problematic dimension to the meaning of television's coverage of South Africa because representations of social upheaval are encoded with historically determined cultural codes that depict blacks as either violent or servile. In other ways, the presence of blacks on national television, especially as nominated spokespersons, contrasts with the stereotypically racist imagery. American network news representations of blacks in South Africa are therefore complex and often contradictory.

INTERNATIONAL NEWS FORMAT

During the two weeks this study examined, there were several news reports of primary importance. Lead stories included Gary Hart's withdrawal from the presidential campaign, Japanese Prime Minister Nakasone's visit to the United States that coincided with a controversial trade sanctions bill, and the start of the congressional Iran-Contra hearings. Since constraints of time and space create an excess of stories, the selection process indicates what events are considered significant.[11] Therefore, for South Africa to appear on CBS six out of ten nights and on ABC seven out of ten nights testifies to the networks' investing great importance in events there. Moreover, the amount of foreign video compared with domestic video or anchor coverage is an important barometer of the networks' economic commitment to a particular region.[12] All of the reports were made by correspondents in Johannesburg, and with only one exception included taped footage. Foreign video testifies to the network's presence on the spot, underscoring both the veracity and the timeliness of the report, and the network's legitimation of South African events as newsworthy.

Thematic unity, visual quality, and drama are characteristic determinants of international news coverage.[13] Similar to news reports about other Third World countries, as studies of Latin America and the Middle East have shown,[14] network news reporting on South Africa conforms to a determining paradigmatic structure of event-oriented drama and action. The news can be more easily simplified into quick explanations required by the limited time allotted when framed as dramatic events. Networks usually devote about ten minutes (45 percent) of the broadcast to international news. This percentage is more than scholars had previously assumed but it is still an "awesomely minuscule window on the world."[15]

Network news must be considered within the larger context of commercial television. News shows are just that, shows following the dictates of narrative entertainment. South Africa's tensions, demonstrations, and upheavals are frequently reported by the networks. Violent events have good visual quality because they are lively and full of action, and conform readily to narrative structures of storytelling. Gitlin calls the crime story the archetypal news story and demonstrates how network news treats other forms of social action within this frame by focusing on arrests, number of injuries, and related statistics.[16] Equating violent resistance with crime makes the "event" easier to explain. During the first week's coverage (April 27 to May 1), attention focused primarily on the demonstrations and their eruptions into violence. Statistics on numbers of injuries and arrests were reported on each segment. Scenes of police in riot gear shooting tear gas at running and screaming crowds, along with burning cars and tires in city streets, pervade the coverage of South African demonstrations.

Hartley describes four narrative moments in a news story: the framing of the story, introduced by the anchor; switching to the correspondent, who restates and expands on the particular problem; verifying the reality of the story through actuality footage and interviews with professionals and others with authoritative status; and the concluding resolution, usually an analysis by either the correspondent or the anchor.[17] This narrative pattern was maintained in all the reports examined between April 27 and May 7. For instance, on April 27, ABC's anchor introduced its report on the violence that erupted during student demonstrations at several South African universities. Switching to the correspondent, Jim Hickey spoke in a voice-over while the video showed students marching and chanting. Hickey elaborated on the locations of these events and statistics about injuries and arrests. He next explained that the demonstrations were in response to government raids on Zambia. In conformance with the narrative structure Hartley outlines, the reality of the story was verified through "actuality" footage of destroyed houses. Then Hickey interviewed an opposition leader and the South African foreign minister. The commentary next discussed the relationship of the raid to election campaigning about security. The video reiterated the verbal text with pictures of the military on parade to signify government security and control. Hickey resolved the narrative threads into a coherent summation in his concluding remark, "Whether it is in neighboring countries or on college campuses, the government is determined to demonstrate control."

Gans maintains that the function of film or video footage is to accompany and illustrate the verbal text.[18] Similarly, Gitlin has called television news an "illustrated lecture," in that "actual pictures are purely decorative.''[19] Assessments like these seriously underestimate the importance of visual material in constructing news messages. Admittedly, the function of film or videotape footage is to illustrate, but it is also readily apparent that stories with accompanying actuality pictures are more likely to get on the air.[20] Censorship restrictions cause problems for news personnel because of dependence on visual images for concise dramatization of events. Therefore, when restrictions were lifted in South Africa, both networks acknowledged the importance of this for their coverage. ABC anchor Peter Jennings stated on April 30, ''If you think there has been more news on the air about South Africa than usual, you are right. Because of court rulings lifting press restrictions, we are actually able to show you what appears to be spreading unrest.'' Because television relies heavily on actuality footage, it reproduces events with good visual quality, in large measure thereby determining what constitutes the news. Moreover, Jenning's use of the term ''show'' reveals his presumption that video shot on location can in fact record the ''spreading unrest.''

The need to visualize the headlines frequently leads to the indexical use of iconic images, that is, to their use as shorthand symbolic references.[21] A clip of blacks throwing stones, or a shot of police with gas masks, is used as a synecdoche for complex processes of social upheaval. This use of film or video is most apparent in extreme situations when the footage is not really applicable or, sometimes, quite unreadable. On April 29, ABC described a police raid on a black trade union building. The picture, however, depicts several policemen standing in a busy street, with no clear relationship to the black trade union. Juxtaposition of the verbal text with this image of policemen suggests that the police serve as an index of black unrest, since, after all, the police are inextricably related to violence.

Since the news conforms to a simplified narrative format, as does entertainment programming, it typically reduces social processes to two opposing positions. Yet, in American news coverage of the Third World, no matter which position the networks support, violence takes precedence.[22] The priority given to violence can be seen in how filmic codes are employed in footage of street action. Tuchman demonstrates that news film follows Western cultural conventions of visual resprensentation.[23] In particular, conventions of single-point perspective, placement, and time are used to construct ''objectivity.'' Footage of street activities usually remains at eye level, with minimal jolting or blurring in order to make it appear natural—and, hence, objective. Gibson explains, "The Naturalist film code seeks to hide the fact that it is film and instead presents itself as unmediated reality."[24]

Sometimes, however, camera personnel will manipulate these codes in order to create a different message. On April 27, ABC showed a line of police in riot gear from a low angle, looking up at the police as they advanced into the camera. This violates rules of distortion and perspective in order to appear more threatening. On April 30, ABC used this same camera angle to show blacks chanting and marching down city streets. Video that exaggerates drama through unusual angles is used in depictions of both government and opposition actions, signifying that instability is the primary interest of the news. Dahlgren explains that depictions of disorder implicitly evoke its bipolar opposite, stability (presumably American society), which is reassuring to viewers.[25] An interesting example of this is ABC's May 7 coverage of street violence following the election. A video clip of cars driving past a burning car suggests an ordinariness to this event that contrasts with American middle-class experiences, for Americans do not usually encounter such visible signs of violence.

In emphasizing singular events, the news prefers crises, usually presented in vivid, often voyeuristic detail.[26] Privileging certain issues and events, of course, also implies significant exclusions, exemplifying what Hartley calls the absent/present paradigm.[27] Coverage of South African student protest movements demonstrates this absent/present paradigm in operation. Labor shortages in the 1970s forced the government to permit increases in technical and vocational education for blacks, though usually in segregated schools. The universities have remained segregated; in 1980, three-fourths of all university students were white. Black South Africans have always been keenly aware that the white minority government uses education to perpetuate segregation. Since 1980, there have been frequent education strikes throughout the country, in large part because of the unified efforts of African, colored, and Indian groups.[28] There are, nonetheless, important differences between various student groups. These differences have become more acute since the rise of black consciousness movements in the 1970s, when groups like the South African Student Organization split away from interracial organizations.[29] News coverage, however, does not examine the presence of blacks in white universities, or why educational arenas spawn political protest and agitation. The simplifying process also collapses various organizations into "student riots," which elides important differences and tensions between them.

It is important to recognize the persistent theme of crisis in news content because it perpetuates stereotypes about the Third World. Focusing on conflicts, with a concomitant lack of attention to social processes, network news presents events in the Third World as a series of spasmodic convulsions.[30] This already problematic reduction of complex issues to simplified stereotypes is made even more troublesome by cultural meanings embedded in representations of race.

REPRESENTATIONS OF RACE

The portrayal of South African blacks on American network news has significant cultural resonance for a country with its own persistent history of racism. In 1987, racial incidents in New York and Georgia, as well as the renewed media attention to white-supremacist organizations, indicated the continued existence of deep racial tensions in American society. There is a distinctive parallel between the South African and the U.S. histories of racial segregation. In both these countries, systems of segregation are structurally embedded in and reinforced by industrial capitalism.[31] This relationship between capitalism and segregation suggests further reasons why U.S. corporations and the U.S. government maintain contradictory attitudes toward South Africa.

Despite the two countries' comparable histories of structural racism, however, the U.S. constitution gives American blacks a legal status denied to South African blacks.[32] Many liberals also cite the U.S. civil rights movement as a significant step toward racial equality. Needless to say, liberal advocacy of racial equality has remained a minority voice in South Africa, where military force is increasingly relied upon to uphold institutional discrimination. In contrast, by the 1980s most American cultural practices, including television, have adopted at least superficially sympathetic attitudes toward black struggles.

Shifting cultural attitudes have resulted in representations of blacks that are often contradictory. Liberal attitudes have produced an overt opposition to South African apartheid, even as structural and cultural assumptions reinforce racism. The networks, perhaps in response to growing opposition in the United States to apartheid, have taken a critical stance against the South African government. Network coverage is frequently harsh, often bordering on caricature (in large measure because of television's process of simplification). Verbal texts are frequently critical of the Botha regime, usually within the guise of statements of fact. For example, on May 4, CBS's correspondent Martha Teichner described the South African president as "P. W. Botha as the world sees him: dour, rigid, easy to hate." Video footage often underscores this negative view of the South African government, usually through depictions of white military forces victimizing blacks. On April 27, ABC showed police shooting tear gas into crowds of students while other policemen with whips ran after unarmed students. The camera angle is from behind the police, clearly revealing whom the police are shooting at. On April 30, CBS reported on a South African neofascist rally with video that prominently focused on red flags bearing swastikas. The visual prominence of this sign, which draws upon cultural memories of Nazi Germany for Western audiences, reinforces CBS's critical stance.

Although the networks are critical of brutalities in defense of apartheid, they do not advocate a violent overthrow of the government. Television news, while attempting to be objective, offers a reformist ideology. Gans calls this "journalistic paraideology," similar to early-twentieth-century Progressivism in its insistence on responsible capitalism that preserves the upper- and upper-middle-class social orders.[33] In television news, different political positions are presented in order to maintain the doctrine of fairness. Political differences, however, remain within the limits and boundaries of the state.[34] After all, as major corporate enterprises that must appeal to as broad a constituency as possible, the news media have a vested interest in maintaining the status quo.[35]

A correspondent's comments are verified by video footage, whose compliance with realistic conventions reinforces the assumption that what we are looking at truly happened at that time, in the way described by the reporter. On May 4, CBS correspondent Teichner reported on Botha's campaign statements claiming that because violence threatened the security of South Africa, only his military force could prevent anarchy and preserve the status quo. Teichner stated that South Africa has the "strongest military force in Africa." Meanwhile, the video "demonstrated" this through pictures of ground missiles being fired and the government's newest South African-built helicopter. Next Botha was seen explaining that continued violence necessitated tightened security, with a jump cut to file footage of blacks demonstrating. Teichner explained that "with uncanny skill P. W. Botha has capitalized on two and a half years of racial unrest to scare white South Africans that a vote for anyone else is a vote for violence and political instability." In rapid succession the video jumped from a close-up of Botha to a view of street violence in which a group of blacks were chanting and dancing around a burning car. Then the video showed policemen on a crowded street who suddenly turned and shot at an unknown assailant or assailants. Next the video showed a group of gun-carrying black men running down the street.

Pictures of military forces and statements about the need for security are juxtaposed in this report with images of blacks engaged in acts of violence. This juxtaposition creates an illusion of simultaneity that implies the two are related, whether or not they happened at the same time. Video footage appears to reinforce rather than contradict Botha's message since, in essence, these images become illustrations for his speeches. The use of file tape, not labeled as such, further exposes the mediation process of television editing. Hence, while network news is sympathetic to black resistance movements, filmic and editing codes reinforce the racist position they are presumably critiquing.

Television's simplification of social processes into events depends on cultural stereotypes that are predictable and easily readable.[36] This leads, in the case of violent conflicts between races, to stereotypically negative images of blacks. Violence is also shown in white areas like Belfast, but when simplification is combined with race, the dangers of stereotyping are exacerbated. Hartmann and Husband examine how British media frame news about blacks, demonstrating that depictions of conflict within a country rife with racial tension perpetuate racist stereotypes.[37] Reinforcement of these stereotypes similarly occurs in reports on racial conflict in other nations. Dominant groups most typically depict subordinate races as "inferior, childlike, and servile, but also as innately aggressive, dangerous and uppity."[38] The routine portrayal of blacks in acts of violence in South Africa reinforces these culturally derived codes. On April 27, CBS reported on a demonstration by white and black students at Cape Town University. Yet in the actuality footage showing the violence, only blacks were shown throwing stones and burning tires. Similarly, on April 30, while both whites and blacks participated in a protest demonstration, ABC focused on a black youth throwing bricks, even though the voice-over commentary ambiguously explained that "some of the students threw rocks and bottles."

Correspondents prefer to interview figures in positions of authority as a verification of their own objectivity.[39] Legitimated newsmakers, professionals, or government officials such as Botha, are identified, or nominated, and allowed to speak for themselves. Unlike nominated, authoritative voices, representative individuals remain unnominated; thus the news distinguishes various states of competence to speak.[40] Unnominated individuals are presented as symbols, as typical members of a group coping with the dilemma being presented in the news story.[41] Conferring professional status on Botha and other government officials legitimizes them in a way that unnominated blacks and mass demonstrators never are.

While blacks are shown rioting, whites are depicted in business suits, voting, listening calmly to speeches, and being interviewed in offices. Frequently whites speak for blacks, instead of blacks speaking for themselves. In this two-week period, ABC interviewed two black persons versus eight whites; CBS interviewed three blacks and seven whites. This type of paternalistic racism pervades representations of both anti- and pro-apartheid advocates. On April 27, ABC reported on a South African raid on Zambia. After panning the destroyed buildings of a village, the camera focused on a group of blacks observing the scene. Correspondent Hickey then interviewed a white liberal opposition leader, Brian Goodall, who suggested that this was a preelection display of strength by the Botha government. Neither black opposition leaders nor the blacks who suffered from this display of militarism were accessed.

When correspondents interviewed representative whites about apratheid, they did not give equal time to black representatives. On April 30, CBS interviewed a representative white farmer who stated, "I'm scared we'll be overrun by blacks," while the camera showed the beautiful mountainous scenery of the Transvaal. Then the video cut to the farmer's barns, which were burned down last year by blacks. Through editing, fear of loss is juxtaposed with the beautiful countryside, implying that the threat of violence includes this pastoral setting. Despite sympathy for blacks, the absence of their opinions (yet their presence in violence visually and verbally) seems to substantiate white fears.

Even when black resistance groups and leaders are presented, depictions of conflict and calls for social change are limited by accepted definitions of social development. Network news privileges black leaders like Zulu leader Mangosuthu Buthelezi and Archbishop Desmond Tutu, who are both moderate, middle-class spokespersons. Reports on radical or extremist organizations are much more infrequent. As Gitlin demonstrates, revolutionaries, no matter what their color, have more difficulty getting on television than do reformers.[42] In the two weeks of this study, the more radical African National Congress (ANC) was not discussed; ANC leader Oliver Tambo was never mentioned, and Nelson Mandela was mentioned briefly only on May 4. Moderate black opposition groups conform more comfortably to culturally acceptable definitions of race relations and social change.

Although South African government censorship attempts to restrict press coverage of violence, this alone does not account for the dominance of whites on network news. Blacks are interviewed, although less frequently than whites, and reports criticizing the South African government's repressive policies continue to be broadcast from Johannesburg. Thus, selection and choice must be accounted for by explanations other than censorship. Gans suggests that reporters privilege those whose speech is closest to the dominant white dialect.[43] Obviously, white Americans can more readily identify with the language and culture of white South Africans. In addition, whites in South Africa maintain most positions generally credited with authority or professional knowledge. Since network news prefers to interview authority figures, all but a few black South Africans are excluded.

Finally, television is a corporate institution that replicates the power hierarchies prevalent in society.[44] Discrimination against blacks in American society has been reinforced on network television, where until recently blacks were not even present.[45] When blacks now appear on television as the star performers on fiction shows, it is usually in situation comedies that reinforce the stereotype of the comedic black. Television is primarily a vehicle for advertising, and traditionally blacks have not been considered important consumers. Thus neither advertising nor television programming has targeted blacks as a significant audience, making it difficult for black performers to be taken seriously or for shows that are culturally meaningful for blacks to be produced. Since news directs its attention to the same audience as entertainment programming, the same advertising and marketing restrictions and demands prevail. As Fiske and Hartley write, "News reporting and fiction use similar signs because they naturally refer to the same myths in our culture."[46] Despite verbal condemnation of apartheid by the networks, pervasive assumptions about authority and reliance on cultural conventions reinforce insidious stereotypes about blacks.

INTERPRETING POLYSEMIC MESSAGES

Television news coverage of South Africa reproduces cultural codes that have historically claimed that blacks, as a race, are dangerous and threatening. At the same time, American networks often overtly criticize the South African government's policy of

apartheid. Journalists' liberal concerns, along with networks' confor-
mity to current national attitudes, in part explain the presence of
positive representations. But, just as negative images are not intentionally produced (both Gans and Tuchman report that news personnel profess and believe in their own objectivity)[47], neither are positive
images. Primarily, the determining framework that constructs "news
events" produces texts that are necessarily open to different readings.
Television is polysemic in order to be appealing or, in the case of
news, "objective" to a mass audience.[48] Although dominant
ideologies are structured into the text, the structure of the text contains unresolved contradictions.

Like fiction programs, news stories repeatedly show a limited
number of famous people and familiar settings. While representatives
do not survive week to week, certain authoritative figures persist
weekly, becoming recognizable to the audience. Fiske and Hartley
describe this process as a "syntagmatic structuring into which
paradigmatic unpredictable events of the day are given meaning."[49]
This structure is especially important in international news, where the
audience is less well acquainted with foreign leaders. The recurring
appearance of political leaders like Botha is reassuringly familiar
amid a bewildering array of foreign names, places, and events.
Familiarity gives national prominence to Botha, but also to black
leaders, since within the dramatic structure of conflict, they, too,
repeatedly appear on network news. Not only Botha, but oppositional leaders like Desmond Tutu, have become familiar figures to the
American public.

Journalists favor government personnel as spokespersons because
their authority is legitimated by their professional status and access to
knowledge. At the same time, however, news organizations feel compelled to interview spokespersons from "both sides" of an issue in
order to conform to definitions of objectivity. Thus, news reports
also access opposition leaders, though of course privileging those individuals who best conform to dominant cultural codes specifying
authority, such as Tutu and Buthelezi. Although interviews with
blacks are less frequent than interviews with whites, this type of
coverage grants Africans a status that runs counter to typically
simplistic representations of blacks as either aggressive or victimized.

Along with paternalism and racist exclusion, television news
sometimes represents blacks who speak articulately on their own
behalf. Positive representations of political struggle are generally constructed through heroic portrayals of leaders like Desmond Tutu. After
the election, for example, on May 7, ABC interviewed Tutu, who

stated, "What we are going to have is an increase in state-sponsored terrorism against the black civilian population of this country." Meanwhile, the camera panned the room crowded with white people who were listening to him. Since the narrative structure requires protagonists, news stories privilege leaders like Tutu, who, as a religious authority, conforms to legitimated codes.

Like other news conventions, these representations are contradictory because they also perpetuate American television's process of elevating individuals (in this case, selected black South African leaders) to celebrity status.[50] This is a problem because it simplifies complex social problems and masks important differences between oppositional groups. On May 4, ABC's report on a student demonstration at Johannesburg University focused on Winnie Mandela, who was supposed to speak at the rally but was barred from participation. Instead of analyzing the students' political objectives, the report concentrated on Mandela.

On the other hand, celebrity status accords a legitimacy to leaders rarely given to representational blacks. This can be seen in the use of different visual codes, based on conventions of objectivity that define social meaning through the construction of visual distances.[51] "Public distance" includes many people and a large area, and is used primarily for depicting masses, not individuals. Rioting blacks and crowds of demonstrators are seen at this public distance. Legitimated newsmakers are most commonly filmed at the "talking distance." At talking distance the camera frames the head and shoulders of the person speaking. This shot is close enough for viewers to see the subject's responses and reactions, yet maintains a degree of distance that is presumed to be objective. President Botha is always filmed at talking distance, whether he is speaking at a political rally or being interviewed in his office. When representative individuals are interviewed, they, too, are framed at talking distance. However, unlike professionals, who are seen behind desks or similar signs of their legitimated status, representatives are positioned in front of an emblematic place, such as the site of a disaster.[52]

Thus, when Tutu was interviewed on both ABC and CBS on May 7, it was significant that he sat in the more intimate setting of a living room rather than in the emblematic space required for representatives. ABC's film of Mandela on May 4 similarly relied on the framing conventions typically employed to represent white leaders. Cutting from the scene of the demonstration at a public distance to a close-up of her at a talking distance accords Mandela the status of a legitimated newsmaker usually reserved for white authorities. In a final shot from behind her shoulder, the camera shows news personnel videotaping and photographing her, further signifying her importance.

CBS's May 6 coverage of the election exemplifies the polysemic nature of news reports. After discussing the conservative outcome of the election, correspondent Teichner examined blacks' reactions to their exclusion from the electoral process. The central segment of the report discussed a straw poll that was conducted by the black newspaper *The Sowetan*. In a voice-over, the reporter explained the poll while the video showed a black woman seated at a computer, then black hands pasting up a newspaper. The setting was a professional modern office, not an industrial work place. Images of technical apparatus encode messages about these subjects' professional status. Next Teichner interviewed the newspaper's black editor, Aggrey Klaaste (seen at talking distance), who observed, "People, it seems to us, are voting like other ordinary men in the street." Klaaste was nominated and granted visual status as a legitimated newsmaker. Even as the voice-over commentary discussed Africans' exclusion from the electoral process, these scenes offered alternative representations to the dominant depiction of blacks rioting in the streets. The last image in this report is a press repetitively printing the front page of *The Sowetan* with the headline "MANDELA WINS." While reporting the results of the straw poll, this sign also subtly alludes to future alternatives to the dominant system of apartheid.

Such alternative depictions of blacks' social position, however, are always mediated by television's persistent interest in violence. In another sequence in the report, blacks were shown in a city street burning tires, with the comment "Sporadic incidents of violence were confined to black areas and did not affect the polling." This focus on blacks' violent activities continually militates against a positive portrayal.

CONCLUSION

In news coverage of South Africa, visual images construct complex messages that primarily reinforce, although at times they challenge, racist stereotypes. To dismiss film and videotape footage as merely "decorative" underestimates the complexity and ambivalence of news broadcasts. Visual texts show the limitations of network coverage, in large part because of television's proclivity for simplification and its fascination with violence. In simplifying the news, television reduces complexities to stereotypes. Stereotypes are harmful to everyone, but especially to blacks, who are excluded from power structures and have limited means with which to counter these stereotypes.

Network news nonetheless produces ambiguous messages. Television coverage of the May 6 election and surrounding protests by disenfranchised blacks exhibits overtly negative attitudes toward the white supremacist government and the institution of apartheid. More significantly, in following conventions of interviewing authority figures from both sides, networks show alternative or conflicting signs. Whether this adds up to sympathy for blacks' struggles for liberation is not clear because so much of the video footage equates blacks with violence and destruction, implying they are the "problem." And yet, while representations of blacks are highly problematic, blacks are being given a voice on American national television. When black leaders are interviewed on network news, television's codes of representation grant them the same status as white South Africans. These images make available, wittingly or not, alternative interpretations of political and social developments.

NOTES

The author thanks Frank and Shirley Wojtal for technical assistance, and Dona Schwartz, Michael Griffin, Tony Smith, and Steven Wojtal for their helpful criticisms and comments.

1. See Leonard Thompson, *The Political Mythology of Apartheid* (New Haven: Yale University Press, 1985), 192–195.

2. See Bernard Magubane, "United States-South Africa Relations and the Implications for Black Liberation," *Journal of Ethnic Studies* 11 (1983):107–133.

3. Milton Krieger, "Still Marking Time: South Africa and the United States," *Journal of Ethnic Studies* 11 (1983):3–19.

4. Magubane, "United States-South Africa Relations."

5. Daniel Riffe, Brenda Ellis, Momo K. Rogers, Roger L. Van Ommeren, and Kieran A. Woodman, "Gatekeeping and the Network News Mix," *Journalism Quarterly* 63 (1986):315–321; David L. Altheide, "Three-in-One News: Network Coverage of Iran," *Journalism Quarterly* 59 (1982):482–486.

6. Gaye Tuchman, "The Technology of Objectivity: Doing 'Objective' TV News Film," *Urban Life and Culture* 2 (1973):3–26; and *Making News: A Study in the Construction of Reality* (New York: The Free Press, 1978).

7. Altheide, "Three-in-One News," p. 483.

8. See, for example, Todd Gitlin, "The Whole World Is Watching: Mass Media and the New Left, 1965–70," Ph.D. diss., University of California, Berkeley, 1977, 321; Glasgow University Media Group, *More Bad News* (London: Routledge & Kegan Paul, 1980), 333.

9. William Adams, "Visual Analysis of Newscasts: Issues in Social Science Research," in *Television Network News: Issues in Content Research*, ed. William Adams and Fay Schreibman (Washington, DC: Television and Politics Study Program, School of Public and International Affairs, George Washington University, 1978), 156–157.

10. See, for example, John Hartley, *Understanding News* (New York: Methuen, 1982); John Fiske and John Hartley, *Reading Television* (New York: Methuen, 1978).

11. Tuchman, *Making News*, p. 44.

12. See James F. Larson, Emile G. McAnany, and J. Douglas Storey, "News of Latin America on Network Television, 1972–1981: A Northern Perspective on the Southern Hemisphere," *Critical Studies in Mass Communication* 3 (1986):169–183.

13. David L. Altheide, "Impact of Format and Ideology on TV News Coverage of Iran," *Journalism Quarterly* 62 (1985):346–351.

14. Waltraud Q. Morales, "Revolutions, Earthquakes, and Latin America: The Networks Look at Allende's Chile and Somoza's Nicaragua," in *Television Coverage of International Affairs*, ed. William Adams (Norwood, NJ: Ablex, 1982), 79–113; Peter Dahlgren, "The Third World on TV News: Western Ways of Seeing the Other." in *Television Coverage of International Affairs*, ed. William Adams (Norwood, NJ: Ablex, 1982), 45–65; Larson, McAnany, and Storey, "News of Latin America on Network Television"; and Altheide, "Three-in-One News."

15. William Adams, ed., *Television Coverage of International Affairs* (Norwood, NJ: Ablex, 1982), 3.

16. Gitlin, "The Whole World Is Watching," p. 51.

17. Hartley, *Understanding News*, p. 118.

18. Herbert J. Gans, *Deciding What's News: A Study of CBS Evening News, NBC Nightly News, Newsweek, and Time* (New York: Pantheon, 1979), 158.

19. Gitlin, "The Whole World Is Watching," p. 321.

20. Altheide, "Impact of Format and Ideology."

21. Glasgow University Media Group, *More Bad News*, pp. 240, 248.

22. Dahlgren, "The Third World on TV News," p. 53.

23. Tuchman, "The Technology of Objectivity."

24. William Gibson, "Network News: Elements of a Theory," *Social Text* 3 (1980):103.

25. Dahlgren, "The Third World on TV News," p. 48.

26. Ibid., pp. 51–53.

27. Hartley, *Understanding News*, p. 42.

28. *Apartheid, the Facts* (London: International Defense and Aid Funds for South Africa, in cooperation with the United Nations Centre Against Apartheid, 1983), 27–28, 97.

29. Motsoko Pheko, *Apartheid: The Story of a Dispossessed People* (London: Marram, 1984), 169–171.

30. Larson, McAnany, and Storey, "News of Latin America on Network Television."

31. John Cell, *The Highest Stage of White Supremacy: The Origins of Segregation in South Africa and the American South* (Cambridge: Cambridge University Press, 1982), 251–253.

32. Thompson, *The Political Mythology of Apartheid*, 189–190; Krieger, "Still Marking Time."

33. Gans, *Deciding What's News*, p. 69.

34. Gibson, "Network News"; Hartley, *Understanding News*, p. 56.

35. Tuchman, *Making News*, p. 163.

36. Altheide, "Impact of Format and Ideology."

37. Paul Hartmann and Charles Husband, "The Mass Media and Racial Conflict," in *The Manufacture of News*, ed. Stanley Cohen and Jock Young (Beverly Hills, CA: Sage, 1973), 270–283.

38. Cell, *The Highest Stage of White Supremacy*, p. 12.

39. Tuchman, *Making News*, p. 85.

40. Hartley, *Understanding News*, pp. 108–111.

41. Tuchman, *Making News*, p. 123.

42. Gitlin, "The Whole World Is Watching," p. 340.

43. Gans, *Deciding What's News*, p. 131.

44. John Fiske, "Television: Polysemy and Popularity," *Critical Studies in Mass Communication* 3 (1986):391–408.

45. Erik Barnouw, *Tube of Plenty: The Evolution of American Television*, rev. ed. (Oxford and New York: Oxford University Press, 1982), 326–327.

46. Fiske and Hartley, *Reading Television*, p. 43.

47. Gans, *Deciding What's News*; Tuchman, *Making News*.

48. Fiske, "Television: Polysemy and Popularity."

49. Fiske and Hartley, *Reading Television*, p. 189.

50. Gitlin, "The Whole World Is Watching," pp. 191–198.

51. Tuchman, "The Technology of Objectivity."

52. Tuchman, *Making News*, p. 123.

11

Propaganda Techniques in Documentary Film and Television: AIM vs. PBS

Martin J. Medhurst

The term "documentary" is perhaps one of the most misunderstood concepts in the lexicon of radio, television, and film. This misunderstanding is based, in part, on an incorrect exegesis of the etymological origins of the word "documentary." Commonsense perception would suggest that the root of "documentary" must be the English term "document," and that the basic meaning of "documentary" must, therefore, derive from one of the two basic meanings of the word "document": the verb form "to document"—to check against appropriate criteria or facts as a way of verifying the authenticity or accuracy of an object: or the noun form as in "this or that document"—a paper bearing original, official, or legal form that can be used to furnish decisive evidence. Neither of these definitions is correct with respect to media studies.

The term "documentary" was first applied to film by the Scotsman John Grierson, who, upon viewing Robert Flaherty's film *Moana*, proclaimed it "a visual account of events in the daily life of a Polynesian youth," which, in Grierson's words, contained "documentary value."[1] Grierson later recalled: "When I used the word 'documentary' of Bob Flaherty's *Moana*, I was merely using it as an adjective."[2] Soon, however, both Grierson and others started to use the word "documentary" as a noun that stood for a particular type of film. Blending the French conception of *documentaires* (travel films) with his own notion of using film as "a medium for reaching public opinion,"[3] Grierson established the documentary film as the type dealing with the "creative treatment of actuality."[4]

For Grierson, both the "creative" and the "actuality" dimensions were crucial for a proper understanding of the documentary form. Documentary film was to deal with real people in real situations, but was to do so with a distinct point of view or purpose in mind. He wrote in the 1933–34 issue of *Sight and Sound*:

I look on cinema as a pulpit, and use it as a propagandist; and this I put unashamedly because, in the still unshaven philosophies of cinema, broad distinctions are necessary. Art is one matter, and the wise, as I suggest, had better seek it where there is elbow room for its creation; entertainment is another matter; education, in so far as it concerns the classroom pedagogue, another; propaganda another; and cinema is to be conceived as a medium, like writing, capable of many forms and many functions. A professional propagandist may well be especially interested in it. It gives generous access to the public. It is capable of direct description, simple analysis and commanding conclusion, and may, by its tempo'd and imagistic powers, be made easily persuasive.[5]

From the outset, therefore, documentary film was anything but the objective, neutral, factual reporting of events as they transpired in real life. Even the films of Robert Flaherty, filled as they were with real people in their natural surroundings, were not in any sense objective, value neutral, or even historically accurate in all respects. They were *creative* treatments of actuality, with emphasis on the inventive powers of the filmmaker.[6] Thus, to assert or presuppose that documentary film or television is or should be objective, totally accurate, or value neutral is to require of the form that it become something other than what it always has been—a vehicle for propagating the particular point of view, values, or social policies of the filmmaker.

The choices, therefore, are not between "objective" and "nonobjective," or "neutral" and "biased," or even "factual" and "valuative." In the final analysis, as Grierson realized, all documentary films are vehicles of persuasion and propaganda. The real question, then, is not whether they are "weighted" toward one viewpoint or another—clearly they are—but how well the filmmaker is able to accomplish his or her rhetorical goals within the confines of the particular medium. In other words, the crucial questions are (1) Is this a good or bad propaganda film? (2) What are the legitimate bases for judging its goodness or badness, its effectiveness or ineffectiveness?

It is my contention that the counterdocumentary produced by Accuracy in Media (AIM), "Television's Vietnam: The Real Story," is a bad propaganda film because it fails to meet many of the widely accepted notions of what constitutes a good propaganda film. The other side of my argument is that the PBS series, "Vietnam: A Television History," is a very good propaganda film because its producers and directors creatively incorporated the techniques of visual rhetoric to promote—successfully, I believe—their point of view.

First, I will lay out the criteria by which good propaganda films are often recognized. I will seek to explicate these criteria by reference to their application in other widely shown and highly respected films. Second, I will apply each of these criteria to both the PBS series and the AIM counterdocumentary, with special attention to the opening segments of both. By first establishing the criteria and then applying each criterion to both the PBS and the AIM films, I will demonstrate that the PBS series is, in fact, better propaganda, a more "creative" treatment of actuality.

TECHNIQUES OF FILMIC PROPAGANDA

There are nine techniques, some unique to the cinema, some shared with other media, that characterize effective propaganda films:

1. Decontextualization of sound and image through condensation and displacement
2. Recontextualization of sound and image through various narrative devices
3. A conscious attempt to appear natural, objective, or fair
4. Use of pathetic figures to evoke strong emotional responses
5. Use of a privileged narrator, often employing the authoritative "voice-of-God" technique
6. Intentional reordering of filmic events for maximum rhetorical impact, without regard for the veracity of the representation or the structural integrity of the raw materials
7. Pursuit of a journalistic "line" or "angle" that often functions at the level of subconscious apprehension but that, upon subsequent viewings, is clearly present
8. Use of asynchronous associative logic that functions through metaphoric and/or metonymic techniques of sound and image
9. Use of visual ambiguity in conjunction with a scripted (planned) narrative logic that suggests an interpretation of the visual confusion on the screen without actually asserting such an interpretation is true. It is up to the viewer to draw the right conclusions from the clues provided.

These nine techniques recur throughout the history of documentary film and can be clearly described through reference to some of the classics of the genre.

Decontextualization Through Condensation and Displacement

One need not look much beyond the point at which Grierson first defined the documentary film to find the first of these nine techniques at work. In *The Plow That Broke the Plains* (1936), often considered the first noteworthy social documentary made in America, the technique of decontextualization through condensation and displacement is clearly present. Pare Lorentz takes stock footage of farmers combining their fields and uses it at crucial junctures in the film as an illustration of the practices that paved the way for the great drought and dust storms. A particular point in time is condensed into a few stock shots that are added to the film and made to stand, synecdochically, for all of the factors that led to the loss of the topsoil and the problems of drought and farm failure. To give the film a sense of historical continuity, the problems are condensed into a few shots that then displace actual time and space considerations in order to forward the narrative structure of the film.

This technique of decontextualization through condensation and displacement was a staple of World War II propaganda films—both those produced by the Axis Powers and those produced by the Allies. Frank Capra's *The Nazis Strike* (1942) and *Divide and Conquer* (1943) are no less dependent on the technique of decontextualization than are the Nazi films *Baptism of Fire* (1940) and *Campaign in Poland* (1940). All create visual synecdoches through use of the condensation and displacement technique, a technique shared with other visual media. Kenneth Burke notes, "Artistic representation is synecdochic, in that certain relations within the medium 'stand for' corresponding relations outside it. There is also a sense in which the well-formed work of art is internally synecdochic, as the beginning of a drama contains its close or the close sums up the beginning, the parts all thus being consubstantially related."[7]

Recontextualization Through Narrative Devices

The persuasive effect of decontextualization is most fully realized when combined with the second technique: recontextualization through one or more narrative devices. The viewer must be told or led in some other manner to a "correct" integration and interpretation of the displaced image in its new context. A proper understanding of the "fit" between and among image sequences on the part of the audience must be achieved if the propaganda is to have the intended effect. Using the examples cited above, it is not merely the decontextualization that achieves the persuasive end, but the combination of the decontextualized image with a narrative reconstruction of the meaning context. Hence, in *The Plow That Broke the Plains* we see the heavy use of the land during World War I while simultaneously listening to the narrator tell us, "Wheat will win the war . . . wheat for the boys over there; wheat for the Allies; wheat for the British; wheat for the Belgians; wheat for the French . . . wheat will win the war." It is these images—reconstructions, to be sure—that are then held up as the reason for the land not being able to recover from the severe drought and windstorms. These images, which came out of a Hollywood warehouse, have been recontextualized to allow the filmmaker to lead his audience to the "proper" conclusion.[8]

The same technique is used in *Divide and Conquer*, where, over stock footage of displaced refugees, the narrator intones: "Unopposed bombing raids sent civilians fleeing in stark terror. They hadn't wanted war. They had done everything to avoid it. Hoping they could escape the Nazi scourge, they had compromised and tragically failed to unite with the other democracies. And now they faced the scourge defenseless and alone." The narrative recontextualizes the images and guides the viewer to the "correct" interpretation and feeling state.

Attempt to Appear Natural, Objective, or Fair

Though documentary films vary radically in their stance toward objectivity of presentation, the most effective propaganda films try mightily to *appear* to be fair, balanced, and unprejudiced. This appearance can be accomplished in many different ways. One way is through the introduction of widely shared value premises, such as "thou shalt not lie," premises that are then shown to be violated repeatedly and without remorse by the antagonist. This is the basic technique of Capra's *Why We Fight* series.

A second way to try to appear objective or fair is by using the technique of historical recall, in which several people conjure up from memory details of the past—the assumption being that a multiplicity of voices testifying to their own existential experiences must necessarily yield a form of historical truth. To have lived through the time period or to have participated in the great events of the day lends an air of expertise, authority, and credibility that is itself a form of perceived objectivity, for the filmmaker, it appears, allows real people to tell their own stories in their own way. This is the technique of *Union Maids* (1978) and *The Life and Times of Rosie the Riveter* (1980).

A third way to give the appearance of fairness and objectivity, if not of nature itself, is through attention to details of place and person that, by their very naturalness and innocence, testify to the care and respect with which the filmmaker treats his subject. The assumption is that that which is natural cannot be other than fair and balanced. It is merely the way God has made the world, and the task of the filmmaker is to record this creation in all its splendor and glory. Thus does Robert Flaherty appear to be the most objective of observers in *Nanook of the North* (1922) and *Man of Aran* (1934), for the elements bear testimony to their own integrity and authenticity, or so it would appear.

Finally, the filmmaker can seek to be perceived as fair and objective by choosing to use a particular type of narrator or on-camera host. Here it is the credibility of the source that, by dint of past associations combined with the appearance of special knowledge about the present, functions as the vehicle of the appeal. Such a person can, by force of personality or intellect alone, assure the audience of the normative value of his or her report. The classic example is Edward R. Murrow, who in such films as *Argument at Indianapolis* (1953) and *Harvest of Shame* (1960) convinced millions that he was merely a journalist reporting the facts as he found them—facts that could, it appeared, speak for themselves.

The techniques by which one may foster the appearance of naturalness, objectivity, and fairness are legion. These are but four of the more prevalent. Yet whatever the technique by which it is achieved, the *appearance* of an unbiased, objective reporting of "the way it is" is integral to the practice of effective film propaganda. The audience must believe that what they are witnessing on the screen is real—that it has actually happened in the manner depicted and that the filmmaker is merely re-presenting and reporting that reality.

Use of Pathetic Figures

The fourth technique of the film or television propagandist is the dramatic use of pathetic events and figures. Pathos is that mode of rhetorical appeal which, according to Aristotle, results from the evocation of the correct emotion or set of emotions from the audience. That which is "correct," under an Aristotelian paradigm, is that which corresponds to the aims and purposes of the persuader. From the outset, documentary filmmakers have made extensive use of this rhetorical resource:

- The Eskimo family huddled together in their igloo in *Nanook of the North* (1922)
- The mourning over the fallen Vakulinchuk in *Battleship Potemkin* (1925)

- The photogenic children playing amid the traffic and smoke of *The City* (1939)
- The psychologically impaired soldiers whose tears and tremors lead us to an emotional apprehension of the terrible costs of war in *Let There Be Light* (1945)
- The women and children being herded like cattle in the photographic stillness of *Night and Fog* (1955).

To be effective, all persuasion, whether by cinematic means or otherwise, must strike a responsive chord in the audience to which it is directed.[9] By leading the viewers to an emotional feeling state, the documentarian can weight, psychologically and emotionally, even the most objective of reports, as Edward R. Murrow demonstrated time and again in both radio and television formats. By gaining control of the viewers' emotions, skilled propagandists can use those emotions to lead the audience to specific ideational conclusions. This premise was, in fact, the theoretical basis behind Sergei Eisenstein's notion of "intellectual montage." Eisenstein noted:

The strength of montage resides in this, that it includes in the creative process the emotions and mind of the spectator. The spectator is compelled to proceed along the selfsame creative road that the author traveled in creating the image. . . . In fact, every spectator, in correspondence with his individuality, and in his own way and out of his own experience—out of the womb of his fantasy, out of the warp and weft of his associations, all conditioned by the premises of his character, habits and social appurtenances, creates an image in accordance with the representational guidance suggested by the author, leading him to understanding and experience of the author's theme.[10]

By knowing the emotional predispositions of the viewers, visual persuaders can use that knowledge to foster acceptance of specific ideational conclusions.

Use of a Privileged Narrator

The fifth technique employed frequently by film propagandists is the privileged narrator or commentator. Though striving to appear fair, neutral, and objective, the privileged narrator "knows" more than the audience and successfully communicates that superior knowledge through intonation, interpretation, and assertion.

Historically, the most widely practiced form of privileged narration has been the voice-of-God commentary employed by 1930s newsreels and World War II documentaries. The prime example of voice-of-God commentary is, of course, the *March of Time* newsreel series, which ran from 1935 to 1951 and featured the voices of Ted Husing, Harry Von Zell, and Westbrook Van Voorhis. Yet the voice-of-God technique is only one of the ways in which intonation asserts privilege (though it is the most obvious, to be sure). At the other end of the scale, so to speak, is what might be called the trans-historical voice.

The transhistorical voice belongs to no one in particular, is without historical referent or ideological insight. Like the wind, it blows where it wills, describing in a flat ("natural") voice whatever happens to appear on the screen. It is disembodied, uncommitted, and transhistorical. It will ever and always be the same, without regard for subject matter, location, or chronological era. Flat and unemotional, the transhistorical voice speaks as though interpretation is unnecessary, as though the "facts" really do speak for themselves if the narrator will but distance himself as far as possible from the specifics of the moment. The narrative voice in the 13-part PBS series is a prime example of this technique.

But intonation is not the only dimension of privileged narration. Though purporting merely to describe "the facts and nothing but the facts," the narrative voice of privilege interprets the facts and events through word choice, rhythm, and syntax. In *Divide and Conquer*, for example, the narrator refers to "the ceaseless barrage of German propaganda," to "one of the most ruthless exhibitions of savagery the world has ever seen," and to the "Nazi master race." Here word choice guides interpretive response.

In *Night Mail* (1936) and *The River* (1937), however, it is rhythmic commentary that interprets for the viewers the images placed before them. As viewers of *The River* watch mules being used to build levees, the commentator rhythmically intones:

> New Orleans to Baton Rouge,
> Baton Rouge to Natchez,
> Natchez to Vicksburg,
> Vicksburg to Memphis,
> Memphis to Cairo—
> We built a dyke a thousand miles long.
> Men and mules;
> Mules and mud;
> Mules and mud a thousand miles up the Mississippi.

Through these and other devices the narrator becomes a privileged spectator whose prescient status, though unacknowledged, is nonetheless real.

Where intonation or linguistic interpretation proves unfruitful, the privileged narrator can always resort to straightforward assertion.

As long as the assertion is not in direct conflict with the images appearing on the screen, the "facts" asserted by the narrator are likely to be accepted at face value. After all, why should the narrator lie? The narrative voice enjoys the privilege that accompanies suspension of disbelief. To assert in such a context is to prove, for the audience is a willing participant in its own seduction.[11]

When Roger Mudd tells us, in *The Selling of the Pentagon* (1971), that Mr. Friedheim, the public information officer for the Pentagon, is a "careful and respected adversary" who "does not tell all he knows" and "wouldn't have his job long if he did," the audience nods in agreement, for the context and the privileged position of the narrator transform assertion into apodictic truth. It matters little that the raw materials have been altered to sustain the illusion of spontaneity. We "know" the truth when we hear it, or at least believe we do.

Reordering of Filmic Events for Rhetorical Impact

The sixth technique employed by cinematic propagandists is the intentional reordering of filmic events for maximum rhetorical impact, without regard for the veracity of the representation or the structural integrity of the raw materials. Here the question is more than just the displacement of one image by another or the recontextualization of the image through narration. Here there is material alteration of the image sequence or sound track.

In *The Selling of the Pentagon*, for example, several sequences are cut and then spliced together with other material to provide alternative answers to questions posed by the on-camera interviewer. The original answers are deleted, and responses to totally different questions are substituted.[12] *Point of Order* (1964), Emile de Antonio's treatment of the Army-McCarthy hearings, provides another case in point. In addition to recontextualizing displaced images and splicing answers from one question to follow a different question, de Antonio manipulates the sound track by placing canned laughter over McCarthy's testimony. The effect is to make it appear that the whole hearing room is laughing at what McCarthy has to say. Again, the structural integrity of both sound and image is violated.

Pursuit of a Journalistic Line or Angle

The reordering of sound and image is often directly related to the seventh technique of filmic propaganda—the pursuit of a journalistic "line" or "angle." Though often done in such a subtle manner as to escape initial detection, the pursuit of a particular line or conclusion often becomes obvious upon second or third viewing. Most audiences do not, of course, have the luxury of multiple viewings. Viewers generally must judge the accuracy, objectivity, and conclusions of a piece of communication more or less immediately, and decide simultaneously how they will react to that communication.

The pursuit of a journalistic line, whether developed intentionally or evolved from unconscious motives, will always be detectable through subsequent structural analysis. Kenneth Burke puts the matter well when he observes of the literary persuader: "The motivation out of which he writes is synonymous with the structural way in which he puts events and values together when he writes; and however consciously he may go about such work, there is a kind of generalization about these interrelations that he could not have been conscious of, since the generalization could be made by the kind of inspection that is possible only *after the completion* of the work."[13]

That such a line or conclusion informs such films as *The City* (1939), *Power and the Land* (1940), *The Battle of San Pietro* (1945), and *Thursday's Children* (1954) is undeniable. Yet it is present even in films that are not obviously didactic, argumentative, or promotional in nature. Thomas Benson's studies of the Frederick Wiseman documentaries *High School* (1968) and *Primate* (1974), and my studies of the feature films *The Exorcist* (1974) and *Hiroshima, Mon Amour* (1959) exemplify this principle at work.[14] Though it is not obvious from a cursory viewing, such films possess a structural logic of their own that, when understood, leads to a clear "line" or "conclusion" that has, in fact, been present all along.

Use of Asynchronous Associative Logic

The eighth propaganda technique available to the filmmaker is what I call the use of asynchronous associative logic. Such a logic usually proceeds by recourse to the rhetorical devices of metaphor and metonym. Generally, a narrative film proceeds by means of synchronization between the sound and image tracks. Thus, when a person is shown speaking, the sound track is usually a transcription of his or her words or a description of what he or she is saying. Likewise, when an image is shown on the screen, the sound track usually has music, commentary, dialogue, or effects related directly to that image. Even when the sound track intentionally clashes with the imagery, establishing an aural-visual counterpoint, the contrast with its attendant meaning is obvious to the educated viewer.

Asynchronous associative logic works in a much different manner. Here the sound and images relate to each other, though not simultaneously. Image follows sound or sound follows image at no particular interval and according to no specific rhythmic pattern.[15] Asynchronous associative logic requires the viewer to attend to relationships based upon structural contiguity (a sort of visual metonym) and ideational similarity (visual and conceptual metaphor).

A good example of this technique occurs in Alain Resnais's classic documentary *Night and Fog* (1955). Over the image of a steam shovel at work the narrator speaks of "friends in high places," a clear reference to business and government officials within Nazi Germany. The next image, however, is that of a tall guard tower overlooking a concentration camp. The previous narrative line about "friends in high places" now takes on a totally different meaning. The asynchronous association of the narration with the imagery immediately following suggests a metaphoric interpretation: government policymakers and cooperative businessmen have led to the death camps; politicians and capitalists are partners in murder.

Asynchronous logic works through metaphoric associations between and among the various artistic elements: image, sound, color, lighting, movement. Metaphoric meanings echo throughout the film, informing subsequent sounds and images, and modifying audience interpretation. Working on both the conscious and the subconscious level, asynchronous association is a powerful technique of suggestion, implication, and coded meaning.[16]

Use of Visual Ambiguity and Narrative Cuing

The ninth technique associated with film or television propaganda is the intentional use of visual ambiguity to allow for multiple interpretations of portrayed events. Like the use of weasel words or doubletalk in spoken language, visual ambiguity allows for a multiplicity of meanings and forces the viewer to turn for interpretive guidance either to the narration or to structural clues within the text. These other elements can then be used to construct a "proper" frame for interpretation of the ambiguous imagery.

Psychologically, the use of visual ambiguity in tandem with structural and narrational markers functions much like the traditional enthymeme.[17] By providing a context for interpretation and creating certain sorts of expectations through narrational clues, the filmmaker can guide the response of the viewer along predetermined lines. The viewer supplies the "proper" meaning for the ambiguous imagery, thereby becoming an active participant in the process of persuasion.[18]

APPLYING THE TECHNIQUES

I turn now to the application of these techniques to the PBS Vietnam series and to the Accuracy in Media counterdocumentary. Rather than apply the techniques one at a time in a lockstep, mechanical fashion, I will trace the narrative development of the opening segments of both films, commenting on the techniques as they manifest themselves diachronically.

Vietnam: A Television History

The 13-hour PBS series "Vietnam: A Television History" opens with an American helicopter sortie that fills the screen like a plague of locusts. Reminiscent of a famous scene from Francis Ford Coppola's *Apocalypse Now*, the helicopters announce the coming of the Americans to the jungles of Southeast Asia. Eerie music fills the air as the filmmaker cuts to shots of American special forces in full camouflage. Strange patterns of facial paint, combined with the cold stares of the soldiers, remind viewers of nothing so much as the occultlike madness that reigned in Colonel Kurtz's camp.

The parallels with *Apocalypse Now* are more than accidental; they are integral to a proper understanding of the themes developed throughout the 13 hours of the series. In the opening shots of the first episode, "Roots of a War," we have already seen a metaphorical expression of the type of battle the filmmaker is inviting us to perceive. It is a war like that depicted in the Coppola film—a war of madness, corruption, drug use, barbarity, and, in the end, meaninglessness.

The metaphorical opening is followed by a series of short clips of Presidents Eisenhower, Kennedy, Johnson, and Nixon articulating their concern over the possible loss of all Southeast Asia. Their comments are interspersed with scenes from the war in Vietnam, as though their rhetoric and the belief system it represents are the animating force behind these scenes of suffering. The "domino theory" is the rationale, we are led to believe, for our involvement in Vietnam.

The narrator first enters the production with these words: "First a handful of advisers. Then the Marines. Finally, an army of half a million. That was the Vietnam War.'' The narrator asserts knowledge that has not been demonstrated by the preceding images and does not summarize what is to follow. As a descriptive definition of the Vietnam War, the assertion is inaccurate, woefully reductionistic, and clearly ethnocentric. The war did not begin with a handful of U.S. advisers, nor did it end with a U.S. army of half a million—facts that the series itself reveals at the end of this episode.

What, then, are we to make of these opening images and narrative devices? I believe that they are structural cues to the "line" or "angle" that the series as a whole seeks to develop. When the narrator continues, "It was an undeclared war. A war without front lines or clear objectives. A war against an elusive (or is it illusive?) enemy.'' He is identifying the basic themes that will be pursued throughout the 13 episodes: the lack of congressional validation for the war effort; uncertainty about war objectives; ambiguity inherent in the situation; and the constant focus on suffering, both that of the Vietnamese people and that of the American soldiers.

The ordering of the shots in this opening segment similarly demonstrates an editorial slant or journalistic line. First, the quotations from American presidents end with Richard Nixon. Yet the Vietnam War continued through the presidency of Gerald Ford, when Saigon fell in May 1975. By ending with Nixon, the filmmakers are able psychologically to transfer negative feelings about his presidency to the "domino theory" and the justification for the war in Vietnam. But there is more.

When the narrator speaks of an elusive enemy, the camera tracks past a bamboo hut partially hidden by the jungle. It appears to be nothing more than a rural village. Visual ambiguity is used to make the viewer wonder how dangerous such a tranquil scene could be. Seconds later we are given guidance—a structural cue—in the "proper" interpretation of this scene when an old Vietnamese woman testifies, "Wherever the Americans went, they burned and destroyed and killed. I didn't see any guerrillas being killed, only villagers.'' The enemy really is more illusive than elusive. Only peace-loving villagers reside in these structures. The ambiguity inherent in the visual portrayal is clarified by this subsequent narrative device.

The first on-camera interview is with an unidentified veteran, and reveals the interplay between the themes of suffering and obscurity of objectives. The veteran says, "We had some precarious situations and we lost some people, but we always won. So to me we were very successful. But as I think of it now, I don't know what we won. We won a box on a map where the next day we left it, and we never came back, maybe.'' Over this testimony, the viewer sees wounded Americans being evacuated from the front. This is the visual correlate of ''success.''

The narrator then observes, ''It was a war that blurred the line between friend and enemy.'' The Vietnamese woman referred to above recites her piece about seeing only villagers killed, which is immediately followed by a second veteran saying, ''An 8-year-old or a 9-year-old can kill you just as quick as 25- or 26-year-old men.'' The effect, of course, is to give credibility to the woman's assertion as well as to the viewer's own reading of the visually ambiguous village. What we have been led to suspect all along has proven to be true—American soldiers felt that eight- and nine-year-olds were their enemies and must, therefore, be killed.

The narrator says, ''It was a war with deep roots, deeper than most Americans knew. Ho Chi Minh and his followers fought for decades—against the French, then against the Americans and their South Vietnamese ally.'' The filmmaker then cuts to the testimony of a South Vietnamese father who, with tears in his eyes, says, ''I always believed in my country. But instead of sending my sons out to defend their country, I sent them out to die.'' Again, the theme of purposelessness, senselessness, and meaninglessness is featured. Now it is not only the Americans who have testified to the war's futility and aimlessness, but the South Vietnamese as well.

This testimony is followed by the first of what will be scores of pathos-inducing shots: teenage boys being measured for their uniforms, uniforms that we have already been told are death garments; a mother crying; and a father planting a farewell kiss on the cheek of his child. Clearly the filmmaker is doing more than reporting. He is inviting us to feel the pain of separation and carefully structuring that pain so that it is clearly understood within the context of purposelessness. The ''line'' being pursued is not hard to fathom: this pain, separation, and death need never have happened. It was a sacrifice without any redeeming value, a waste of precious human lives.

The narrator tells the viewer, ''It was a war that turned South Vietnam inside out; a war that changed the GI's who fought it.'' The director then cuts to a former GI, who says, ''For a box of Tide you could get a carton of prepacked, prerolled marijuana cigarettes, soaked in opium. For ten dollars you could get a vial of pure heroin. You could get liquid opium, speed, acid, anything you wanted.'' Here is how the American GI has been ''changed.'' He is portrayed as a dope user whose Vietnam experience was both physically and psychologically destructive. Condensed into the testimony of this young man are the experiences of over 2.5 million American servicemen, all of whom are represented by a few comments about the ready availability of drugs.

As the focus turns to the role of the media in covering the war, we see American troops engaged in a fire fight, and are told by one soldier that "the whole thing stinks." The narrative device of letting the participants speak for themselves helps to structure audience perception and confirm the narrator's privileged point of view. The narrator thus appears merely to be repeating what everyone (it seems) already believes.

The only note of discord in the first eight and a half minutes of this cinematic frontispiece is Ronald Reagan's assertion, "It's time that we recognized ours was, in truth, a noble cause." Not only has every piece of visual and verbal evidence presented contradicted this assertion, but Reagan, as a U.S. president, is structurally related to Eisenhower, Kennedy, Johnson, and Nixon—the leaders who promulgated the policies that led us into this meaningless war. Just to make sure that everyone understands that Reagan's viewpoint is not to be taken too seriously, the narrator immediately follows with "Vietnam. A noble cause? A shameful venture? The questions continue, because for America the Vietnam War is not over." As the narrative voice proposes these alternative interpretations, thus once again striving to appear impartial and balanced, the visuals show us a disabled veteran in a wheelchair and a placard that reads: "We killed. We bled. We died. For Worse Than Nothing." Visually, the choice between "noble cause" and "shameful venture" has already been made.

After noting that Vietnam is still at war "in Cambodia and with China," the narrator brings the introductory segment to a close with both a statement and a question: "Two and a half million Americans fought in Vietnam, and fifty-eight thousand Americans died there. Why?" Viewers are left with the question and the stark image of the Vietnam Veterans Memorial staring them in the face. Thus ends the introductory segment to what has been called "a landmark in American broadcast journalism."[19]

Television's Vietnam: The Real Story

The 55-minute counterdocumentary produced by Accuracy in Media (AIM) was described in substantially different terms. Lawrence Lichty, director of media research for the PBS series and a well-known communications professor, labeled the AIM film "a very good example" of a "bad propaganda film."[20] Other reviewers were less charitable. *New York Times* columnist Anthony Lewis said that the AIM film was "a doctrinaire harangue posing as a news documentary."[21] The editorial page of the *Sacramento Bee* called it "little more than a propaganda hit piece."[22]

Time and again the notion that the AIM film was "propaganda" while the award-winning PBS series was "documentary" was repeated by reviewers, editorialists, and letter writers. But what is the cinematic evidence for such a charge? How does the AIM film compare with the PBS series if judged by the nine techniques described in this chapter? A detailed analysis of the opening segment allows for a clear comparison.

There is little doubt that in terms of purely visual interest, the AIM film cannot stand comparison with the $5.6 million PBS production. The editing is stilted, the compositional qualities of the framing often lacking, the narrative continuity uneven, and the footage largely uninspiring. Yet the question with which we are concerned is not so much one of aesthetics as of propagandistic techniques and persuasive effect.

The AIM film opens with a voice-over narration by Charlton Heston. "This is the Vietnam Veterans Memorial," he states, as the viewer sees the black marble slabs inscribed with name after name of the dead. A man makes a carbon print of a name as the camera pans the grounds surrounding the memorial, finally coming to rest on the Washington Monument. This opening, too, is metaphoric, for we are visually told that the Vietnam War was a fight for freedom and independence, just as Washington fought our first war for those same goals. The two memorials participate in the same essence, represent the same spirit.

Heston wastes no time in announcing the point of view to be represented in the film. He unequivocally states that the PBS series " 'Vietnam: A Television History' was flawed by serious errors and distortions," and that the AIM program is "dedicated to setting the historical record straight." Here is the first significant point of departure between the two films. While the narrator of the PBS series seeks to give the appearance of a neutral observer, Heston reveals his ideological bias at the outset.

From the standpoint of effective propaganda, AIM has already hurt its cause, for to announce a persuasive or argumentative intent is to lose the advantage that attends the perception of objectivity or neutrality. As Joseph Goebbels observed, "Propaganda becomes ineffective the moment we are aware of it."[23] We are aware of the persuasive motives of AIM from the outset.

The AIM critique is centered on four promises allegedly made by PBS in its original funding proposal to the National Endowment for the Humanities: (1) to supply information for the historical record; (2) to provide an antidote to the misuses of history; (3) to contribute to healing and to national esteem; and (4) to contribute to historical methodology. On all four counts AIM finds the PBS series deficient.

Yet, again, from the point of view of effective propaganda, the clarity, conciseness, and boldness with which AIM challenges the PBS objectives tend to dissipate AIM's effectiveness, if effective propaganda is the goal. The last thing that the professional propagandist wishes to do is foster a debate. As Richard Taylor notes, "One of the guiding principles for the successful 'propagandist' is surely to make the attitudes that he wishes to spread appear as uncontroversial as possible. The whiff of controversy would invite the possibility of debate and open those same attitudes to contradiction."[24] This is precisely what the AIM film does. It introduces specific arguments and attempts to build, through testimony, evidence, and reasoning, good counterarguments. That the result of this approach was, in fact, an expanded public debate is evidenced, among other things, by the many editorials, news stories, commentaries, and letters to the editor that followed its airing on the PBS network.[25]

So, from the very outset, the AIM film places itself at a grave disadvantage with respect to its propagandistic potential. This is not to say that there are no propaganda techniques employed, for clearly there are. It is to contend, however, that these techniques are largely vitiated by the argumentative form within which they are encompassed.

Having introduced and dismissed each of the four PBS contentions, the director cuts back to Heston, now seated. As narrator, Heston's main function is to introduce the various interviewees and to tie each segment together with a dramatic rendering of the script. As a dramatic narrator, Heston's performance is nearly perfect. But from a propagandistic point of view, both the selection of Heston the personality and his pointedly dramatic tones and evocative facial expressions work against the persuasive potentialities inherent in the subject matter.

Heston's political views are well known. His support of Ronald Reagan and his ongoing battles with left-wing actor Ed Asner and other leaders of the Screen Actors Guild are public knowledge. If one were looking for a personage who could connote fairness and objectivity, Heston would certainly have to be one of the last people to whom one would turn. Likewise, if persuasion of the ignorant or uncommitted is the goal, the seemingly neutral tone and disembodied presence of the PBS narrator is much more likely to be accepted at face value than the obviously committed and dramatically colored narration of the AIM film. Once again, as effective film propaganda, the PBS series is far superior.

The AIM film does, of course, have its moments. When AIM chairman Reed Irvine speaks of "the repression and misery that caused an estimated two million Vietnamese, Cambodians, and Laotians to flee their countries," we are shown touching shots of the boat people as they struggle against the elements. When historian Stephen Morris argues that Ho Chi Minh was "primarily a Communist," we see shots of the Communist Party Congress in Moscow with Ho prominently featured, along with other leaders of world Communism.

Yet, for the most part, the visuals are uninspiring. Without access to the stocks of newsreel acquired by PBS, the AIM producers had to rely to a much greater degree on still photos and voice-over commentary. This constraint naturally led to a disproportionate use of two persuasive techniques: decontextualization through condensation and displacement, and recontextualization through narrative devices. A good example of these techniques at work occurs midway through the AIM program when Charlton Heston challenges the PBS portrayal of South Vietnamese President Diem.

Heston charges that the third episode of the PBS series, "America's Mandarin," tells us that "Ngo Dinh Diem was an American puppet." As we watch the PBS footage of Diem deplaning and being greeted by Eisenhower, Heston interprets what we are seeing in the following manner: "The message is that Diem, the puppet, has come to Washington to see the man who pulls the strings." Yet nothing in the visuals necessarily suggests such a reading, and when they are viewed within the context of the PBS narration, Heston's interpretation is positively refuted. It is a clear example of the technique of decontextualization and recontextualization through narrative interpretation. The same technique appears two or three more times in the AIM film.

Perhaps the most effective technique used in the AIM counter-documentary is the introduction of pathos-inducing visuals: a small Vietnamese child making the sign of the cross; the lines of coffins and wailing relatives following the Hue massacre; the contemplative music, poetic narration, and moving shots of the boat people as they are rescued from the high seas, many having to be removed by stretcher because they are so weak; and the piles of bones and skulls from Kampuchea. These moments, though few, are effective uses of one specific propaganda technique—pathetic appeal.

However, once one notes the decontextualization/recontextualization techniques and the use of pathetic figures, one is hard pressed to find other clear uses of any of the other six techniques. There is no attempt to be neutral or to present a supposedly objective point of view; the narrator neither asserts nor implies any special privilege save that of his clearly stated ideological bias. His is neither the voice-of-God nor the transhistorical voice, but merely the voice of the theater transplanted to the small screen; there does not appear to be any material alteration or reordering of imagery or sound, though slow-motion techniques are employed from time to time, with mixed results; though there is clearly a line or conclusion being pursued, it is far from the subconscious or unconscious one of the propagandist. The AIM line is neither subtle nor structural. It is obvious and easily detected. Apart from the opening shots, there is no use of asynchronous logic or metaphorical or metonymic techniques. Likewise, there is no use of visual ambiguity. Both sounds and images are crisp, clear, and concise. Emphasis is on simplicity and clarity of presentation. No hidden or subconscious meanings lurk here.

One can, of course, disagree with the evidence presented, or the interpretation of the evidence offered, or the final conclusions drawn by the AIM experts, but one is hard pressed to label this film as propagandistic. If it is propaganda, then surely Professor Lichty is right when he calls it "bad propaganda." As propaganda, the AIM film fails nearly all of the theoretical axioms concerning how such films should be produced, distributed, and promoted. From the standpoint of purely cinematic or televisual persuasion, the AIM documentary employs only two or three of the nine dominant techniques of visual propaganda. While its membership in the documentary genre demands that it be considered a form of propaganda, it does not follow that it is therefore effective propaganda.

From the standpoint of persuasive technique, and especially when compared with the PBS series, the AIM counterdocumentary is only marginally effective. The clarity of argumentative stance, combined with the controversial nature of its sponsor and the well-known political persuasion of its on-camera narrator, dictates against easy acceptance. Quite to the contrary, the AIM counterdocumentary invites a public debate by the very boldness of its vision and the clarity of its articulation.

CONCLUSION

The terms "documentary" and "propaganda" are often considered mutually exclusive by consumers of media fare. Yet, historically, the documentary form has been characterized by the "creative treatment of actuality," with such creativity being fostered through recourse to nine dominant techniques of cinematic persuasion. Nearly every award-winning documentary has made heavy use of one or more of these techniques. It is therefore meaningless to speak of documentary film or television in terms of "objectivity," "neutrality," or self-evident "facts," as though the sounds and images speak for themselves. They do not.

Documentary film and television, like all film and television, is an artistically structured, goal-oriented enterprise that can best be understood in terms of the persuasive techniques employed and the relative effectiveness or ineffectiveness of those techniques, both within the individual work and among works of the same type. The first step in criticism is to recognize the techniques; the second, to evaluate their use in specific contexts.

It is the argument of this chapter that the 13-part PBS series, "Vietnam: A Television History," is a more effective vehicle for cinematic persuasion than is the AIM counterdocumentary, "Vietnam: The Real Story." The basis for this judgment lies in the application of the nine dominant techniques of cinematic and televisual propaganda to each film, and the consequent judgment concerning the frequency with which such techniques are employed and the effectiveness of their instantiation as visual persuasion.

Having identified the techniques and applied them to two of the more controversial documentaries of recent years, a central question remains: Should educators, journalists, and others concerned with matters of public communication applaud good (effective) propaganda or bad, and upon what moral or ethical theory should such a choice be based? This is not primarily a political question, but an ethical one: subtle, psychological persuasion in the guise of neutrality, or clear, ideologically based argument that invites public debate? To explore the implications of this question and the conclusions and entailments that specific answers to it would suggest is, of course, beyond the scope of this chapter. Nevertheless, the question remains. And it is a crucial question, for upon the answer to it rests our ability to construct truly rhetorical audiences and a fully democratic citizenry.

NOTES

1. John Grierson, cited in *Grierson on Documentary*, ed. Forsyth Hardy (New York: Praeger, 1966), 13.

2. Grierson, cited in Elizabeth Sussex, *The Rise and Fall of British Documentary* (Berkeley: University of California Press, 1975), 3.

3. *Grierson on Documentary*, p.15.

4. Ibid., p.13.

5. John Grierson, "Propaganda: A Problem for Educational Theory and for Cinema," *Sight and Sound* 2 (1933–34):119.

6. For an excellent description of the way Robert Flaherty manipulated his raw materials, see the four articles devoted to *Nanook of the North* in *Studies in Visual Communication* 6 (1980):2–76. See also the classic study of Flaherty's life, Arthur Calder-Marshall, *The Innocent Eye: The Life of Robert J. Flaherty* (London: W. H. Allen, 1963).

7. Kenneth Burke, *A Grammar of Motives* (1945; repr. Berkeley: University of California Press, 1966), 508.

8. See Robert L. Snyder, *Pare Lorentz and the Documentary Film* (Norman: University of Oklahoma Press, 1968), 31–32; Richard Dyer MacCann, *The People's Films: A Political History of U.S. Government Motion Pictures* (New York: Hastings House, 1973), 68–69.

9. See Tony Schwartz, *The Responsive Chord* (Garden City, NY: Anchor/ Doubleday, 1974).

10. Sergei Eisenstein, *The Film Sense*, trans. and ed. Jay Leyda (1942; repr. New York: Harcourt, Brace & World, 1975), 32–33. On the concept of "intellectual montage" see Eisenstein, *Film Form: Essays in Film Theory*, trans. and ed. Jay Leyda (New York: Harcourt, Brace & World, 1949), 82–83.

11. Bill Nichols, "The Voice of Documentary," *Film Quarterly* 36 (1983): 17–30; Jeffrey Youdelman, "Narration, Invention, & History: A Documentary Dilemma," *Cineaste* 12 (1982): 8–15.

12. See Frank J. Kahn, ed., *Documents of American Broadcasting*, 2nd ed. (New York: Appleton-Century-Crofts, 1973), 447–452.

13. Kenneth Burke, *The Philosophy of Literary Form* (1941; repr. Berkeley: University of California Press, 1969), 20.

14. Thomas W. Benson, "The Rhetorical Structure of Frederick Wiseman's *High School*," *Communication Monographs* 47 (1980): 233–261, and "The Rhetorical Structure of Frederick Wiseman's *Primate*," *Quarterly Journal of Speech* 71 (1985): 204–217; Martin J. Medhurst, "Image and Ambiguity: A Rhetorical Approach to *The Exorcist*," *Southern Speech Communication Journal* 44 (1978): 73–92, and "*Hiroshima, Mon Amour*: From Iconography to Rhetoric, " *Quarterly Journal of Speech* 68 (1982): 345–370.

15. For a close textual analysis of a documentary film that *does* follow a specific rhythmical pattern, see Martin J. Medhurst and Thomas W. Benson, "*The City*: The Rhetoric of Rhythm," *Communication Monographs* 48 (1981): 54–72.

16. See Bill Nichols, *Ideology and the Image: Social Representation in the Cinema and Other Media* (Bloomington: Indiana University Press, 1981), 104–169.

17. On traditional notions of the enthymeme, see Lloyd F. Bitzer,"Aristotle's Enthymeme Revisited,"*Quarterly Journal of Speech* 45 (1959): 399–408.

18. See Martin J. Medhurst and Michael A. DeSousa, "Political Cartoons as Rhetorical Form: A Taxonomy of Graphic Discourse," *Communication Monographs* 48 (1981): 197–236; Bruce E. Gronbeck, "Narrative, Enactment, and Television Programming," *Southern Speech Communication Journal* 48 (1983): 229–242.

19. Judy Woodruff, citing unidentified reviewer, in *Inside Story Special Edition: Vietnam Op/Ed* (New York: The Press and the Public Project, 1985), 3.

20. Lawrence Lichty, cited in *Inside Story Special Edition*, p.5.

21. Anthony Lewis, "If the Press Were Tame," *New York Times*, June 27, 1985, p.A23.

22. Editorial, *Sacramento Bee*, June 28, 1985, p.B2.

23. Joseph Goebbels, cited in Richard Taylor, *Film Propaganda: Soviet Russia and Nazi Germany* (London: Croom Helm, 1979), 230.

24. Taylor, *Film Propaganda*, p.26.

25. See, for example, Richard Zoglin, "Taking A.I.M. Again at Viet Nam," *Time*, July 1, 1985, p.47; *Inside Story Special Edition*, p.46.

12
TV's World of Sports: Presenting and Playing the Game
Jimmie L. Reeves

> How we play the game may turn out to be more important than we imagine, for it signifies nothing less than our way of being in the world.
>
> George B. Leonard[1]

In many ways and to varying degrees, our lives, like our living rooms, are arranged around the flow of television. However, care must be taken in making sense of the relationship between TV and the world of everyday life. Although TV is *of* the commonsense world—an integral part of our daily experience—it is also distinct from it. Clearly, television does much more than merely record or reflect social reality. With its kaleidoscopic stream of programming, television processes and re-presents social reality by translating the conflicts and contradictions of the modern world into terms that are accessible and forms that are comprehensible to a vast, heterogeneous audience. In framing, focusing, and narrating the commonsense world, then, television is also engaged in an ongoing rewrite—or re-*vision*— of the American way. In this rewriting ritual, television contributes to the reproduction, maintenance, repair, and transformation of social reality.[2]

As the symbolic place where social agendas are collectively scrutinized, evaluated, and reckoned with, TV speaks to us always of "the appropriate." Operating as our culture's central symbol system, TV claws everything toward its vortex, rejecting only that which threatens its profits and its culture.[3] But, in its representation and negotiation of meaning, TV is far from being a "fair," or even a "neutral," mediator. Certain social agendas, in the world according to TV, receive favorable treatment; other agendas are trivialized and misrepresented; still others, too threatening to accept as legitimate, are rejected as "inappropriate."

Commercial American television, then, is vitally concerned with the routine commodification and communication of shared beliefs.[4] It accomplishes this marketing of meaning through a versatile array of expressive forms and discursive strategies. Without a doubt, TV's supreme message-product is prime-time consensus narrative: a storytelling enterprise that, according to David Thorburn, is characterized by the "ambition or desire to speak for and to the whole of its culture, or as much of 'the whole' as the governing forces in society will allow."[5] Outside the prime-time domain of network television, TV often attempts to appeal to more specific, though still large, segments of the mass audience. In contrast with consensus narrative, fringe entertainment forms such as the music video, the Saturday morning cartoon, and the daytime soap opera endeavor to "speak for and to" particular age and gender groups, taste factions, and socioeconomic classes.[6]

But television's processing of social reality is not restricted to discourse that is traditionally labeled "fiction." News, advertising, educational, and variety programs also articulate, privilege, and perpetuate certain commonsense views and values. The primary emphasis in this study, however, is on how television's sports arena assists in the social construction of reality, for television's sport forms are not neutral forces in society.[7] Just as Hollywood's gangster films and TV's situation comedies represent value-laden systems of expression, so popular sport forms speak to us always of shared beliefs, of status, and of "the appropriate." As Clifford Geertz suggests in his famous "thick description" of the Balinese cockfight, sport forms render "ordinary, everyday experience comprehensible":

What it (the cockfight) does is what, for other people with other temperaments and conventions, *Lear* and *Crime and Punishment* do; it catches up these themes—death, masculinity, rage, pride, loss, beneficence, chance—and, ordering them into an encompassing structure, presents them in such a way as to throw into relief a particular view of their essential nature. . . . An image, fiction, a model, a metaphor, the cockfight is a means of expression; its function is neither to assuage social passions nor to heighten them (though, in its playing-with-fire way it does a bit of both), but, in a medium of feathers, blood, crowds, and money, to display them.[8]

In treating television's sport forms as ritual communication, this study proposes that the American football game, like the Balinese cockfight, is a means of displaying unwritten rules regulating mundane existence.

SPORT AS LIVING DISCOURSE

Of course, in our society, sport's status as ritual communication must be reconciled with its status as big business. And the nation's sports industry, like the entertainment and information industries, must constantly be attuned to changes in the culture or risk losing popularity, relevance, and revenues. Those in charge of "regulating" popular sport forms, then, are often required to act as cultural interpreters. This interpretive role is perhaps most evident during moments of scandal when sports commissioners and league officials must answer widespread criticism with public relations ploys. Here, the mandatory drug-testing programs unveiled in the wake of the cocaine-related deaths of Len Bias and Don Rogers stand as prime examples of the world of sports responding to the world of public opinion.

To the chagrin of sports purists, these same regulators constantly rewrite the rules governing many of our most hallowed American sports. Today, these revisions are often geared toward attracting a larger portion of TV's restless, action-oriented audience—an audience not so much concerned with a sport's sacred traditions as with its profane excitement. Taking a purist's position, Cary Schneider lists and laments the changes instituted to accommodate television: the tie breaker in pro tennis; the designated hitter rule, the extension of the season into October, and the scheduling of World Series night games in pro baseball; and in pro football, sudden-death overtime, as well as rules favoring a high-powered passing offense. According to Schneider, "The facts are immutable: television demands action and spectacle whether the source be the athletes, spectators, cheerleaders, ball girls or giant chickens in the stands. Whatever gets in the way of action must be eliminated."[9] Although television has undeniably sparked the changes outlined by Schneider, such "history minded" purists suffer more from nostalgia than from insight. The purist, in naturalizing a purely historical phenomenon, fails to recognize that sports are—and always have been—volatile, changing forms of cultural expression.

Sports' mutability is especially apparent in the intriguing history of professional wrestling. At the end of the nineteenth century, professional wrestling was as "authentic"—that is, as genuinely competitive—as professional baseball or football is today. Similiar to modern amateur wrestling in terms of style, holds, and strategy, matches during this "authentic" stage frequently lasted for hours in one- and two-hold stalemates. Although watching two giants frozen in sincere hammerlocks must have been poor spectator fare, for a while "authentic" professional wrestling managed to attract a loyal following. This early success was sustained primarily by the talents and fame of two excellent athletes, Frank Gotch and Tom Jenkins, who together dominated wrestling from the 1890s to 1913. However, after their retirement the "authentic" form of pro wrestling could not compete for the spectator dollar with more action-oriented pro-sports.

Although it's not clear exactly how pro wrestling's transformation from "authentic" to "stage-managed" sport was accomplished, by 1930 its essential redefinition was complete. The economic imperatives associated with luring crowds back to the arena resulted in stylistic, promotional, and structural modification of the sport form. The sport's gymnastic style, theatrical contrivances, and control by regional promoters are all very evident today in televised events. But they were instituted and conventionalized years before the introduction of television. So, while pro wrestling would not reach its peak of popularity until the early years of television, sports purists cannot hold television accountable for the sport form's theatrical transformation.[10]

The point is—sport lives. Like language, sport is in a constant state of flux. Sport forms respond to technological advances, to ideological developments, to competition for shifting spectator attention. Thus sport forms—at least those that survive and thrive—both adapt and evolve according to changing social, economic, and technological conditions. To freeze a sport's development in order to maintain its "purity" is to sign its death warrant—static sports soon lose their cultural relevance.

TELEVISION'S SPORTS NARRATION

In its rewriting of culture, television's sports discourse is perhaps most closely related to its news discourse. Where television's prime time consensus narrative is carefully and completely scripted prior to production, sports and news programs process events that are not entirely "prescripted." Consequently, narration in both sports and news discourse is more interpretive than creative. Traditionally delivered using the direct mode of address, sports narration, like news narration, strives to make sense of events that are beyond the direct control of the narrator.[11]

Where the news arena focuses on the new, the relevant, and the unknown of the "reported world," the sports arena focuses on the "world of sports"—a matrix of distinct, yet interconnected, sport forms active in the culture. As is the case in most representational discourse, the behind-the-scenes labor of producers, directors, sound technicians, video editors, and camera operators is masked, or made invisible, by conventional production techniques. Unless the conventions are violated, either by error or by design, the visual processing of the sporting event generally remains inconspicuous, submerged in the subconscious muck of the taken-for-granted.

While we may not always be aware of how the television production crew frames and focuses our view of the sporting event, we are generally aware of two distinct planes of symbolic action that coexist in sports discourse: the presentational plane and the performance plane. Although athletic figures appearing on the performance plane are the main focus of attention in the sports arena, their actions are interpreted and filtered by broadcast professionals and sports experts speaking on the presentational plane. Like all performance, athletic action in the sports arena is dialogic—that is, it has a dynamically open orientation.[12] As a symbolic event, the sports performance takes on meaning only in relation to other performances. And the meaning context framing athletic figures in action extends well beyond the "here and now" of a particular televised event. Spectator expectations are born in the realm of past performance, nurtured by anticipation of future performance, and moderated in the realm of present performance.

Consequently, a great deal of sports narration is devoted to placing a relevant performance in dialogue with other performances. For instance, Walter Payton's present performance is put in dialogue with Jim Brown's past performance when Frank Gifford compares their running styles. And when John Madden, during a Chicago Bears game, predicts that Mike Ditka and company will return to the Super Bowl, the present team performance is placed in dialogue with an anticipated future team performance. To assist in the dialogic presentation of sporting events, athletic performances are converted into records—the most strike outs, the most yards gained, the most passes completed, the fewest errors. This statistical conversation, in turn, becomes privileged male knowledge, knowledge that is gathered, compared, and debated. This statistical knowledge is, in fact, a major component of the "language" of sports narration, giving interpretive accounts of sporting events the window dressing of "objectivity."

Just as the ideology of journalistic objectivity governs the telling of news stories, so a related ideology—the ideal of free and open competition—exerts a strong force in sports narration. In fact, competition has become such a naturalized aspect of sport in our culture that sport is commonly reduced to its vulgar competitive elements. Leonard argues that this distortion of sports is a relatively recent ideological development: "In less than a generation, the prevailing sports ethos in America has shifted from, 'It's not whether you win or lose, it's how you play the game,' to 'Winning isn't everything. It's the only thing.' " [13]

Where journalistic objectivity is premised on reportorial "fairness," free and open competition is premised on the "fairness" of rules and their "objective" enforcement. According to this myth, the rules are vehicles whereby just and fair competition can be realized; they are assumed to be logical, almost natural, manifestations of the particular sport. Game officials, in "objectively" applying those rules to maintain order, are portrayed as competent, neutral agents dedicated to the task of ensuring that the best person or team wins. After all, to have faith enough in a contest to wager on its outcome, one must accept the premise that both the rules and the officials are fair and impartial—and that every participant in the contest expends maximum effort to win. To have faith in the ideal of competition, then, requires a fundamental suspension of disbelief.

Many athletic performers who attain sports stardom are models of competition. Blessed with extraordinary ability, they channel their talents toward the winning of team or individual contests. Representing excellence, they achieve stardom by "maximizing" an "expert" social type.[14] The greatest, fastest, meanest, tallest, smartest, strongest—all are superlatives attached to star performers who give concrete form to competitive excellence. Beyond the field of play, the sports star's symbolic power is almost always translated into sales power. Star performers from every major professional sport are co-opted into TV's advertising arena to front a variety of consumer goods. In fact, today product endorsements represent a major portion of the star's earning power. In interpreting the meaning of sports stardom, then, we must somehow come to terms with the star's dual status as commodity and communication.

The Lombardian warp to sports connected with the ideology of competition is also a strong force in the sports arena's presentational plane. Some narrators/presenters are sports insiders—experts at competition. Others are well-informed professional types possessing detailed empirical knowledge of the relevant statistics associated with a particular sport form. John Madden qualifies as an expert at competition who fronts his commentary as a football "insider." Representing an expert type from within the special realm of professional sport experience, his "insights" carry the credibility of authoritative language. A favorite Madden phrase, "I've been there, I know what it's like," speaks of his past performances as a professional football coach who has accumulated firsthand experience pacing the sidelines during sudden-death overtime, arguing with officials after a questionable call, and riding off the field on the shoulders of his players after a Super Bowl victory.

Howard Cosell, on the other hand, spoke as a well-informed television professional—a voice that was not as valued or credible in commonsense America as the insights of a sports veteran. Popularly perceived as a "know-it-all" critic with no feel for the harsh reality of the trenches of professional sport, Cosell achieved a perverse stardom as the man we "love to hate." The style of his intrusive narration made sportscasting strange. In the tradition of pro wrestling's announcers, who describe even the most mundane match as a "clash of titans," Cosell overdramatized the sporting event to such an extent that the presentational plane overwhelmed the performance plane.

Despite being the focus of widespread hostility, Cosell became a formidable figure in the sports arena. The magnitude of his enduring unpopularity gave his appearance and performance immense power. His figure was as recognizable and significant, in its own way, as Johnny Carson's, Walter Cronkite's, or J. R. Ewing's. As the sports arena's premier star presenter, Howard Cosell held a position comparable with Carson's place in television's variety arena. Just as Carson's blessing is important to an entertainer's achieving stardom, Cosell's blessing was, until recently, important to an athlete's rise to sports stardom.

Indeed, the innovative sports narration of "ABC's Monday Night Football" was designed around Cosell's distinctive performance. In foregrounding opinionated expert dialogue over the "objective" direct address of traditional play-by-play narration, the bantering of the most memorable stars of "Monday Night Football"—Howard Cosell, Don Meredith and Frank Gifford—was both controversial and tremendously successful.[15] The dialogue between Cosell and Meredith, mediated to a certain extent by Gifford, made even the most lopsided contest watchable. In fact, the experience of watching "Monday Night Football" sans Cosell is comparable with what it might be like to watch "All in the Family" without Archie Bunker, "Dallas" without J. R. Ewing, or "Dynasty" without Alexis Carrington. Cosell, like Walter Cronkite, was family—but whereas "Uncle Walter" was blood kin and a welcome visitor in our homes, "Uncle Howard" was the unwelcome in-law.

CENTRIFUGAL FORCES IN THE WORLD OF SPORTS

> I returned, and saw under the sun that the race is not to the swift nor the battle to the strong, neither yet bread to the wise, nor yet riches to men of understanding, nor yet favor to men of skill; but time and chance happeneth to them all.
>
> Ecclesiastes, 9:11

While the unifying force constituted by the ideal of free and open competition has firm control of sports' heartland, there are certain forces in television's world of sports that subvert the competition ethic. To discuss these decentralizing forces, I again return to the exception to the rule in sport forms: professional wrestling.

Widely condemned as "false" or "pseudo" sport, television pro wrestling constantly challenges the ideal of free and open competition. In a sport without statistics, the win-loss percentage of a wrestling star is not relevant knowledge. In wrestling it's how one plays the game that truly counts: a hero in defeat is still heroic; a villain triumphant is still to be despised. And in this privileging of character at the expense of authenticity, pro wrestling lampoons naive ideals associated with the winner-take-all justice of the competition ethic. Pro wrestling champions a much richer brand of justice—a justice from character, not conquest.

People don't bet on the outcome of wrestling matches, obviously, because wrestling requires the suspension of disbelief of a moviegoer, not a gambler. However, in our culture, the wrestling fan is typically ridiculed as a gullible and stupid creature, while the gambler is frequently honored as daring and clever. Assuming that some wrestling fans actually believe matches are authentic (and there's reason to believe most don't),[16] one wonders who is the more deceived: the wrestling fan who believes in the spectacle of good versus evil, or the gambler who trusts the arbitrary, amoral order of legitimate spectator sports.

A subversive sport form, wrestling completely calls into question assumptions about rules and rule enforcement attached to the ideal of competition. In wrestling the rules are obviously and painfully arbitrary and unevenly enforced; they generally work in favor of the villain and against the hero. The referee, though usually sincere and well-intentioned, is frequently distracted and often blind to villainous violations the partisan crowd can easily spot. Typically, the hero respects the rules until it becomes obvious to all that obedience will ultimately result in defeat; then, in a wonderful eruption of chaos, the hero takes the law into his own hands—and, sometimes, justice emerges from the fray. In wrestling, justice doesn't "trickle down" through the system. Instead, justice results from individual action and an eventual disregard of arbitrary rules impeding vindication. In wrestling, as in life, law and order do not equal justice and equality.[17]

Although now located on television's wild fringes, professional wrestling was a prime-time spectacle during the 1950s. In those early years of broadcast television, a wrestler named Gorgeous George became a pivotal figure in TV's world of sports. Pioneering a brand of sports stardom that acts as a centrifugal force[18] in sports discourse, George's performance emphasized character more than athletic excellence. His success did not go unnoticed by performers in more legitimate sports. Indeed, George provided inspiration to the greatest sports star of modern times—Muhammad Ali.

In his autobiography, Ali addresses the prefight routine that became his signature. It was before a fight with the forgettable Bill McDonald that he first talked openly about beating an opponent. Ali remembers that his now famous badgering immediately created a great deal of controversy:

Word got around that "Cassius is bragging." But when they came to the gym, they gave me all the attention I wanted. I kept calling out, "I'm The Greatest! I can't be beat!" I'd seen good fighters carry on bloody brawls with hardly anybody caring which one won or lost. At least now they were interested in my fights, even if they wanted to see me lose, something I had some control over.[19]

According to Ali, a performance by Gorgeous George was an epiphanic experience for him—one that illuminated the subtle dynamics of hype:

When I flew into Las Vegas, I found I was on the right track. I was awed by the glitter and the girls and the gambling, but mostly I was struck by Gorgeous George. He was doing what I had been doing. I was fascinated.

Gorgeous came into the TV studio where Duke Sabedong, my opponent, and I were being introduced. He made his entrance combing his long blond hair like a movie idol, two pretty girls holding up the end of his ten-foot-long robe so it wouldn't drag. "Look at my velvet skin," he purred. "Look at my pretty hair. If that bum messes up my hair tomorrow night, I'll annihilate him!" When he snatched the microphone, the announcer cautioned him, "Hold it, Gorgeous. This is not your show!" "It is my show!" George said, and he walked in front of the stage and spoke into the mike. "I want all of you out there to come to the Sports Palace early because I'm gonna mop the floor with this bum. If he beats me, I'll cut off my golden hair and throw the hair out in the audience and go bald."

Instead of resting for my fight the next night, I was at the Sports Palace along with a standing-room-only crowd, wanting to see what would happen to George. I saw how his strategy had worked, just as mine had been working.[20]

George and Ali's "strategy" boils down to individualizing the sports performance. In observing that "good fighters carry on bloody brawls with hardly anybody caring which one won or lost," Ali arrived at a key element of television stardom: the TV star must emerge from the background of social type to trigger audience identification/recognition/care.[21] The same strategy is evident in the controversial performance of pro football's Mark Gastineau. Where other great defensive ends got lost on the crowded field, Gastineau's now illegal war dance brought to the fore and underscored the excellence of his play. And in pro tennis, John McEnroe's obnoxious antics at center court have contributed mightily to individualizing his performance—making winning strange by making winning ugly.

The importance of Gorgeous George, then, is that he was the first of TV's sports stars to establish that personality, character, and color are as interesting to audiences and as crucial to media stardom as run-of-the-mill competitive superiority. And the genius of the tremendously successful Lite Beer advertising campaign is akin to the genius of Gorgeous George and Muhammad Ali. In resurrecting unglamorous but colorful athletes from days past to hawk the product, Lite Beer rediscovered that a sports performer could be memorable without corroborating statistics—that, contrary to the ideal of competition, how one played the game was as important to the spectator as winning or losing. Bob Uecker, for instance, was far from a model of excellence in professional baseball, but he has parlayed his failed athletic career into a kind of marginal sports stardom—inverting the ideal of competition. Uecker's popularity typifies the kind of centrifugal stardom exploited by the Lite Beer commercials.

The collision of these two forms of sports stardom is perhaps most evident in the four stars of the Chicago Bears' 1986 Super Bowl team: Walter Payton, Coach Mike Ditka, Jim McMahon, and William "The Refrigerator" Perry. Payton, in breaking Jim Brown's NFL career rushing record, established himself as a model of competitive excellence. However, in maximizing an expert type, Payton doesn't make excellence strange; his performance generally reinforces the ideal of free and open competition—and, ironically, he's not as recognizable off the field as some of his less accomplished teammates. Similarly, Ditka is primarily a model of coaching excellence who reinforces the ethic of competition. Where the coaching performances of Woody Hayes, Bobby Knight, and even Bum Phillips often challenge the competition ethic by making winning strange, Ditka's coaching doesn't. But the centripetal stardom of Payton and Ditka is more than offset by the centrifugal stardom of McMahon and Perry. McMahon's self-consciously "outrageous" behavior on the sidelines and off the field, and Perry's extraordinary size, coupled with his unconventional performance as a running back in short yardage situations, have made the two centrifugal sports stars who have defamiliarized competition. Though less accomplished than Ditka and Payton, both McMahon and Perry are more recognizable off the field because their stardom is not based so much on competition as on character. And both have enjoyed tremendous success in commodifying their stardom: McMahon in Honda Scooter commercials and Perry in fast food commercials.

As sports discourse, then, stardom can either reinforce or militate against the ideal of free and open competition: The sports stardom of athletes who represent models of excellence tends to reinforce the ideal; the TV stardom of those who make excellence controversial tends to subvert the ideal. Generally, star performers like Walter Payton, who only represent models of excellence, encounter a fleeting stardom that doesn't extend much past their active careers. These stars are, ultimately, only as good as their statistics—and once those statistics are no longer relevant, once their records have been broken, they recede into the annals of sports trivia. Centrifugal sports stars, on the other hand, can become sports legends if their performances are controversial enough for them to remain the site of conflicted meanings in the culture. Clearly, in giving bodily expression to cultural contradictions related to the civil rights movement and the Vietnam War, Muhammad Ali has achieved the status of sports legend. Sharing roughly the same symbolic space as the Reverend Dr. Martin Luther King Jr., Ali became known around the world and will be remembered long after Walter Payton is confused with Gale Sayers and Vince Lombardi with Guy Lombardo.

INTERPRETING THE WORLD OF SPORTS

> In any society, not only its story systems but many other practices and institutions will be devoted to articulating an ideology that affirms existing cultural arrangements and values.
>
> David Thorburn[22]

Just as certain stories in the prime-time domain of the major broadcast networks can be treated as consensus narrative, so major sport forms—football, baseball, and basketball—can be interpreted as "consensus sports." And many of Thorburn's observations regarding consensus narrative apply to consensus sport. Consensus sport, too, "operates at the very center of life of its culture."[23] These sport forms also articulate "an ideology that affirms existing cultural arrangements and values." As this study suggests, in communicating the ideology of free and open competition, sports discourse provides some of television's most deeply conservative, even reactionary, programming.

Ironically, its conservative character makes the world of sports a symbolic place where common sense is most profoundly tested and contested on television. When a greedy owner makes private property strange by moving a beloved franchise to another city, when a baseball executive suggests that blacks don't have the intelligence to manage in the major leagues, when a university must disband its football program because of institutionalized cheating, the culture at large is forced to reconsider and renegotiate values associated with a "free" market economy. In other words, precisely because of its conservative character, a crisis in the world of sports represents an ideological rupture, a moment when people confront cultural contradictions normally masked by the routines of everyday life.

In interpreting the world of sports, we must avoid the nostalgia of the sports purist and recognize that sports are, and always have been, products of history, not of nature. On American television, sports are big business—and entertainment, and politics, and perhaps even religion. In making sense of TV's sports discourse, then, we must embrace sports' dual status as commodity and communication. But, in recognizing its symbolic and economic dimensions, we must be careful not to reduce television's world of sports to a single, monolithic message. As this analysis indicates, there are forces at work in the world of sports—fringe sport forms and centrifugal sports stardom—that undermine the competition ethic. Critical inquiry focusing on TV's sports arena must move beyond the obvious, and not too remarkable, truth that popular sport forms tend to reinforce the status quo. Although questions of how sport forms may enforce a dominant ideology are certainly still relevant, critical studies must also address even more complex questions regarding how the world of sports can challenge, alter, and even transform the world of everyday life. As this analysis also suggests, studies taking a dialogic approach to interpreting sports discourse are uniquely equipped to address both the struggle for dominance and the struggle for freedom expressed in sports' ritual representation of shared beliefs.

NOTES

The author thanks Richard F. Allen for sharing insights into the significance of professional wrestling's status as a theatrical sport form.

1. George B. Leonard, "Winning Isn't Everything. It's Nothing," *Intellectual Digest,* October 1973, reprinted in *Jock: Sports and Male Identity,* ed. Donald F. Sabo and Ross Runfola (Englewood Cliffs, NJ: Prentice-Hall, 1980), 265–266.

2. This is essentially a paraphrase of James W. Carey's "ritual view of communication," a view that defines communication as "the symbolic process whereby reality is produced, maintained, repaired, and transformed." See Carey's "A Cultural Approach to Communication," *Communication 2* (1975):10. Critical scholars on both sides of the Atlantic have adapted the ritual view of communication to the study of TV's central place in modern, technological societies. In Britain, John Fiske and John Hartley's "bardic" model and Roger Silverstone's "mythic" model represent ritual views of television. See Fiske and Hartley, *Reading Television* (London: Methuen, 1978); Silverstone, *The Message of Television: Myth and Narrative in Contemporary Culture* (London: Heinemann Educational Books, 1981). In the United States, Horace Newcomb and Robert S. Alley's "choric" model is also derived from the ritual view. See their *The Producer's Medium* (New York: Oxford University Press, 1983).

3. This description of television "clawing back" everything toward its central position is derived from Fiske and Hartley's elaboration of the "bardic" model. According to Fiske and Hartley:

The bardic role is normally a positive and dynamic one. It is to draw into its own central position both the audience with which it communicates and the reality to which it refers. We have tried to articulate this positive role by means of the term *claw back.* The bardic mediator constantly strives to claw back into a central focus the subject of its messages. (*Reading Television*, pp.86–87)

4. The need for critical studies to account for the commercial dimensions of mass communication is perhaps most clearly stated in Eileen R. Meehan, "Conceptualizing Culture as Commodity: The Problem of Television," *Critical Studies in Mass Communication* 3, no.4 (December 1986):448–457.

5. David Thorburn, "Television as an Aesthetic Medium," *Critical Studies in Mass Communication* 4, no. 2 (June 1987):167–168.

6. For a more elaborate discussion of fringe television, see Jimmie L. Reeves and Horace Newcomb, "Fringe Television: A Challenge to Prime-Time Criticism," *Southern Speech Communication Journal* 52, no. 4 (Summer 1987):339–348.

7. As Horace Newcomb puts it:

It [sport] is quickly transformed into a vehicle for cultural values, and we translate the playing field into an image for "real life." The virtues of practice, hard work, dedication, desire, competitive spirit, fair play, "good sportsmanship," and a host of other commodities are pointed out to generation after generation of young people. (*TV: The Most Popular Art* [Garden City, NY: Anchor/Doubleday,1974], 193.)

8. Clifford Geertz, "Person, Time and Conduct in Bali," *The Interpretation of Cultures: Selected Essays* (New York: Basic Books, 1973), 443–444.

9. Cary Schneider, "The Astroturfing of American Sports," *Film Comment* 15, no.4 (July-August 1979): 60–62.

10. See Richard F. Allen and Jimmie L. Reeves, "A Critical Analysis of Televised Professional Wrestling," paper presented at the Popular Culture Association meeting, Wichita, Kansas, April 1983. This interpretation of the history of pro wrestling is derived from *The Concise Encyclopedia of Sports*, ed. K. W. Jennison (New York: Franklin Watts, 1970), 163; F. G. Menke, *All-Sports Record Book* (New York: A. S. Barnes and Co., 1950), 1011.

11. Barbara S. Morris and Joel Nydahl present a sophisticated method for approaching television's narration and visualization of unscripted events in their "Toward Analysis of Live Television Broadcasts," *Central States Speech Journal* 34, no.3 (Fall 1983): 195–202.

12. This dialogic view of TV's sports discourse is based on the translinguistics of M. M. Bakhtin. This theory of language is best presented in Bakhtin's masterful essay "Discourse in the Novel," *The Dialogic Imagination*, ed. Michael Holquist, trans. Caryn Emerson and Michael Holquist (Austin: University of Texas Press, 1981), 259–422. For a discussion of how Bakhtin's work applies to the interpretation of television discourse, see Horace Newcomb, "On the Dialogic Aspects of Mass Communication," *Critical Studies in Mass Communication* 1, no.1 (1984): 34–50.

13. Leonard, "Winning Isn't Everything," p. 259.

14. Richard Dyer, in his study of movie stardom, argues that cinematic stars become the object of audience identification by maximizing, inflecting, or resisting social typification. See his *Stars* (London: British Film Institute, 1979), 111–113. For an analysis of how the "well-informed," the "expert," and the "layman" social types relate to television stardom, see Jimmie L. Reeves, "Television Stardom: A Ritual of Social Typification and Individualization," *Sage Annual Review of Communication Research* 15 (1988): 146–60. This organization of social types according to the social distribution of knowledge is derived from Alfred Schutz and Thomas Luckmann, *The Structures of the Life-World*, trans. R. Zaner and H. Englehardt (Evanston, IL: Northwestern University Press, 1973).

15. Tim Brooks and Earle Marsh's description of the "Monday Night Football" phenomenon supports this analysis:

It was around Cosell's caustic personality that the announcing team was organized. Whereas the traditional way of covering football was with two people, a play-by-play announcer and color man who added insights and observations, ABC decided to put three people in the booth. Keith Jackson did the play-by-play during the first season, with Frank Gifford assuming that role in 1971. The other two commentators, Cosell and Don Meredith, were there to inform, observe, and entertain. It was this last aspect of their work that offended sports traditionalists. (*The Complete Directory to Prime Time Network TV Shows: 1946–Present*, rev. ed. [New York: Ballantine Books, 1980], 938)

16. Richard F. Allen, in a qualitative study of the live wrestling audience, discovered that many of the most animated fans made occasional comments indicating they recognized the contrivances of the action in the ring. See his "Professional Wrestling: Toward an Understanding of a Complex Form," paper presented at the Popular Culture Association meeting, Toronto, 1984.

17. See Allen and Reeves, "A Critical Analysis of Televised Professional Wrestling." This interpretation of pro wrestling as a subversive sport form obviously has been strongly informed by Roland Barthes's essay "The World of Wrestling," *Mythologies*, trans. Lavers (New York: Hill and Wang, 1972). 15–25.

18. This way of thinking about the operation of meaning in sports discourse is based on the translinguistics of M. M. Bakhtin. Bakhtin saw the meaning-making process as animated by a clash of two opposing social forces: the centrifugal forces of social stratification and diversification, and the centripetal forces that tend toward social unification and systemization. Michael Holquist, one of Bakhtin's American translators, describes the unifying forces' relation to the centrifugal forces as "akin to the interworkings that anthropologists nominate as the activity of culture in modeling a completely different order called nature." *The Dialogic Imagination*, p. xix.

19. Muhammad Ali with Richard Durham, *The Greatest: My Own Story* (New York: Random House, 1975), 106–107.

20. Ibid., p. 107.

21. This is, again, derived from Richard Dyer's observations concerning movie stars: "What is abundantly clear is stars are supremely figures of identification . . . and this identification is achieved principally through a star's relation to social type." *Stars*, p. 111.

22. David Thorburn, "Television as an Aesthetic Medium," p. 168.

23. Ibid.

IV

AUDIENCE AS TEXT

13

Invisible Fictions: Television Audiences, Paedocracy, Pleasure

John Hartley

PASSPORT CONTROL

Although television as an institution is dependent upon audiences, it is by no means certain what a television audience is. However, it seems that this is not the only uncertainty facing those working in the field of television studies. E. Ann Kaplan, for instance, in her introduction to *Regarding Television,* remarks:

The structure, form, content and context for British television are so radically different from those of its American counterpart that everything has to be rethought by critics in this country [the USA]. Television scholarship is simply not exportable in the easy manner of film criticism.[1]

The idea that international television criticism is a contradiction in terms is not confined to the American side of the Atlantic. In fact, it has been taken even further by the British writer John Ellis, who suggests not only that television scholarship is unexportable but also that one nation's television is "incomprehensible" to observers from other nations. In the preliminaries to his *Visible Fictions,* Ellis confesses that at the time of writing he had never visited the United States. He continues:

This really demonstrates an insuperable problem with all writing about broadcast TV: unlike cinema, which in its commercial sectors has a highly integrated international

This chapter is a revised version of a paper given as the centerpiece address at the Fourth International TV Drama Conference, Michigan State University, May 1985. I wish to thank the organizers of that conference for giving me the opportunity to focus on these matters.

aspect, broadcast TV is an essentially national activity for the vast majority of its audience. Broadcast TV is the private life of the nation-state . . . incomprehensible for anyone who is outside its scope.[2]

Neither Kaplan nor Ellis qualifies these remarks with customary scholarly caution. Both write in absolute terms: television is incomprehensible for those outside its scope; television criticism is simply not exportable; everything has to be rethought; the problem is insuperable; it applies to all writing about broadcast television; television is essentially national. Furthermore, their remarks are not isolated. Quite a lot of media criticism in recent years has been conducted around a perceived gulf, as wide as the Atlantic Ocean, between American and Anglo-European perspectives.[3] This gulf, once invoked, is made to explain such divisions as those between empirical and theoretical approaches; so-called transmission and ritual models of communication; liberal-pluralist and Marxist theories; even the disciplinary location of media studies—in America it's a social science; in Britain it's in the humanities.

If these divisions really constitute an insuperable problem, then of course international television scholarship does become impossible. Or, more accurately, the kind of criticism that constructs as its object an *essential* form, on the model of "cinema" or "literature," becomes impossible. What the uncertainties noted above do imply is that there is no such thing as "television"—an abstract, general form with invariable features. Neither does television have any *essential* mode of production, distribution, and consumption—despite the very obvious fact that many television shows, series, and formats display exactly that "highly integrated international aspect" claimed by Ellis for cinema.

As for television studies, a certain uneasiness with the erection of essential, national boundaries around television scholarship has been voiced by Willard Rowland and Bruce Watkins in their introduction to *Interpreting Television*. They discuss "this old and contentious issue," largely with reference to a myth of American "dependence" on European thought, and show that although that dependence is mythical, the consequences of reiterating the myth have been real enough. They argue that although it is tempting, it is inadequate to categorize current research by means of a "bi-polar, European/critical versus American/liberal dichotomy." They conclude that "it is becoming increasingly difficult to speak about any pure national or even regional tradition of thought, especially in communication and cultural studies."[4] If it is indeed difficult to speak of pure, national traditions of thought in this context, it may be easier, and certainly more productive, to speak of impurity. It may even be possible to see in impurities not a problem but a fundamental criterion for cultural studies.

The productivity of impurity, of transgressing national boundaries unawares, has been amply illustrated, paradoxically enough, by John Ellis. Having erected pure—insuperable—boundaries between British and American television, and between British and American writing on television, he then subverts this line of thinking completely:

Sudden exposure to the often bizarre practices of broadcast TV in another country can stimulate fresh thinking about the whole phenomenon of TV. This is the case with Raymond Williams's concept of "flow" which resulted from his culture shock on seeing US TV. Seeing another country's broadcast TV has the effect of "making strange" something we normally take for granted: TV, normally habitual and bound into the life of the nation, suddenly becomes an alien and inexplicable series of events.[5]

Thus, transgressing the frontiers of the familiar, the national, produces culture shock—the bizarre, the alien, the inexplicable—and this turns out to be the very condition for understanding, stimulating fresh thinking by breaking habitual bonds. Even so, it has to be noted that some bonds remain taken for granted: Ellis is still presuming that there is such a thing as "the whole phenomenon" of television, in the teeth of his own evidence to the contrary.

TELEVISION: ANOTHER COUNTRY?

Since the concept of the nation seems to play such an important role in specifying both television and TV scholarship, it would seem to be a good idea to look at what the concept of the nation might mean. However, it wouldn't be such a good idea to substitute for the essentialism of "television" another kind of essentialism—for instance, the notion of an essential "America" or "Britain" or "Australia" or even "the nation." Nations cannot be understood "purely," that is, from their own supposed intrinsic or essential features. Neither television nor nations can be understood at all, in fact, except in relational terms. They have no pure, intrinsic properties but only differences from other, related domains. Benedict Anderson has argued that they are by definition limited, or impure, because each nation is defined by *other* nations:

Even the largest of them, encompassing perhaps a billion living human beings, has finite, if elastic boundaries, beyond which lie other nations. No nation imagines itself coterminous with mankind [*sic*]. The most messianic nationalists do not dream of the day when all the members of the human race will join their nation in the way that it was possible, in certain epochs, for, say, Christians to dream of a wholly Christian planet.[6]

It follows that nations can only be defined by what they are not; their individual identity consists in the recognition and establishment of finite boundaries that are simultaneously elastic. This formula generates, of course, a well-known definition not only of nations but also of signs; like signs, nations are constructs. But, like signs, nations are constructs not of any external, referential world but of *discourses*; Anderson calls nations "imagined communities." They are communities because everyone has confidence in the existence of others within their nation; they are imagined because there is absolutely no external warrant for this confidence:

An American will never meet, or even know the names of more than a handful of his [*sic*] 240,000,000-odd fellow Americans. He has no idea of what they are up to at any one time. But he has complete confidence in their steady, anonymous, simultaneous activity.[7]

Where does this confidence come from? Among other sources, Anderson mentions the newspaper as a mechanism for providing imaginary links between members of a nation. Newspapers are at one and the same time the ultimate fiction, since they construct the imagined community, and the basis of a mass ritual or ceremony that millions engage in every day: "What more vivid figure for the secular, historically clocked, imagined community can be envisioned?" asks Anderson.[8] Of course, a more vivid metaphorical figure for the imagined communities of nations can indeed be envisioned. It's called television. Indeed, like newspapers, television may be more than merely a metaphor for imagined communities; it is one of the prime sites upon which a given nation is constructed for its members. And, as we have seen, the nation is, concomitantly, one of the sites upon which television has been constructed as a concept.

Like nations, television as an institution is limited, impure, with no essence but only difference from other television, other forms, other institutions. Nevertheless, television does frequently transgress national boundaries—the idea of its essential nation-ality is as imagined, or fictional, as the idea of the nation itself. Certain program types, especially sporting championships, Olympic Games, news pictures, beauty and other contests, and awards ceremonies within the general showbiz domain, together with the more recent genre of "aid" shows, may be seen more or less simultaneously by hundreds of millions of people, sometimes making it possible for producers to dream, as it were, of a wholly tuned-in planet. As well, television transgresses national frontiers in more routine ways, notably at the level of transnational ownership and control of both production and distribution, and at the level of international sales of individual shows and series. It follows that if television can be imagined as an "essentially national activity," as Ellis puts it, it can only be so imagined on behalf of the experience of audiences: the audience is constructed as comprising those for whom television is indeed the "private life of the nation-state." In short, one unwarranted, invisible fiction—the imagined communitiy of the nation—is used to invent and explain another—the television audience.

INVISIBLE FICTIONS

Television is, like nations, a construct of specific institutions; what it "means" turns on how those institutional discourses construct it for their own specific purposes. Among the institutions that construct television discursively, three stand out: the television industry (networks, stations, producers, etc.); political/legal institutions (usually formalized as regulatory bodies, and intermittently as government-sponsored inquiries and reports); and critical institutions (academic, journalistic, and—surprisingly rarely—self-constituted audience organizations or pressure groups). Each of these institutions is, of course, marked by internal contradictions, hierarchies, and historical shifts, and by manifold differences from each of the others. However, despite the fact that they don't speak with one voice, all three tend to legitimate their actions and interventions in the name of the same imagined community. All claim to speak, albeit with quite different voices, on behalf of the audience.

It follows that audiences are not just constructs; they are the invisible fictions that are produced institutionally in order for various institutions to take charge of the mechanisms of their own survival. Audiences may be imagined empirically, theoretically, or politically, but in all cases the product is a fiction that serves the needs of the imagining institution. In no case is the audience "real," or external to its discursive construction. There is no "actual'" audience that lies beyond its production as a category, which is merely to say that audiences are only ever encountered per se as *representations*. Furthermore, they are so rarely *self*-represented that they are almost always absent, making TV audiences perhaps the largest "community" in the world that is subject to what Edward Said has dubbed the discourse of "orientalism,"[9] whereby disorganized communities which have never developed or won adequate means of self-representation, and which exist almost wholly within the imagination and rhetoric of those who speak on their behalf, become the "other" of powerful, imperial discourses.[10]

What kind of fiction is the orientalized audience imagined to be? In the critical domain, two influential recent developments in the theoretical conceptualization of audiences seem noteworthy. The first, elaborated in relation to cinema and associated largely with the journal *Screen* in the 1970s, is applied by John Ellis to television. Here the audience is imagined as "the subject," positioned or constructed as a textual/institutional effect of television. However, Ellis's "viewer" is far from being an effect of television; Ellis's viewer is an effect of Ellis's stated project, which is to produce an argument about the general aesthetics of broadcast television in comparison with those of cinema. Ellis is preoccupied with the idea that television has, or might have, a "specific signifying practice," and that such a thing is what unifies television. Hence the argument is driven, ineluctably, it seems, to imagining a unified viewer to go with this unified signifying practice:

The viewer is constituted as a normal citizen. This is the position constructed for the TV viewer by the processes of broadcast TV; many viewers occupy the very position which TV addresses, even if they would never consider themselves to be such a strange being as a normal citizen.[11]

A strange being indeed, and one produced by that totally unwarranted confidence in the existence of the nation noted above. Indeed, Ellis's viewer is imagined as coterminous with the ideal bearer of the concept of the nation: the "normal citizen." Not content with imagining the "normal citizen" as a fictional construct or textual position produced by television's signifying practice, however, Ellis then asserts (on their behalf, without consultation) that "many viewers occupy [this] very position." Thus Ellis's viewer is an invisible fiction, a construct that is a figment of the argument's imagination.

The second influential recent approach to audiences is that of David Morley in and following his study *The "Nationwide" Audience*. Morley's work was ground-breaking when it appeared, offering the hope of integrating theoretical approaches such as those of both *Screen* and the Centre for Contemporary Cultural Studies in Birmingham, in their different ways, with the more traditional concerns of empirical audience research. Thus, although Morley is astute and convincing in his account of theoretical issues, his work retains a commitment to an "actual" audience that—the research paradigm requires it—is an independent entity. Empirical research is based on the presumption that audiences are not merely the product of the research into them but exist prior to, apart from, and beyond the activities of both television and television research. Unlike Ellis, but like traditional audience researchers, Morley sets off in search of the audience. Unlike traditional researchers, however, he tramps the country seeking not preferences, attitudes, opinions, and tastes but the relation between television and class. Thus he seeks his audience among already constituted groups which he feels able to identify in class terms—groups of students taking courses in various different kinds of educational establishments. The shop stewards, trade-union officials, bank managers, apprentices, and students of various other kinds are described in terms of their class "background," though no warrant is ever offered for the very precise labels Morley uses. He never explains how be distinguishes between, for instance, "skilled working class," "skilled upper working class," "upper working class," and "working class."[12] The fact that some of his chosen groups were unfamiliar with the chosen show (*Nationwide*), because he showed them a different regional version or because they habitually watched the other channel, is not deemed significant. And the fact that the show was screened to them in a setting that is itself discursively productive in ways that necessarily affect what the "social subjects" said about it was, says Morley, merely "situational."[13]

Clearly, then, for Morley an audience is an audience, whether it is "responding" in an educational/work setting or "decoding" in a family/home context. For Morley, the "cultural and linguistic codes a person has available to them" is a matter not affected by a "situation" in which those persons are watching a program dealing with financial and union issues during courses in banking or trade-union studies. And an audience's cultural competence to "decode" is not significantly affected by the fact that they've never seen the show before. An audience is an audience at home or at work, despite the fact that Morley's groups are carefully chosen and sorted into class "backgrounds" rather than being interviewed at home. Clearly, Morley's audience, too, is an invisible fiction produced by his project, which was itself a product of academic/critical institutional discourses. His audience is no more real than Ellis's, and no more independent of the research than any other experimental subject.

It's Morley's *method* that is empirical, not the audience he constructs for his research.

A PAEDOCRATIC REGIME

Even innovative and critical work such as Ellis's and Morley's, whether theoretical or empirical in mode, is not exempt from a tendency to essentialize the audience. Ellis makes it essentially a "normal citizen." Morley's "social subject" is more complex, being inflected by class differences in particular, but even so his project assumes that audiences have intrinsic (observable) properties, and his very title implies that they are to be found with essentially the same properties "nationwide." If audiences can be understood in this way in critical, academic discourses, then the tendency to imagine them as independently existing, essential entities that are also nations is abundantly amplified in the practical discourses of the TV industry and of its regulatory bodies. This is no doubt partly because both the industry and its regulatory bodies are obliged not only to speak *about* an audience but—crucially, for them—to talk *to* one as well: they need not only to *represent* audiences but to enter into *relations* with them.[14]

The way in which corporate executives and professional producers imagine audiences is particularly important, since it determines to some extent what gets on air, and it may help to explain why the industry acts as it does. Conversely, the way in which regulatory bodies imagine the audience may help to account for some of the things that don't get on the air. Turning, first, to the industry, it is clear that as far as private opinions of producers are concerned, there may be as many views of the audience as there are personnel, and certainly such views will display contradictory aspects. However, insofar as audiences can be understood as imagined communities that are also nations, then it is relevant to ask what system or manner of rule or government—what *regime*—characterizes such communities. In other words, it isn't the personal opinions of individuals which are at issue here but an institutional system—a construction of the audience that organizes the industry's practices and serves its institutional needs and purposes. The institutional needs and purposes of the television industry are survival and profitability, to be achieved (hopefully) by audience maximization and by minimizing risks and uncertainties.

Audiences are *paedocratized* to serve these needs. For the industry, television is a *paedocratic regime*. The audience is imagined as having childlike qualities and attributes. Television discourse addresses its viewers as children. It is itself characterized by childlike preoccupations and actions. This regime does not govern all television everywhere all the time, of course. But there may be a "law" which states, "The bigger the target audience, the more it will be paedocratized." Thus American network television is the most paedocratic regime of all. However, smaller networks and stations are by no means exempt from the tendency to paedocratize audiences, if only because they buy network products and operate according to models of popular television generated by the networks. Indeed, it isn't the absolute size of a target audience that determines whether or not it will be paedocratized but rather the proportion of the population (local, state, or national) that might conceivably be attracted: the higher the proportion, the more paedocratic the regime.

What do those who work at the center of U.S. network television imagine about the audience? How do they fill out their invisible fictions with plausible attributes? Often the fiction is invested with those attributes that best explain or justify the professional's own practices. Many examples can be found in Todd Gitlin's excellent study, *Inside Prime Time*. In fact, Gitlin saves one of these comments for the last paragraph of the book, where it refers not just to audiences but to the whole television industry, and it serves as an epigraph not only for the industry's view of its practices but for Gitlin's too. Gitlin cites Michael Kozoll, cocreator of "Hill Street Blues":

Which truth to conclude with . . . ? Let the last word go to Michael Kozoll. . . . Halfway through the second season [of "Hill Street Blues"], Kozoll said he had finally found the metaphor for television he had long been seeking. Doing episodic television, he said, is like raising a retarded child. By which he meant that there are only so many things it will ever learn to do, no matter how much you love the child, no matter how much effort and care and intelligence you lavish upon it. It will never shine. One could add: Its little accomplishments are also miraculous.[15]

So says Todd Gitlin, whose pessimism about television seems matched only by his pessimistic and very conservative view of "retarded" children. Elsewhere, however, Gitlin cites Marvin J. Chomsky, director of "Attica," "Holocaust," and "Inside the Third Reich," who justifies network paedocracy by reference to the need to win ratings:

Our audience is the guy who's used to walking around and getting a beer. We've got to reach him. He's a guy who hasn't made much of a commitment to give his rapt attention to what we're offering, right? We're going for the eighty million who will watch something. An infant in a cradle likes to watch things that move. So, there you are. We go in for close-ups and we try to find the conflicts.[16]

This "conventional wisdom"[17] is perhaps best exemplified in the work of Aaron Spelling ("in a class by himself," says Gitlin, for network successes), producer of "The Rookies," "S.W.A.T.," "Starsky and Hutch," "Charlie's Angels," "The Love Boat," "Fantasy Island," "Vega$," "Hart to Hart," "T. J. Hooker," and "Dynasty," among other top-rated shows. Spelling has called his products "mind candy" and "fast-food entertainment." His shows have "tennis-match dialogue" and "show and tell" plots—"on a Spelling show any plot point important enough to be signalled once is signalled twice."[18] Gitlin cites a lengthy insider's anecdote which is designed to show that even the smallest details of scripting, representation, and semiosis are determined by the concept of a childlike audience. In particular, narrative suspense is constructed according to the conventions of children's theater. The insider explains Spelling's methods thus:

The villain walks . . . onstage and says "Heh-heh-heh! I have the secret match-book, and I am going to hide it. I am going to put it behind this basket, and the heroine will never find it. Heh-heh-heh!" And he walks off. Now the heroine comes out and says, "Where oh where is the secret matchbook?" And all the kids in the audience say, "It's behind the basket! It's behind the basket!" That's what Aaron does. He believes that's what the American audience is, you see.[19]

Gitlin comments, "By any Network standard, it all works." Indeed, according to Gitlin, "Spelling embraced the form's simplifications so fervently he left his personal impress on the medium," in the shape of "two-generation pairings" of a fatherlike "sage and authoritative elder" overseeing a team of youthful, siblinglike peers who in turn oversee the rest of the diegetic world, "patrolling the street nasties and keeping recalcitrant, childish reality under control."[20] In short, the mechanisms of representation, together with the diegetic world that they produce, are paedocratically organized to communicate with an audience which is itself believed to relate to television paedocratically.

CHILD'S PLAY

Why do industry professionals invent the audience in the image of a retarded child, or of an infant in the cradle—with or without a beer—who is just about sharp enough to spot the movement of moustache-twirling villainy? One reason is that audiences are, literally, unknowable. Gitlin quotes Scott Siegler, then CBS vice-president for drama development: "Because it's a mass audience—it's an unimaginably large audience—the audience tastes are so diffused and so general that you've got to be guessing."[21] But guess they must, since communication depends on what Valentin Vološinov has identified as dialogic orientation toward an addressee. For Vološinov, this fundamental characteristic of communication applies to books (and, we may add, allowing for technological developments, to television and the electronic media) just as much as it does to interpersonal speech. He calls such public performances "ideological colloquy of large scale,"[22] and producers can't escape it: Not only must their programs talk about something, they must also talk to someone. Since that someone is unimaginable, with attributes that are diffused and general, it is perhaps not surprising to find the image of a child, or an infant, being used to humanize the unknown interlocutor with 80 million or more heads.

There are, in fact, other options open to broadcasters, but for historical and political reasons these options have narrowed. In the past, and in other discursive regimes, audiences have been hailed variously as "workers," "citizens," "the people," but such appellations have been abandoned for most purposes in Western mainstream media, probably because of the leftist rhetorical connotations that such terms have been invested with since at least World War II. Similarly, there are unacceptable rightist connotations in some mobilizations of national identity, so care has to be exercised in this area; patriotism and commitment to what even Superman calls the American way may be understood as an automatic, natural reflex—but the knee jerk must not be mistaken for the goose step.

Thus broadcasters have to maintain an uneasy equilibrium; without being too populist or too nationalistic, they must strive to be popular, and speak to, for, and about the nation. In addition, their popularity is organized not around citizenship or jingoism, but primarily around pleasure; the chosen path to survival and profitability is entertainment, understood as universally intelligible narrative fiction and spectacle. What this means in practice is that broadcasters tend not to insist on allegiances and identities that might be constructed on other sites but, on the contrary, to persuade audiences to abandon any such allegiances and identities, especially those of class (rendered as "demographics" in television, of course), ethnicity, and gender. Other "variables," such as region, age, education, family structure, even nation itself, may be significant, but the whole point of popular television is to cut across such divisions and to reconstitute the people involved into one unified constituency: the audience.

The mechanism broadcasters have hit upon to do this impossible job is that of paedocracy. This isn't to say that television is merely infantile, childish, or dedicated to the lowest common denominator—those would be certain mechanisms for losing the audience. On the contrary, broadcasters paedocratize audiences in the name of pleasure. They appeal to the playful, imaginative, fantasy, irresponsible aspects of adult behavior. They seek the common personal ground that unites diverse and often directly antagonistic groupings among a given population. What better, then, than a fictional version of everyone's supposed childlike tendencies which might be understood as predating such social groupings? In short, a fictional image of the positive attributes of childlike pleasures is invented. The desired audience is encouraged to look up, expectant, open, willing to be guided and gratified, whenever television as an institution exclaims: "Hi, kids!"

FAMILY-CIRCULAR ARGUMENTS

The paedocratic regime is not confined to the imagination of broadcasters, nor to the American networks. Broadcasters are encouraged in this view of audiences and the television medium itself by regulatory bodies that lay down broadcasting policy and program standards. Such bodies tend to express little uncertainty about the audience and its attributes; indeed, so strong and obvious is this knowledge that it is used to account for the "nature" of television, presumably on the principle that you grow to be like the people you live with. Here, for instance, is the Annan Committee, a royal commission whose report, *The Future of Broadcasting,* published the results of the biggest-ever government-sponsored inquiry into television in Britian. The report is prefaced with this definition of television:

We ourselves agree that it is in [television's] nature to communicate personalities more successfully than ideas, emotional reflexes better than intellectual analysis, specific detail better than universal principles, simplicity better than complexity, change, movement and disorder better than permanence, tranquillity and order, consequences better than causes. The broadcast audience does not require education or even literacy to understand and enjoy programmes.[23]

This is another version of the "retarded child" model of television, and once again it is a fictional imagining. Television doesn't have an essential "nature," so—like "the nation"—it is explained anthropomorphically (paedomorphically) by investing it with the very attributes that the Annan Committee imagines belong to preliterate children: personality, emotional reflexes, specific detail, simplicity, change, movement, disorder, consequences, nonliteracy, lack of education.

Reserving to itself the opposing (parental) attributes—ideas, intellectual analysis, universal principles, complexity, permanence, tranquillity, order, causes, literacy, education—the Annan Committee goes on to speak on behalf of the audience, which, like a preliterate child, may not need education but does require protection:

The audience for a programme may total millions: but people watch and listen in the family circle, in their homes, so that violations of the taboos of language and behaviour, which exist in every society, are witnessed by the whole family—parents, children and grandparents—in each other's presence. These violations are more deeply embarrassing and upsetting than if they had occurred in the privacy of a book, or in a club, cinema or theatre.[24]

The television family is not just orientalized; it is tribalized. The image of a three-generation family sitting in a circle round a television set under the spell of taboos is a complete fiction. Three-generation families are statistically quite rare; where they exist, there's no evidence that they watch television together (quite the reverse, in many cases); television cannot be watched in a "circle"; there are no universal "taboos." Even so, this strange, tribal family is imagined as paedocratic: all its members are defined in terms of their relationships with children; they are not people, or even adults, but "parents," "grandparents."

The child-orientated sensibilities of this family circle are not its own private affair; on the contrary, for the Annan Committee they are matters of the highest public policy. This is because "whatever is published is presumed to be in some way approved or at least condoned, by the society which permits its publication."[25] The Annan Committee doesn't say exactly who does the presuming, approving, condoning, or—more important—the permitting, nor does it extend its notion of privacy ("the privacy of a book") to watching television in the privacy of the home. It simply equates television with "the society," and then closes the circle by equating "society" with the "whole family," which, as we've seen, is governed by children.

Along the way, a potentially useful model of the relationship between television and its audience is invoked, then ignored in favor of protective paedocracy. This is the model of broadcasting as *publication*. But the model of book and magazine publishing is not followed through. Instead, the "privacy of a book" is imagined as essentially a solitary affair, while television, as a social phenomenon, is understood to require a "permit" from "society." Of course, publishing is just as social as broadcasting, but printed publications can cater for a much wider range of political, personal, sexual, aesthetic, generic, and other tastes—with or without "violations" of "taboos" —than broadcasting ever has, without each item ("whatever is published") being seen as approved of by the whole "society." Publishing has had its own long history of regulation and censorship, but never in modern times has *everything* been subject to permit. If broadcasting is a form of publication, the question arises: why is it treated so differently? But the question does not occur to the Annan Committee, so strong is the image of the "embarrassment" that would ensue if children were to be seen by their parents and grandparents witnessing "violations" of language and behavior (another interesting question they do not address is exactly who is imagined to be "upset"—the parents or the children). Such is the power of paedocracy.

Turning from policy recommendations to the regulations that enforce them, and turning from Britain to Australia, it is clear that the "publication" of television is governed by children down to the most surprising details. The Australian Broadcasting Tribunal issues a manual to broadcasters ("licensees"). Having equated the "Australian community" and the "general public" with "adults and children," the writers of the *Manual* go on to warn licensees of their "overriding obligation" to "avoid televising program material which can give offence to sections of the public or can be harmful to the young people who make up a large part of the audience at certain times of the day."[26] Once again, it turns out that "the Australian community" as a whole is governed by that "large part" of the audience comprising "young people"—the tail wags the dog. This is especially evident in the standards laid down for "family programmes," whose "special provisions" are the following:

(a) The selection of subject matter and treatment of themes should be wholesome and fresh in outlook. The more sordid aspects of life must not be emphasised.

(b) The following in particular should be avoided—

(i) torture or suggestion of torture;

(ii) horror or undue suspense;

(iii) the use of the supernatural or superstition so as to arouse anxiety or fear;

(iv) any matter likely to lead to hysteria, nightmares or other undesirable emotional disturbances in children;

(v) excessive violence.

(c) Morbid sound effects intended to anticipate or simulate death or injury should not be used.

(d) Particular attention should be paid to the treatment of child or animal characters, as a child's imagination can be readily over-stimulated by suggestions of ill-treatment of such characters.

(e) Particular attention should be paid to the use of correct speech and pronunciation; slang and incorrect English should be avoided, except when necessary for characterization.[27]

Like their British counterparts, the writers of the ABT manual are confident they can speak on behalf of "a child's imagination," and they are equally certain that they know what goes on in that imaginary, tribal "family circle." Below is one of the regulations covering advertising (now under review):

Because some products (especially those of a personal nature) are considered unsuitable as topics for conversation in the family circle, licensees should exercise discretion in accepting advertisements for them; if such advertisements are accepted, great care should be taken in selecting times appropriate for their transmission. Products of a particularly intimate nature which are not freely mentioned or discussed in mixed company should not be advertised through television. Illustrated advertisements for brassieres, girdles, briefs or similar items of underwear making use of live models should not be televised between 6:00 a.m. and 8:30 a.m. or between 4:00 p.m. and 7:30 p.m. on weekdays or at any time before 7:30 p.m. on Saturday, Sunday, or weekdays which are not schooldays.[28]

REGIMES OF PLEASURE

Broadcasters are required to conform to a fictional image of the family circle and to an extraordinarily outdated notion of "mixed company" on pain of losing their license to broadcast. However, a more constant threat for television networks is losing not their license but their market share. Does it follow, then, that audiences do in fact exert a powerful influence on broadcasters in the form of demand? Television as an industry is subject to certain market forces, but the institutional organization of the industry seems designed not to enter into active relations with audiences as already constituted trading partners, but, on the contrary, to *produce* audiences—to invent them in its own image for its own purposes.

Certainly the relationship of the television industry to its audience is not the classic market relation of supply and demand. This is because television, as one of the culture or consciousness industries, is not like the traditional producer of goods or services which are then sold to a market. Television shows are not commodities in the usual sense—they are "nonmaterial" commodities—and audiences don't buy them. The exchange is not goods for money, but symbols for time. If, as Nicholas Garnham has put it, culture is "above all the sphere for the expansion of difference,"[29] then it follows that the use value of cultural commodities like television shows is very hard to pin down or to predict. Television executives do their best. Todd Gitlin cites a list of the "mysteries" that executives offered to him as explanations for a show's success: "whether a concept was 'special,' 'different,' 'unique,' even (wonder of wonders) 'very unique'; whether a show had 'chemistry'; whether it 'clicked'; whether 'it all came together.'"[30] But clearly the demand for novelty or difference, for the "very unique," is so unspecific that it barely counts as demand at all. The only discipline such demand imposes on the industry is that of variety: television, like other culture industries, cannot standardize its product but must offer a repertoire. Further, such demand cannot be stabilized. Despite the tendency to minimize uncertainty and risk by the use of repeats, long-running series (in both drama and news), recombinations of successful formulas, and spin-offs, uncertainty remains: out of around 3,000 new ideas put up to each of the three American networks each year, about 100 will be commissioned to the script stage; of these, 25 will go to pilot stage; after testing of the pilots, perhaps 5 or 10 new series will go on the air; of these, perhaps 1 will go to a second season.[31] In the face of such uncertainties, television networks are driven to ever higher production costs per item in order to maintain novelty and difference, which in turn means that they are driven to seek ever larger audiences to justify the unit costs.

But for their part, audiences treat television shows not as scarce commodities but as public utilities for which they are not prepared to pay. Like other cultural goods, such as radio shows, advertising, and free newspapers, television shows are not purchased. Furthermore, they are not consumed; they are not used up in the act of reading or viewing. This means both that the products of the past are available for reconsumption and that audiences are apt to use television when and how they like, and (despite piracy laws) to save what they like for reconsumption—an increasing tendency since the introduction of video recorders. This means it is hard for the industry to maintain scarcity (and thus price), especially given the need for audience maximization.

In this context—where the industry's product cannot be standardized, where demand cannot be predicted or stabilized, where the commodity is "nonmaterial" and neither purchased nor consumed, and where vast capital investment is required to manufacture goods that are then virtually as free as the airwaves that carry them—in this context audiences are not television's real market. There is one sense, of course, in which audiences are literally the product of the television industry: in the commercial sector, networks sell access to their audiences to advertisers; in the public sector, the corporations must convince their funding agencies that an agreed proportion of the public is tuned in often enough to justify the enterprise. Thus audiences—or, more accurately, ratings—are the key to profitability and survival in the television industry, and access to them is the key to power.

It follows, as Garnham has argued, that in line with other cultural industries, but unlike traditional manufacturing industries, distributors (networks) are more important in television than manufacturers (producers), just as publishers are more powerful and profitable than authors. However, it does not follow that audiences have power over networks; they are created, organized, and maintained *by* networks, and not vice versa. Indeed, the real relations of broadcasters are not with audiences as such but with other professionals in the industry: with advertisers, funding agencies, suppliers and—it's about as close as they get—with audience research organizations. In this context, the "power" of the audience is contained within the networks themselves, taking the fictionalized form of ratings and of those imaginary, paedocratized representations of the audience that the networks promote throughout the industry. Networks minimize their risks by stabilizing not demand but supply, but neither networks nor producers know what will "sell"; they don't know who they're talking to and they don't "give the public what it wants" because they don't know what the public wants. This structural uncertainty at the heart of the television industry means that networks and producers alike are afraid of the audience: afraid of offending it, of inciting it, of inflaming it—above all, of losing it.

At the level of programming, in the "ideological colloquy of large scale," this structural uncertainty is reproduced as a constant effort to reconcile an irreconcilable contradiction. On the one hand, audiences must be appealed to and won; they must voluntarily forgo other activities and choose not only to watch television but to watch this channel, during this time slot, today. On the other hand, audiences must be disciplined and controlled; they must learn to recognize that what's offered is, despite its requisite novelty or difference, just that kind of pleasure for the enjoyment of which they have both forgone other activities and invested scarce time resources. A further contradiction facing broadcasters is that between the audience as an unimaginably large mass and the audience as an individual viewer. Without having the slightest notion of each or any viewer's identity, the ideological colloquy has to address each in order to amass all.

In practice, such contradictions produce what can be called television's regimes of pleasure. Like other publishing forms, television channels provide a montage or repertoire of different kinds of elements in order to convert as wide a spectrum of the public as possible into the audience. Far from seeking to fix just one "subject position," least of all that of Ellis's "normal citizen," television as a cultural form has developed a heterogeneity of modes of address, points of view, program genres, styles of presentation, and codes of recognition.[32] Television is characterized, in effect, by excess, providing audiences with an excess of options which can nevertheless be easily recognized, and offering an excess of pleasures (one of which is to choose between those offered), which can nevertheless be disciplined into familiar, predictable forms. Thus, in order to produce an audience, television must first produce excess.[33] But, like the audience whose demand it is supposed to represent, pleasure is a diffuse and irrecoverable concept; it must be regimented in various ways in order for the television industry to be able to supply it, and so to survive, profitably. Thus television is a pleasurable institution, but one offering a complex of channeled, disciplined pleasures which are driven toward corporately achievable forms; television operates *regimes* of pleasure.

ILLEGAL IMMIGRANTS?

But all the time the efforts of television networks and producers to regiment the audience are subverted by the audience's own excess—its tendency always to exceed the discipline, control, and channeling of television's regimes, and its tendency always to exceed the imagination of television's corporate executives. Thus the interests of audiences and television are in principle opposed. Television as an industry needs regimented, docile, eager audiences, willing to recognize what they like in what they get; and audiences, for their part, need a relationship with television in order to exist at all as audiences, but that relationship is not organized, or even represented very directly, in the institution. Their interests are discernible only as random: childish, unfocused desires for excess, transgression, novelty, difference; for play, escape from categorization; and occasionally for that characteristic childish demand—"Do it again!"

The politics of television, then, consist in a very unequal struggle between different interests within a wholly fictional (that is, discursively/rhetorically/textually imagined) community. Since audiences don't exist prior to or outside television, they need constant hailing and guidance in how-to-be-an-audience—hailing and guidance that are unstintingly given within, and especially between, shows, and in the metadiscourses that surround television, the most prominent among which, of course, are those publications aptly called television guides. Thus television is not just a regime, or a complex of regimes, of pleasure; it is a pedagogic regime as well. What this means, in effect, is that television producers haven't got the courage of their convictions. For, if television audiences are subject to a *pedagogic* regime of pleasure, then it follows that they do not live, while acting as audiences, in a democracy. But neither do they live in a paedocracy, since a pedagogic regime cannot be governed *by* childlike qualities; on the contrary, it constitutes government *over* them.

In fact, the paedocratic regime of television discourse is itself, in the end, an invisible fiction, because audiences have no voice of their own to speak within the institution. Like the discourse of orientalism, paedocracy too often functions within the industry not to explain audiences but to explain them away, to contain their potential threat, to render obvious their need for protection, regulation, rule. The paedocratized image of television audiences that circulates within the industry and among its academic and regulatory observers as an obvious truth is not necessarily devoid of force for those who "actually" watch television—but its primary function as a discourse is to serve the purposes of the professionals engaged in professional survival. For them, any irruption of "actual" audiences would spoil their routine assumption of the power to speak on behalf of a disorganized community which hitherto has existed almost wholly within their own imagination and rhetoric.

Thus it is true that television networks act, as Todd Gitlin has put it, "in loco parentis" for the audience, but it is not the childishness of the audience that produces this situation; nor is it, as Gitlin is tempted to conclude, "a projection of their own childishness."[34] On the contrary, it is a system for imagining the unimaginable; for controlling the uncontrollable. Luckily for the networks, few among the audience seem to have bothered much about it, at least until now.

NOTES

1. E. Ann Kaplan (ed.), *Regarding Television: Critical Approaches—An Anthology* (Frederick, MD: University Publications of America, 1983), xi.

2. John Ellis, *Visible Fictions: Cinema, Television, Video* (London: Routledge & Kegan Paul, 1982), 5.

3. See, for instance, Raymond Williams, *Television: Technology and Cultural Form* (London: Fontana, 1974); James Carey, "Mass Communication Research and Cultural Studies: An American View," in *Mass Communication and Society,* ed. James Curran, Michael Gurevitch, and Janet Woollacott (London: Open University/Edward Arnold, 1977); Stuart Hall, "The Rediscovery of 'Ideology': Return of the Repressed in Media Studies," in *Culture, Society and the Media,* ed. Michael Gurevitch, Tony Bennett, James Curran, and Janet Woollacott (London: Methuen, 1982); "Ferment in the Field" (special issue), *Journal of Communication* 33, no. 3 (1983).

4. Willard D. Rowland, Jr., and Bruce Watkins (eds.) *Interpreting Television: Current Research Perspectives* (Beverly Hills, CA: Sage, 1984), 33, 25.

5. Ellis, *Visible Fictions,* p. 5

6. Benedict Anderson, *Imagined Communities* (London: Verso, 1983), 16.

7. Ibid., p. 31.

8. Ibid., p. 39.

9. Edward Said, *Orientalism* (London: Routledge & Kegan Paul, 1978).

10. Edward Said, "Orientalism Reconsidered," *Race and Class* 27 (1985): 7.

11. Ellis, *Visible Fictions,* p. 169.

12. David Morley, *The 'Nationwide' Audience* (London: British Film Institute, 1980), 40, 42, 46, 68.

13. Ibid., p. 27.

14. Cf. John Hartley and Martin Montgomery, "Representations and Relations: Ideology and Power in Press and TV News," in *Discourse and Communication,* ed. Teun van Dijk (Berlin and New York: Walter de Gruyter, 1985), 233–269.

15. Todd Gitlin, *Inside Prime Time* (New York: Pantheon, 1983), 324.

16. Quoted in ibid., p. 188.

17. Ibid.

18. Ibid., pp. 136, 137.

19. Quoted in ibid., p. 138.

20. Ibid., p. 139.

21. Quoted in ibid., p. 22.

22. Valentin Vološinov, *Marxism and the Philosophy of Language* (New York: Seminar Press, 1973), 95.

23. Annan Committee, *Report of the Committee on the Future of Broadcasting* (London: Her Majesty's Stationery Office, 1977), 25.

24. Ibid., p. 246.

25. Ibid.

26. Australian Broadcasting Tribunal, *Manual* (Canberra: Australian Government Publishing Service, 1984), II.

27. Ibid., p. 15.

28. Ibid., p. 27.

29. Nicholas Garnham, "Concepts of Culture: Public Policy and the Cultural Industries," *Cultural Studies* 1, no. 1 (January 1987): 23-37 (first issued as a pamphlet by the Greater London Council, 1983).

30. Gitlin, *Inside Prime Time,* p. 26.

31. Ibid., p. 21.

32. Cf. Ien Ang, "The Battle Between Television and Its Audiences: The Politics of Watching Television," in *Television in Transition,* ed. Philip Drummond and Richard Paterson (London: British Film Institute, 1986). 250-266.

33. Cf. John Hartley, "Encouraging Signs: Television and the Power of Dirt; Speech and Scandalous Categories," in Rowland and Watkins, *Interpreting Television,* pp. 119-141, and "Out of Bounds: The Myth of Marginality," in *Television Mythologies: Stars, Shows & Signs,* ed. Len Masterman (London: Comedia, 1985), 118-127, where this argument is developed more fully.

34. Gitlin, *Inside Prime Time,* p. 300.

Selected Bibliography

Adams, William, and Fay Schreibman, eds. *Television Network News: Issues in Content Research*. Washington, DC: Television and Politics Study Program, School of Public and International Affairs, George Washington University, 1978.

Adler, Richard P., ed. *Understanding Television: Essays on Television as a Social and Cultural Force*. New York: Praeger, 1981.

Adler, Richard P., and Douglass Cater, eds. *Television as a Cultural Force*. New York: Praeger, 1976.

Allen, Robert C. *Speaking of Soap Operas*. Chapel Hill: University of North Carolina Press, 1985.

————. ed. *Channels of Discourse: Television and Contemporary Criticism*. Chapel Hill: University of North Carolina Press, 1987.

Alvarado, Manuel, and Edward Buscombe. *Hazell: The Making of a TV Series*. London: British Film Institute, in association with Latimer, 1978.

Ang, Ien. *Watching Dallas: Soap Opera and the Melodramatic Imagination*. Trans. Della Couling. London: Methuen, 1985.

Baggaley, Jon, and Steve Duck. *Dynamics of Television*. Farnborough, England: Saxon House, 1976.

Baggaley, Jon, with Margaret Ferguson and Philip Brooks. *Psychology of the TV Image*. Westmead, England: Gower, 1980.

Barnouw, Erik. *The Image Empire: A History of Broadcasting in the United States, Vol. III, From 1953*. New York: Oxford University Press, 1970.

————. *The Sponsor: Notes on a Modern Potentate*. Oxford and New York: Oxford University Press, 1978.

————. *Tube of Plenty: The Evolution of American Television*. Rev. ed. Oxford and New York: Oxford University Press, 1982.

Bennett, Tony, Susan Boyd-Bowman, Colin Mercer, and Janet Woollacott, eds. *Popular Television and Film*. London: British Film Institute, in association with Open University Press, 1981.

Berger, Arthur Asa. *The TV-Guided American*. New York: Walker and Co., 1976.
_____ , ed. *Television in Society*. New Brunswick, NJ: Transaction Books, 1987.
Bluem, A. William. *Documentary in American Television: Form, Function, Method*. New York: Hastings House, 1965.
Brunsdon, Charlotte, and David Morley. *Everyday Television: 'Nationwide.'* London: British Film Institute, 1978.
Cantor, Muriel G. *The Hollywood TV Producer: His Work and His Audience*. New York: Basic Books, 1971.
_____ . *Prime-Time Television: Content and Control*. Beverly Hills, CA: Sage, 1980.
Cater, Douglass, and Richard Adler, eds. *Television as a Social Force: New Approaches to TV Criticism*. New York: Praeger, 1975.
Conrad, Peter. *Television: The Medium and Its Manners*. Boston: Routledge & Kegan Paul, 1982.
D'Agostino, Peter, ed. *Transmission*. New York: Tanam Press, 1985.
Donner, Stanley T., ed. *The Meaning of Commercial Television: The Texas-Stanford Seminar, 1966*. Austin: University of Texas Press, 1967.
Drummond, Phillip, and Richard Paterson, eds. *Television in Transition: Papers from the First International Television Studies Conference*. London: British Film Institute, 1985.
Dyer, Richard. *Light Entertainment*. London: British Film Institute, 1973.
The Eighth Art: Twenty-Three Views of Television Today. New York: Holt, Rinehart and Winston, 1962.
Elliot, Philip. *The Making of a Television Series: A Case Study in the Sociology of Culture*. London: Constable, 1972.
Ellis, John. *Visible Fictions: Cinema, Television, Video*. Boston: Routledge & Kegan Paul, 1982.
Emery, Fred, and Merrelyn Emery. *A Choice of Futures*. Leiden, Netherlands: Martinus Nijhoff Social Sciences Division, 1976.
Epstein, Edward Jay. *News from Nowhere: Television and the News*. New York: Random House, 1973.
Esslin, Martin. *The Age of Television*. San Francisco: W. H. Freeman, 1982.
Ettema, James S., and D. Charles Whitney, eds. *Individuals in Mass Media Organizations: Creativity and Constraint*. Beverly Hills, CA: Sage, 1982.
Feuer, Jane, Paul Kerr, and Tise Vahimagi, eds. *MTM: Quality Television*. London: British Film Institute, 1984.
Fiske, John. *Television Culture: Popular Pleasures and Politics*. London: Methuen, 1987.
Fiske, John, and John Hartley. *Reading Television*. London: Methuen, 1978.
Fowles, Jib. *Television Viewers vs. Media Snobs: What TV Does for People*. New York: Stein and Day, 1982.
Gans, Herbert J. *Deciding What's News: A Study of CBS Evening News, NBC Nightly News, Newsweek, and Time*. New York: Pantheon, 1979.
Gitlin, Todd. *The Whole World Is Watching: Mass Media in the Making & Unmaking of the New Left*. Berkeley: University of California Press, 1980.
_____ . *Inside Prime Time*. New York: Pantheon, 1983.
_____ , ed. *Watching Television*. New York: Pantheon, 1986.
Goethals, Gregor T. *The TV Ritual: Worship at the Video Altar*. Boston: Beacon Press, 1981.
Grote, David. *The End of Comedy: The Sit-Com and the Comedic Tradition*. Hamden, CT: Archon Books, 1983.

Hammond, Charles Montgomery, Jr. *The Image Decade: Television Documentary, 1965-1975*. New York: Hastings House, 1981.

Hanhardt, John G., ed. *Video Culture: A Critical Investigation*. Layton, UT: Gibbs M. Smith, Inc./Peregrine Smith Books, in association with Visual Studies Workshop Press, 1986.

Hartley, John. *Understanding News*. London: Methuen, 1982.

Hazard, Patrick D. ed. *TV as Art: Some Essays in Criticism*. Champaign, IL: National Council of Teachers of English, 1966.

Himmelstein, Hal. *On the Small Screen: New Approaches in Television and Video Criticism*. New York: Praeger, 1981.

_____ . *Television Myth and the American Mind*. New York: Praeger, 1984.

Hobson, Dorothy. *Crossroads: The Drama of a Soap Opera*. London: Methuen, 1982.

Intintoli, Michael James. *Taking Soaps Seriously: The World of Guiding Light*. New York: Praeger, 1984.

Kaminsky, Stuart M., with Jeffrey H. Mahan. *American Television Genres*. Chicago: Nelson-Hall, 1985.

Kaplan, E. Ann, ed. *Regarding Television: Critical Approaches—An Anthology*. Frederick, MD: University Publications of America, 1983.

MacCabe, Colin, ed. *High Theory/Low Culture: Analysing Popular Television and Film*. Manchester, England: Manchester University Press, 1986.

MacDonald, J. Fred. *Blacks and White TV: Afro-Americans in Television Since 1948*. Chicago: Nelson-Hall, 1983.

_____ . *Television and the Red Menace: The Video Road to Vietnam*. New York: Praeger, 1985.

Marc, David. *Demographic Vistas: Television in American Culture*. Philadelphia: University of Pennsylvania Press, 1984.

Comic Visions: *Television Comedy and American Culture*. Winchester, MA: Unwin Hyman, in press.

Masterman, Len. *Teaching About Television*. London: Macmillan, 1980.

_____ , ed. *Television Mythologies: Stars, Shows & Signs*. London: Comedia Publishing Group/MK Media Press, in association with Marion Boyars, 1984.

Modleski, Tania, ed. *Studies in Entertainment: Critical Approaches to Mass Culture*. Bloomington: Indiana University Press, 1986.

Morley, David. *The 'Nationwide' Audience: Structure and Decoding*. London: British Film Institute, 1980.

_____ . *Family Television: Cultural Power and Domestic Leisure*. London: Comedia Publishing Group, 1986.

Newcomb, Horace. *TV: The Most Popular Art*. Garden City, NY: Anchor Press/ Doubleday, 1974.

_____ , ed. *Television: The Critical View*. New York: Oxford University Press, 1976; 2nd ed., 1979; 3rd ed., 1982; 4th ed., 1987.

Newcomb Horace, and Robert S. Alley. *The Producer's Medium: Conversations with Creators of American TV*. New York: Oxford University Press, 1983.

O'Connor, John E., ed. *American History/American Television: Interpreting the Video Past*. New York: Ungar, 1983.

Ravage, John W. *Television: The Director's Viewpoint*. Boulder, CO: Westview Press, 1978.

Rose, Brian G., ed. *TV Genres: A Handbook and Reference Guide*. Westport, CT: Greenwood Press, 1985.

Rowland, Willard D., Jr., and Bruce Watkins, eds. *Interpreting Television: Current Research Perspectives.* Beverly Hills, CA: Sage, 1984.

Schwartz, Tony. *The Responsive Chord.* Garden City, NY: Anchor Press/ Doubleday, 1974.

———. *Media: The Second God.* New York: Random House, 1981.

Silverstone, Roger. *The Message of Television: Myth and Narrative in Contemporary Culture.* London: Heinemann Educational Books, 1981.

Smith, Ralph Lewis. *A Study of the Professional Criticism of Broadcasting in the United States, 1920–1955.* New York: Arno Press, 1979.

Smith, Robert Rutherford. *Beyond the Wasteland: The Criticism of Broadcasting.* Rev ed. Annandale, VA: Speech Communication Association; Urbana, IL: ERIC Clearinghouse on Reading and Communication Skills, National Institute of Education, 1980.

Stein, Ben. *The View from Sunset Boulevard: America as Brought to You by the People Who Make Television.* New York: Basic Books, 1979.

Tuchman, Gaye. *Making News: A Study in the Construction of Reality.* New York: Free Press, 1978.

Tulloch, John, and Manuel Alvarado. *Doctor Who: The Unfolding Text.* London: Macmillan, 1983.

Verna, Tony. *Live TV: An Inside Look at Directing and Producing.* Boston and London: Focal Press, 1987.

Williams, Raymond. *Television: Technology and Cultural Form.* New York: Schocken Books, 1975.

Zettl, Herbert. *Sight Sound Motion: Applied Media Aesthetics.* Belmont, CA: Wadsworth, 1973.

Index

About the Editors and Contributors

GARY BURNS is assistant professor of communication studies at Northern Illinois University.

ROBERT J. THOMPSON is assistant professor of communication studies at the State University of New York, Cortland.

ARTHUR ASA BERGER is professor of broadcast communication arts at San Francisco State University.

MIKE BUDD is professor of communication at Florida Atlantic University.

MARSHA F. CASSIDY is adjunct professor of communication and theater at the University of Illinois, Chicago.

WENDE VYBORNEY DUMBLE is a graduate student and associate instructor in the department of rhetoric and communication at the University of California, Davis.

JOHN FISKE is professor of communication arts at the University of Wisconsin, Madison.

JOHN HARTLEY is senior lecturer in communication studies at Murdoch University in Australia.

WENDY KOZOL is a graduate student in the American Studies Program at the University of Minnesota, Minneapolis.

MARTIN J. MEDHURST is associate professor of speech communication and theater arts at Texas A&M University, College Station.

MEG MORITZ is assistant professor of journalism and mass communication at the University of Colorado, Boulder.

JIMMIE L. REEVES is assistant professor of communication at the University of Michigan, Ann Arbor.

MURRAY SMITH is a graduate student in the department of communication arts at the University of Wisconsin, Madison.

CLAY STEINMAN is associate professor of communication at Florida Atlantic University.

HERBERT ZETTL is professor of broadcast communication arts at San Francisco State University.